LOVE
to
LEARN

LOVE
to
LEARN

**The Transformative Power of Care
and Connection in Early Education**

ISABELLE C. HAU

PUBLICAFFAIRS

New York

PublicAffairs
Hachette Book Group
1290 Avenue of the Americas, New York, NY 10104
www.publicaffairsbooks.com
@Public_Affairs

Printed in the United States of America

First Edition: February 2025

Published by PublicAffairs, an imprint of Hachette Book Group, Inc. The PublicAffairs name and logo is a registered trademark of the Hachette Book Group.

The Hachette Speakers Bureau provides a wide range of authors for speaking events. To find out more, go to www.hachettespeakersbureau.com or email HachetteSpeakers@hbgusa.com.

PublicAffairs books may be purchased in bulk for business, educational, or promotional use. For more information, please contact your local bookseller or the Hachette Book Group Special Markets Department at special.markets@hbgusa.com.

The publisher is not responsible for websites (or their content) that are not owned by the publisher.

Library of Congress Cataloging-in-Publication Data

Names: Hau, Isabelle C., author.
Title: Love to learn : the transformative power of care and connection in early education / Isabelle C. Hau.
Description: First edition. | New York, NY : PublicAffairs, 2025. | Includes bibliographical references and index. |
Identifiers: LCCN 2024034376 | ISBN 9781541703773 (hardcover) | ISBN9781541703797 (ebook)
Subjects: LCSH: Affective education. | Early childhood education—Social aspects. | Student-centered learning. | Teacher-student relationships.
Classification: LCC LB1072 .H385 2025 | DDC 370.15/34—dc23/eng/20240820
LC record available at https://lccn.loc.gov/2024034376

ISBNs: 9781541703773 (hardcover), 9781541703797 (ebook)

LSC-C

Printing 1, 2024

CONTENTS

Contents

INTRODUCTION

Planting the Seeds of Connection

Truly wonderful, the mind of a child is.

—Yoda, *Star Wars: Episode II—*
Attack of the Clones, 2002

Unlocking the potential within every child fundamentally hinges on one key factor: the profound impact of early relationships. From the moment we take our first breath, the connections we form with those around us shape the very core of who we become. It is within these initial interactions that the seeds of learning, growth, and fulfillment are sown. When children feel loved, safe, and valued, when they have the space and time to play and explore while being supported by nurturing, positive relationships, they learn.

In recent decades, the scientific community has converged to acknowledge that early relationships are critical to healthy brain development, academic prowess, resilience, and lifelong flourishing. We are starting to better understand the intricate dance between nature and nurture, and how a nurturing environment—beginning with the soothing touch of a caregiver's hands and the resonance of their voice—can mold neural connections and lay the foundation for a lifelong love of learning. We are uncovering the neurobiological processes that underpin the emotional bonds crucial for cognitive and social-emotional development. In essence, loving relationships make us more intelligent and also contribute to our overall well-being and longevity. This impact is so profound that it prompted the American Academy of Pediatrics to issue a call to action to the pediatric community in 2021, asking it to prioritize early relationships by partnering with families and communities.[1] In a 2023 advisory paper primarily focused on teens and adults, US Surgeon General Vivek Murphy also warns of the deleterious impact of our existing "epidemic of loneliness and isolation" and details the healing effects of social connections and community.[2]

The significance of nurturing early relationships might appear self-evident, a truth that resonates intuitively with anyone who has embraced the role of parent or caregiver, or indeed anyone who has experienced childhood. Then why, one may wonder, write an entire book to explore this seemingly innate wisdom?

Because loving relationships are precisely what so many children are missing, with grave implications for them and for the world. Before the COVID-19 pandemic, one in five young learners in the US did not have a single caring adult in their life.[3] In 2020, 44 percent of high school youth reported having no source of supportive relationships—either adults or peers, a reduction by half from a decade earlier.[4] Astoundingly, at the height of the COVID-19 pandemic, eight in ten infants born at the New York-Presbyterian Morgan Stanley Children's Hospital did not exhibit a strong emotional connection with their mother, according to the COMBO study at Columbia University.[5] And the situation is getting worse.

The incidence of relational deprivation that starts early in life is rising. Kids are growing up in smaller families with fewer siblings, and in more single-parent households. They have fewer adult family friends and mentors. They have less contact with grandparents and other adult relatives. They spend 60 percent less face time with friends than children did a decade ago.[6] They play outside less—half as much as their parents' generation did.[7] They find themselves increasingly immersed in solitary realms of screens, a modern sanctuary where parents seek refuge as well. Teen loneliness has doubled over the past decade.[8] Many kids are overscheduled and too busy to build friendships, a consequence of a stronger focus on high achievement and a race to college that starts ever younger. Others experience chaotic childhoods, too often characterized by neglect.

The global COVID pandemic exacerbated these concerns. Young children are more isolated. They are experiencing more emotional distress and mental health issues. Families and educators are impacted as well. We now have evidence that the seclusion and anxiety wrought by the pandemic exacerbated speech delays in young children.[9] At the same time, Stanford researchers demonstrated that isolation and stress accelerated the maturation of teens' brains.[10] Until now, such accelerated changes in "brain age" had only been seen in children experiencing chronic adversity, such as neglect and family dysfunction. Only time will tell if these brain changes will endure and what their implications might be.

Not only is life expectancy regressing as a result of the pandemic's health toll, but human intelligence may be too. We have emerging evidence of a decline in human IQ for the first time in the one hundred years since the IQ test was invented—a significant change regardless of the fact that IQ is an imperfect view of human intelligence.[11] At the root of these issues is a seismic, growing, silent, and invisible early relational crisis with long-term insidious negative impact. Yet we rarely speak about this crisis, let alone call for solutions to it.

To reverse these effects, this book offers a bold vision: a future where learning is relational and love is a literacy. This vision involves a paradigm shift, a move away from what we've called child-centered education and toward relationship-centered learning, a shift in focus from bolstering

GPA and IQ to bolstering what I refer to as relational intelligence or RQ. And it requires us to focus not just on what we can do to nurture the babies of tomorrow but also on supporting school-aged children already affected by society's prioritization of academic achievement over relational competencies, children whose brains are still developing.

Relational intelligence can be defined as a human's ability to understand, navigate, and effectively interact with others in various social and interpersonal situations. It encompasses a set of skills and behaviors that enable individuals to build and maintain healthy relationships, experience and demonstrate empathy, communicate effectively, resolve conflicts, and show sensitivity to the needs and emotions of others. Relational intelligence plays a vital role in forming meaningful connections, fostering teamwork, and adapting to diverse social contexts, ultimately contributing to successful personal and professional interactions. At the core of relational intelligence is love—everyday micromoments of positive connections with others that foster feelings of joy, trust, and understanding; deepen social connections; promote overall well-being; and shape our biology and our ability to learn. Relational intelligence is closely related to social intelligence, a concept first introduced by American psychologist Edward Thorndike in 1920. Both social intelligence and relational intelligence involve understanding and interacting with others. Social intelligence is more about general social skills and navigating social environments, while relational intelligence focuses on building and maintaining deep, meaningful relationships.

After years of COVID-triggered social disruptions, school closures, isolation, and loneliness, parents and educators alike are noticing a decline in children's social skills and prosocial behaviors. Parents of school-aged children are worried that their children have become more socially awkward around others since the pandemic, and they want schools to incorporate activities that teach social skills. Educators are reporting a surge in social and behavioral concerns.[12] If you, like me, are a parent, you may have noticed some of these impacts on your children and worried about how you can help them practice or develop the skills they have had little opportunity to foster.

Some of you may think that this is all warm and fuzzy, unscientific and sentimental stuff. Yet relationships literally change the brain. Neuroscience shows that not only do children of nurturing caregivers have larger brains and better life outcomes; the opposite is true as well: children raised in neglect have smaller and less powerful brains. A child without a secure attachment is twice as likely to develop mental health issues. (A child is considered securely attached when they feel protected by their caregiver—whether parent, grandparent, nanny, early childcare provider, educator, or other primary caregiver—and can depend on them to return.) And timing matters. When parental nurturing starts later in a child's life, research suggests that the benefits in brain growth still exist but are reduced. I will detail the study findings in later pages. We will also see that it is the entire web of human relationships around a child that matters, not just parents.

I understand the impact of early relational support firsthand. Early childhood education changed the trajectory of my life. When I turned three, my parents received a devastating diagnosis, the kind most families never want to get. A psychology test revealed that I had low academic aptitude, suggesting limited school and career pathways. I was a late crawler, a late walker, a late talker, a late everything. This initial test led to batteries of other tests and recommendations for specialized interventions.

Fast-forward several years. I graduated as valedictorian of my high school and attended Harvard University. Even then, as an "at-risk" late bloomer, a product of below-average public schools in rural southern France, and a first-generation immigrant with a thick foreign accent, no one would have imagined I was destined to become a global financier, a pioneering impact investor, and an education thought leader.

I have often wondered how my life would have turned out under different familial and educational circumstances. How did I manage to flourish despite those early identified learning differences? What exactly did my parents and teachers do to help me thrive developmentally? Could I use that knowledge to help create a path for other children to learn and thrive? This question would guide my professional journey.

I have devoted my career to understanding, researching, and innovating to build a bright future of learning where each child thrives. As the executive director of the Stanford Accelerator for Learning, I lead a large initiative at Stanford University where I partner daily with research scholars, students, educators, and school and community leaders to leverage the latest advances in brain and learning sciences, data, and technology to create more effective and equitable learning solutions for all. Before that, I led the US education initiative with the Omidyar Group, the philanthropy of eBay founder Pierre Omidyar and his wife, Pam. There, I connected people, ideas, and resources to successfully deploy education initiatives that have yielded significant outcomes in early childhood education. I invested in and scaled organizations and ecosystem efforts now collectively delivering positive impact to millions of learners. Throughout those experiences, I had the privilege of meeting educators, families, and little learners in nearly every state in the US and many other countries. All these experiences helped me reach the conclusion that the secret recipe to learning and thriving starts with a simple key ingredient: early loving relationships. This is not to say that early loving relationships are the only ingredient in a complex and multifaceted learning journey. Many children are deeply loved and yet will experience lifelong learning differences and require specialized supports to thrive. Rather, I am seeking to emphasize how relationships are essential, yet too often taken for granted and not sufficiently elevated in our understanding of how to foster a child's curiosity, motivation to learn, and self-confidence.

For me, it all started at home, where as an infant I was cuddled in my parents' arms and enveloped by their affection. This period laid the foundation for the warm and loving relationship with my family I have forged over the years. Pictures from that time depict a happy, smiley, chubby *bébé*. In France, paid parental leave is guaranteed for moms (and since 2001 for dads as well). At the end of my mother's sixteen-week maternity leave, my parents sent me to childcare in a small, homelike setting, called a *crèche*. The crèche was in a house conveniently located next to where our family lived and where my parents worked. It had a garden outside where my little friends and I could enjoy the sunshine and play. As a shy, introverted, nonverbal child, I vividly remember the soothing voice of my first-ever childcare teacher, Mrs. Combes, as she read stories and sang lullabies. I would learn much later that this soothing effect is called bio-behavioral synchrony, which refers to the way in which our behavior and biology become synchronized with those of the people we interact with, an innate and critical human feature that helps us to build connections with others.

The test results on my developmental delays coincided with my transition from an enriching childcare environment to the commencement of my journey in a public preschool. In France, universal public education officially starts at age three with *maternelle* ("maternal care"), a preschool system for children ages three to six. In this inclusive setting, I blossomed. Was there a particular turning point? My early memories are vague, but I do recall a special moment at age five with my preschool teacher Mrs. Lenoir. She undoubtably taught me a lot—in science about butterfly formation and plant biology, in reading and number skills development, and in creative expression through arts and crafts. Most importantly, she believed in me—this shy little girl who was at risk of developmental delays—and gave me my first leadership opportunity.

As in most preschools, we celebrated the end of the year by putting on a show for families. The theme was Snow White and the Seven Dwarfs, and Mrs. Lenoir assigned me the starring role. I played Snow White, leading a group of little ones from younger classes who played the dwarfs. This experience of dressing up and embodying a major role was transformational in building my self-esteem. Even many years later, I can recall this moment of suddenly feeling *seen*. Mrs. Lenoir believed in me, which in turn helped me believe in myself. I never looked back, and I flourished from there. Whether the turning point was this particular moment or, more likely, a buildup of many special teaching instances, we will never know. What is certain is that Mrs. Lenoir had a profound positive impact on me.

I share this story to highlight the transformational power of early experiences, particularly relationships with adults, in a young child's journey. Over the years, I have heard countless stories like mine of how a family member, a teacher, a mentor, or a coach meaningfully impacted someone's trajectory. Next to immediate family, teachers have the most influence on people's lives as they grow up. In fact, a majority of Americans report that a teacher had a significant positive impact on their life.[13]

The human brain is wired with a sophisticated neural network that gives us extraordinary potential to communicate, memorize, think in an orderly manner, create, invent, imagine, feel with a large set of emotions, empathize, and relate to others. But at birth, our neural network is immature, and in many ways premature. Even full-term babies are born without a fully developed brain; 70 percent of our brain's growth happens postbirth.[14]

This immaturity at birth—which makes human babies highly vulnerable to impoverished and toxic environments and relationships, and completely dependent on others for survival—may be surprising relative to the maturity at birth of the brains of other mammals. Many other species can walk, graze, or hunt to feed themselves right after birth. Why, evolutionarily, wouldn't the human brain be fully developed in the safe and warm environment of a mother's womb instead of requiring a postpartum "fourth trimester," when brain development accelerates? Did Mother Nature lose her mind?

Certainly not. The prematurity of the brain is actually *necessary* for human development. Humans, unlike other mammals, are able to reason, imagine, and create. We are able to form larger social networks than other species. We are able to innovate, dream, and conceive new possibilities. We can act morally and ethically, and adapt to new environments and circumstances. All these abilities are rooted in the fact that we begin life with a brain that is not yet fully developed, and that instead grows in the context of our relationships with others—through observation, imitation, inference, and, most importantly, emotional connection. In turn, this feature is rooted in our origins as a hunter-gatherer species. Our survival—whatever culture we come from or inhabit, and regardless of our economic, social, or political views or circumstances—has long depended on human connections and groups. This is a trait of our species.

This fundamentally human neural plasticity in the early years of life is both an extraordinary opportunity and an astounding vulnerability. It is during our first few years that we build the foundations for intelligence and humanity, and the quality of those foundations depends on the quality of our relationships. The brain develops based on what it receives.

Our society has often framed its responsibility for the next generation in terms of K–12 education. We focus our policies and spend our taxpayer dollars on supporting an educational system, and argue over what schools should be, or what and how teachers should teach. But no change in policy, pedagogy, or curriculum can ever really change the game for our students if we don't address the root causes of their learning problems. What we need is a fundamental paradigm shift to focus our support on the early years, and more specifically on the relationships that nurture our little learners. A majority (58 percent) of all US children ages three through five are not fully healthy and ready to learn, according to the US government.[15] UNICEF reports that a majority of children globally do not have access to early childhood programs.[16] The health and learning readiness gaps that build up before age five fuel the achievement gaps in K–12 education.[17] Most young children who start behind are more likely to stay behind or fall further behind. And too many kids already start behind.[18]

In embarking on this paradigm shift, we must acknowledge that little learners develop in a variety of environments outside K–12 classrooms: at home, on the playground, at preschool, in childcare, and through circles of relationships with family, friends, mentors, coaches, teachers, neighbors, faith leaders, and others. Therefore, our vision for investing in relational intelligence as the bedrock for learning needs to be multipronged.

There are many challenges to transforming our approach, which I will address throughout this book. In spite of them, I am optimistic. In particular, I believe we are at the cusp of a societal redefinition of kinship that will permeate learning. Family structures are dramatically evolving. Intergenerational solidarity is on the rise. This involves the sharing of resources, experiences, and values across different age groups, fostering a sense of connection, empathy, and responsibility between older and younger generations that promotes well-being, social cohesion, and the transfer of wisdom and knowledge.

Working at Stanford University, I came to understand that we are in the midst of a major scientific and technological revolution. In many ways, our scientific understanding of how relationships drive human learning is still rudimentary. Yet major scientific breakthroughs over the past decades are rapidly expanding what we know. New research exploring mirror neurons, brain and biosynchrony, biomarkers, the biochemistry of love, and more—research that is powered by new technologies, big data, and artificial intelligence—increasingly informs our collective understanding of why and how our brains are wired to connect.

We all worry about the effects of technology in general, and social media and artificial intelligence in particular, on our children. But technology is also powering human connections. Public and private funding directed to endeavors and institutions that are devoted to young children is increasing, and there is a growing recognition of the importance of care, play, and social-emotional learning. The business world is recognizing emotional intelligence (EQ) and even the love quotient (LQ). Love quotient, a term first coined by Jack Ma, the billionaire founder of Alibaba, and described by Chris Wise, an expert in organizational leadership, refers to one's ability to be loving and kind to self and others.[19] Alongside EQ, LQ is increasingly considered to be as important as or more important than IQ. As artificial intelligence progressively impacts our world, our unique human ability to relate and connect with others—our relational intelligence, or RQ—needs to be elevated. Innovative approaches to relationship-centered learning and intergenerational approaches to parenting and teaching are emerging—and sometimes scaling.

Our new generation of the littlest learners—those born after 2015, many of whom have yet to be born—is unnamed. Some have called this group Generation Alpha, to restart on the alphabet sequence after Gen Y (Millennials) and Gen Z. Others have named it Generation Glass in light of their exposure to screen time starting at a young age. Others have suggested Gen C, with *C* standing for "COVID," given that most of these children lived a disproportionate share of their early lives during the pandemic or in a world fundamentally changed by it. Instead, I optimistically suggest we call the new generation Gen R, the Generation of Relationships, and aim to raise them in a world refocused on the value of loving connections. Just as we have the concepts of "zero emissions" and "zero waste" in respect to climate change, we should aim for "zero human-potential waste"—a world where every Gen R child learns through loving relationships, thrives, and reaches their full potential.

The time is ripe. Whether you are a parent or grandparent eagerly seeking guidance, an educator passionate about enhancing learning and inspiring students, a community leader, child advocate, or policymaker seeking solutions to intractable social problems, or simply a lover of knowledge and human potential, *Love to Learn* invites you to embark on a transformative journey. I hope that the stories of perseverance, empathy, and creativity woven throughout the book, which showcase innovations anchored in the latest neuroscience and technology, will provoke and encourage you to question how we raise our children, how we run early learning and school settings, and how we construct care-full communities. Together, let us deepen our understanding, ignite our collective imagination, and embrace the power of early relationships in nurturing a lifelong love of learning.

A few words about the organization of the book:

Part I makes the case that there is a relational crisis in early childhood and that it is an urgent, endemic issue. Chapter 1 dispels multiple deep-seated myths to explain the critical role of relationships in early childhood. Chapter 2 illuminates how the circles of children's relationships are shrinking. Chapter 3 highlights how these smaller social networks stunt children's potential. Chapter 4 turns to adults, squeezed and screened, who are physically present yet increasingly emotionally absent for our little learners.

Part II explores how scientific research on the impact of relationships on human thriving, and on the new technologies shaping our lives, is well ahead of our relational practices. Chapter 5 outlines the scientific advances in our understanding of how relationships fuel learning. Chapter 6 looks into the positive and negative implications of artificial intelligence for relational intelligence and bonding, while Chapter 7 addresses the problematic impact of tech on relationships. Chapter 8 ties it all together, making the case that love is the silver bullet in education—the heartbeat of life and learning—and that the future belongs to those with high relational intelligence.

Part III outlines hopeful innovations and potential solutions. Chapter 9 explores pioneering relationship-centered solutions for increasingly diverse families. Chapter 10 focuses on fostering children's friendships through play, time, wisdom, and care. Chapter 11 reframes schools as relational hubs and teachers as relational brain builders, and Chapter 12 imagines communities healing, weaving, and belonging.

Part IV does not exist yet. It is for you, me, and all of us to write. Like the fourth trimester for a newborn, it will, I hope, be a new period for the formation of neural connections, discoveries, and development in which we all work to create a bright future for our next generation.

I mention many organizations throughout the chapters. All of them are listed (with their websites) in the Resources section located in the back of the book.

As you read, I invite you to think about three key loving relationships in your life that made a difference in your learning, and to connect how they supported your learning journey to the ideas in this book. Who are the people who changed things for you, like Mrs. Combes and Mrs. Lenoir did for me? What did you learn from them? What made them so special to you? I also invite you to consider: Who is learning from you? How could the young children in your life learn more from you?

The twelve chapters of this book cover a lot of territory. You will join me in Silicon Valley, but also in Tangelo Park, Florida; Hawai'i; and Minnesota—as well as in Bedford Hills Correctional Facility, New York; in Walmart stores; and even in France, Japan, and Kenya. But we need to start our journey in Boston, at my alma mater Harvard, where a retail store tycoon had the foresight at the peak of the Great Depression to invest part of his wealth in studying what drives human flourishing.

PART I

THE EARLY CHILDHOOD RELATIONAL CRISIS

In order to develop normally, a child requires progressively more complex joint activity with one or more adults who have an irrational emotional relationship with the child. Someone's got to be crazy about that kid. That's number 1. First, last and always.

—Urie Bronfenbrenner, "What Do Families Do?"
Institute for American Values, 1991

CHAPTER 1

The Predictive Value
of Early Relationships

*Every child who winds up doing well has had at least one stable
and committed relationship with a supportive adult.*
—JACK SHONKOFF, NATIONAL SCIENTIFIC COUNCIL
ON THE DEVELOPING CHILD, 2015

*Relationships are to [child] development what location is to
real estate: We need relationship, relationship, relationship.*
—JAMES P. COMER, *CHILD BY CHILD:
THE COMER PROCESS FOR CHANGE IN EDUCATION*, 1999

In 1938, during the Great Depression, scientists began one of the longest and arguably most important longitudinal research projects ever undertaken. At a time of economic gloom, they appropriately wanted to understand what leads to a good life. The project was initially funded by a department store magnate, William T. Grant, who established his philanthropic foundation to study human well-being in 1936 with an inspiring mission statement still featured on his foundation's website: "What I have in mind is to assist, by some means, in helping people or peoples to live more contentedly and peacefully and well in body and mind through a better knowledge of how to use and enjoy all the good things that the world has to offer them."[1]

Named after its benefactor, the Grant Study tracked 268 men in hopes of uncovering secrets to leading healthy and happy lives. Harvard researchers picked a close-to-home cohort population: Harvard college students. Between 1939 and 1944, study participants, all undergraduates, underwent various interviews, questionnaires, and physical tests, providing a vast amount of data. The study would become known as the Harvard Study of Adult Development.[2] It tracked a wide range of metrics on the physical health, mental health, and education of the initial participants. However, as is often the case in longitudinal research, funding was discontinued after ten years. The study struggled. A group of researchers barely kept it alive by circulating occasional questionnaires until, in the 1960s, it caught the attention of a young psychiatrist named George Vaillant. He saw its potential. After all, one of those original participants had been President John F. Kennedy. Vaillant revitalized and expanded the study, and became its chief supporter and storyteller.

The initial cohort of study subjects was the opposite of diverse. Harvard was still an all-male institution (women would be added to the survey later), and socioeconomic and racial representation were nearly nonexistent in its student body. To mitigate those concerns, a second study was added in the 1970s enrolling 456 twelve- to sixteen-year-old boys from Boston's poorest and most troubled families. Today, few of the original participants of the first or second cohort are still alive; their children, or the second generation, are now being interviewed every two years.

The study has yielded surprising results. It is not money or fame that drives well-being. As it turns out, the key driver of human flourishing is close relationships. Social ties are a better predictor of a long and happy life than social class, IQ, or even genes—and this is true across socioeconomic, gender, and ethnic groups.

The current director of the study, Bob Waldinger, is a Zen priest and a professor of psychiatry at Harvard. He understands that while taking care of one's physical health is important, tending to relationships is a form of self-care as well. His 2015 TEDx talk, "What Makes a Good Life?," has been viewed by tens of millions and expanded into a book.[3] (When I met him during a conference at Stanford University, he shared that the talk had been recorded in a small location in Brookline, Massachusetts, and that he expected to get only a few thousand views.) His talk focuses on the following three points: First, *social connections* are essential for our overall well-being, and loneliness can have detrimental effects on our health, happiness, and lifespan. Second, the *quality* of those relationships, not only the quantity, matters. Individuals who have stronger social connections tend to be happier, be healthier, and live longer than those who have weaker connections. And third, strong relationships not only benefit our *physical health* but also protect our *cognitive health.*

Waldinger has reached another profound conclusion that the short TEDx talk did not touch on, which is that the quality of childhood relationships matters long into adulthood. Men who had "warm" childhood relationships with their mothers earned a lot more money on average than men whose mothers were uncaring. Conversely, men who had poor childhood relationships with their mothers were much more likely to develop dementia when old. And not only mothers matter. The warmth of childhood relationships with fathers correlates with lower rates of adult anxiety. George Vaillant, the study's originator, summed it up nicely: "Happiness is love. Full stop."[4]

Although this famous Harvard study is a national treasure, it also has serious limitations due to its initial sample. Do the conclusions expand to a broader set of children and families? What happens to children who have odds against them? Why do some succeed despite adversity? These are questions that few have studied as rigorously as developmental psychologist Emmy Werner, one of the more preeminent modern researchers of child resilience.

Werner was a child of war. Born into a Jewish family in Germany in 1929, she survived World War II in Europe and made the study of resilience the through line of her lifelong research. After immigrating to the United States, she started her work at the University of Minnesota Institute of Child Development, where she was hired to be an interviewer in a study of adolescent youth in southwestern Minnesota. At the time, the research results underscored the likelihood that if you were an adolescent experiencing adversity, you were going to continue to struggle as an adult. But Werner grew increasingly intrigued in studying the exceptions to this rule.

Werner paired with Ruth Smith, a licensed psychologist from Hawai'i. They began a longitudinal study observing all children born on the island of Kauai in 1955 (numbering 698) and followed them across thirty-two years.[5] They aimed to understand why some children are able to succeed despite facing adversity. Their findings have since transformed our understanding of resilience and the importance of relationships in learning and thriving.

The island of Kauai would have been a "most-wanted" destination for any three-decade research study, but it was a particularly ideal location for a longitudinal study. The island has a tight-knit community where people tend to stay put—the population is less mobile relative to that on the continental United States—making it possible to follow an entire birth cohort over its lifespan. Kauai is also ethnically diverse, comprised of both native Hawaiians and people whose families migrated to the island from the Philippines, China, Japan, and elsewhere beginning early in the nineteenth century.

As the study began tracking the multiracial cohort of children, Werner and Smith found that 30 percent of them either were born and raised in poverty; had experienced pre- or perinatal complications; lived in families troubled by chronic discord, divorce, or parental mental health issues; or were raised by mothers with less than eight years of education.

Among the children who encountered four or more of these risk factors by age two, approximately two-thirds went on to develop learning or behavioral issues by age ten and had records of delinquency and/or mental health concerns by age eighteen. Astonishingly, though, Werner and Smith found that the other third of children exposed to these risk factors managed to do well. These individuals were referred to as the "vulnerable but invincible." By the time they reached their thirties, none of them faced unemployment, legal issues, or dependence on social services. They exhibited substantially lower divorce rates, mortality rates, and instances of chronic health problems in comparison to individuals of the same gender who grew up in more economically stable and secure households. Furthermore, their educational and career achievements were on par with, or even surpassed, those of children raised in more financially stable and consistent family environments.

How did these people thrive in spite of their early circumstances? Although surrounded by potentially debilitating "risk factors," the part of the cohort that showed the most resilience had access to buffering elements that Werner and Smith called "protective factors."

One protective factor in particular was found to be determinative. Resilient children invariably had at least one supportive relationship. For many of the children in the Kauai study, it was the presence of at least one caring, committed adult— someone who provided the anchor that helped them weather life's adversities and taught them how to survive and thrive—that made the difference. Interestingly, the study also showed that this adult did not need to be a parent. It could be a different family member—an aunt, a grandparent—or another adult in the community: a teacher, coach, faith leader, or mentor.

While Werner and Smith showed that relationships matter throughout the lifespan, their findings, like those of the Harvard Study of Adult Development, highlighted the importance of a child developing trust in adults during the early years. But although these discoveries have been celebrated in the research community and are known to many professionals in the fields of social work, mental health, and education, our society has failed to acknowledge in policy and practice the degree to which social interaction influences learning. Why have we largely ignored these findings? I have spent the past decade investigating this question. And what I found can be distilled into five core reasons, each a myth that has survived for too long:

1. Learning starts in kindergarten.
2. People learn and succeed on their own.
3. Kids naturally bounce back.
4. Intelligence—and potential—is fixed.
5. Too much love spoils babies.

These myths have clouded our vision when it comes to nurturing our youngest learners. They are rooted in a mass education system born out of the Industrial Revolution and a traditional view of women's societal role as caregivers. They also result from a major gap between scientific progress over the past few decades highlighting the importance of the early years and the inadequate investments we make in supporting children and their families in the early years. They serve as rationalizations for a lack of political will to prioritize our youngest. If we now know that 90 percent of brain growth happens in the first five years, why are we investing less than 1 percent of our gross domestic product in those early years?[6]

Let's unpack these myths one at a time.

GRAPH 1

Disconnect Between Early Brain Development and Public Funding
Why Underfunding Before Age 5 Undermines Lifelong Potential

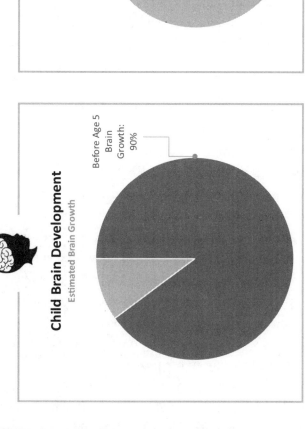

Child Brain Development
Estimated Brain Growth

Before Age 5 Brain Growth: 90%

Public Funding
Percentage of GDP Spending

Before Age 5 Early Care and Education: < 1% GDP

Sources:

- Brown, T. T., and Jernigan, T. L.,. "Brain Development During the Preschool Years." *Neuropsychology Review* 22, no. 4 (2012): 313–333. https://link.springer.com/article/10.1007/s11065-012-9214-1.
- 2022 GDP spending on public education: early care and education: 0.4% GDP; K–12: 3.5% GDP; postsecondary education 2.5% GDP. Institute of Education Sciences, *Report on the Condition of Education 2022*, https://nces.ed.gov/pubs2022/2022144.pdf.

Myth 1: Learning Starts in Kindergarten

Like most new parents, Teresa Hunter of Virginia Beach, Virginia, knew there was a lot she didn't know about how to care for a baby. One perplexing question for her was: What kind of conversation was she supposed to have with her two-month-old? Even though her baby didn't speak yet, was she already supposed to help her baby learn? If so, how should she talk to her little one, and how much?

The parenting class Hunter joined was offered by LENA (Language Environment Analysis), a nonprofit organization "on a mission to transform children's futures through early talk technology and data-driven programs."[7] LENA encouraged Hunter to talk and read to her baby. The instructor gave her a "talk pedometer," a device that would count both the number of words Hunter spoke in her child's presence and the number of conversational interactions between them. The device is like a Fitbit for child language. Just as a Fitbit recommends ten thousand steps per day and tracks them, the talk pedometer encourages caregivers to strive for the benchmark of forty conversational turns per hour, then counts and reports the number of child-parent verbal exchanges.[8] "At first it was weird," Hunter tells me, with a laugh.

Teresa Hunter and her husband, Isaiah, were some of the first participants in the Virginia Beach LENA class. Their daughter, Ivy, now five, was just a few months old at the time. "We didn't really know what we were doing," she shares, and when her home visitation nurse told her about the program, she was intrigued, because it gave parents "the power to increase our babies' brain development." Parents pick one day a week to record at home using the talk pedometer, and they get back a report showing how their level of conversation compares to that of other families with a child in their age group. The Hunters were able to observe Ivy's language learning progress, as well as to connect their own parenting behavior to her progress.

Studies show a correlation between how much adults speak to a young child and the child's higher IQ later in adolescence.[9] But we are naturally poor estimators of how much we talk to our kids. Most of us tend to overestimate. In fact, those of us who talk the least tend to over-estimate the most.[10] The millions of parents without a Fitbit-like device may not know how much they speak, whether their child is learning, or how to interact as a parent.

The learning process that happens in the brain is not directly visible, touchable, or even audible. In the absence of immediate feedback about how learning happens, and despite scientific evidence suggesting otherwise, we continue to operate as if children start learning when they go to school—meaning in kindergarten for most children—and to treat the early years as if they were an inconsequential or foreordained phase of human development. The myth that society has no role to play in a child's development before kindergarten, and our underinvestment in the early years, undervalues the critical role early learning plays in shaping long-term outcomes.

While many of us who are parents or grandparents have a general understanding that what happens in a child's early years can last a lifetime, we don't always appreciate at what age babies and toddlers can begin to feel complex emotions. Many parents don't realize how deeply children can be affected by the way parents interact with them in the first months of life. In a national survey looking at parents' knowledge of early childhood development, nearly two-thirds of parents indicated an understanding that a child's brain develops most rapidly during the first three years of life. Yet more than a third said the time of most rapid brain growth is at ages three to five years, a significant underestimation of the importance of the earliest years. When asked at what age the quality of a parent's care begins to have long-term impact on a child's development, a majority of parents said six months or older, when in fact it starts at birth, and the evidence is mounting that the prenatal period is also foundational. A third of parents believe that talking to children starts to benefit their language skills when they are a year old or later, when in fact it begins at birth, if not in the womb.[11]

Parents aren't the only people underestimating the time frames for impacting children's development. When most of us think of early childhood education, we think of babysitting and daycare: a place where a child is clean, safe, and fed. The language we use colloquially reflects the way we think about early learning—or at least reinforces its low priority as a matter of public policy. We call early learning environments "daycare" and "childcare" as opposed to "learning centers," and those educating our little learners "babysitters" or "nannies" as opposed to "teachers," "educators," "childminders" (a UK term), or "relational brain builders." We refer to "preschools" as if learning environments for children under age five were not schools. Our childcare educators are in the bottom 2 percent of the compensation scale—paid less well than dog walkers and baristas.[12] I often hear this question either explicitly or sometimes implicitly: Why should we train or compensate our early educators well if their work involves changing diapers and watching babies nap? Historically, caregiving and education roles, especially in the early childhood sector, have been undervalued and associated with "women's work." This appraisal has also contributed to the lower perceived value of early childhood education and professional caregiving.

This myth that children start learning in school could not be further from the truth. Not only do we start learning *early*; we learn *the most* in the early years. We are all born billionaires; an infant is born with a treasure chest of a hundred billion neurons. This is about the same as the number of stars in the Milky Way. It is not, however, the number of neurons but the neural connections between them that distinguish a young child's brain from that of a teen or an adult. Synapses, the sites of communication between neurons, undergo dynamic processes of construction, reinforcement, weakening, and pruning, with three particularly active periods in our human lives: the early years, adolescence, and parenthood (yes, our brains change when we become parents; we will come back to that). Synapses facilitate the transmission of information and drive memory and learning. At birth, we can count a few synapses. Postbirth, the process of making connections meaningfully accelerates. Within the first three years, the rate of synapse formation increases to over one million neural connections per second.

The possibilities of associations between those billions of neurons are nearly infinite. People's young brains are highly malleable, a state called brain plasticity or neuroplasticity. The shaping of our brains is powered by human interactions. "Serve and return" relationships during the early years of life are thus foundational for brain development and learning. The term "serve and return" was promoted by Jack Shonkoff at the Harvard Center on the Developing Child to express the tennis-like back-and-forth exchanges between a child and an adult caregiver. For Shonkoff, serve and return interactions are "critical because the brain is wired to expect this kind of back-and-forth interaction. It's really the way the brain builds its circuits, the way the brain develops the capacity for different skills."[13] These nurturing exchanges between adult and child have a positive impact on a child's intelligence and are highly predictive of future academic success.[14] As a child grows, the brain eliminates excess neural connections in a process known as synaptic pruning, which boosts cognitive efficiency and adaptability, particularly during adolescence and early adulthood.

Now that Ivy is five years old, Hunter tells me, she has a strong grasp of language skills and regularly engages in conversation at an impressive level. "If you want to know about LENA, just look at my baby," Hunter says. "She talks about things you wouldn't think she'd know at this age." A child like Ivy, who has been actively engaged in conversations with caregivers since before age five and enters kindergarten ready for school, has an 82 percent chance to master basic skills by age eleven, whereas the odds drop to approximately 45 percent for a child who is not kindergarten ready.[15] The quality of learning in early childhood is linked to outcomes in areas including high school completion, college graduation, employment, health, and even stable romantic relationships in adulthood.[16]

Language is a uniquely human and crucial competency, and the need to develop it is one obvious reason why starting early matters in a child's learning journey. As a nonnative English speaker, I have long been fascinated by the process of language acquisition. How does a child learn a language? What is the optimal period to learn it? How many languages can a child learn without confusion? I have come to understand the "double seven" rule of thumb: before age seven is the ideal time to start learning a language to ever become fluent, and a child has the ability to learn at least seven languages at once without confusion.[17] (By the way, we don't really know the upper limit on the number of languages a child can speak. A few legendary people are hyperpolyglots—people who speak more than a hundred languages.)

My children are being raised in a trilingual environment where they speak English, French, and Mandarin. My kids have turned into natural polyglots, switching back and forth with a perfect accent from one language to another. Their facility with languages has involved minimal effort or talent on their parents' part. Dad speaks Mandarin and Mom speaks French. We both speak English. And my kids are not special. More than half the children on this planet speak more than one language on any given day. I recall an experience early on with my eldest daughter. She was twelve months of age and had mastered only a few words. She had just finished a bowl of grapes and wanted more. She suddenly oscillated between the three languages, successively trying the word "grape" in English, *raisin* in French, and *putao* in Chinese, optimizing for whichever language might result in her desired outcome. She had absorbed the concept that different human beings speak different languages, and that those different words represented the same object. A couple of years later, at age three, she came to me one day and, with her most serious look and in an authoritative tone, declared, "Mom, your English is not very good." She was referring to my strong accent when I speak English, one that I've never lost after nearly twenty-five years living and working in the US.

How can my children be perfectly multilingual when I, as an adult, still struggle to enunciate simple words in English such as "three" or "free," or any word containing *th-* for that matter? Well, our brains have "windows" or "sensitive periods" when our neural systems are more sensitive to new competency and skill acquisition. Many of those windows open early in life, and development within those time periods is catalyzed by social connections.

Pat Kuhl, a linguistics expert and professor at the University of Washington, has long been studying this matter, through brain scans and other experiments. In her 2010 TEDx talk, "The Linguistic Genius of Babies," Kuhl explains that babies learn a language by listening to the humans around them and "taking statistics" on the sounds they need to know.[18] Brain scans show how six-month-old babies use sophisticated reasoning to understand their world. Babies under eight months of age from different cultures can detect sounds in any language from around the world, but adults cannot. Kuhl has even shown that babies' abilities to discriminate phonemes as early as seven months old is a predictor of future reading skills for that child at age five.[19] Kuhl also highlights that after age seven, our prowess in learning a language starts declining and continues to decrease significantly with every two to three years of age.[20] After puberty and certainly in adulthood, as I experienced, it becomes more challenging to acquire language fluency. We clearly have an optimal window within which to learn languages, and this window is early in life.

Kuhl ran a fascinating experiment with nine-month-old babies from English-speaking families across two groups.[21] One group of English-raised infants spent the sessions with a native Mandarin Chinese speaker who sang, played, and spoke to them. The other group did the same activities in English only. After twelve sessions, the researchers measured how well the English-raised babies could distinguish Mandarin Chinese sounds. The American babies who had spent time with the caregiver who spoke Mandarin had basically become native listeners, able to recognize as many sounds as infants who were raised in Mandarin-speaking environments. Kuhl then ran a second pair of experiments in which a native speaker of Mandarin employed the same songs, activities, and chatter, but did so virtually, on a screen. Babies in the screen group did not make progress. Kuhl's findings show that infants are highly social learners—they learn by being connected to people. Face-to-face interactions engage the social brain, which is crucial for helping children learn to communicate in their native and non-native languages. Language learning is not just a technical skill, but a special gift that is passed down through social interactions.

In a similar vein, an experiment conducted at the Max Planck Institute for Human Cognitive and Brain Sciences, in Leipzig, tracked brain activity in babies and showed that starting at four months of age and in less than fifteen minutes of listening, babies are able to know if a sentence from any language is syntactically correct.[22] The researchers also showed that language acquisition is highly dependent on the caregiver's mood and intonation. A more positive caregiver tone at two months postpartum fosters advanced development in speech sound processing by the time the infant reaches six months.[23] Positive loving interactions accelerate skill acquisition in children.

We start learning early and through others. This is true not only for language acquisition; it also applies to early math skills. Did you know that newborns even in their early hours postbirth already possess an approximative sense of numbers? This seems hard to believe, doesn't it? But researchers had babies—all younger than *five days old*—listen to identical sound suites, composed of either four sounds ("tuuu tuuu tuuu tuuu" or "ra-ra-ra-ra") or twelve sounds. The infants were then placed in front of images with four or twelve points each. To the greatest surprise of the researchers, fifteen out of sixteen babies focused longer on images containing the same number of sounds they had heard. This experience suggests that newborns are able to detect quantities, both orally and visually. And against most expectations, they are able to connect the visual and auditive information received.[24]

Preschool-aged children have demonstrated even greater arithmetic capabilities, based on innate numeration intuition. When asked,

"Sarah has 21 candies and gets 30 more. John has 34 candies. Who has more?" most five-year-old children are able to provide a correct answer, even though they have not yet learned the mathematical concepts.[25] Maybe their skill is related to the fact that the question involves candies? But I digress.

As is the case for language, social interactions also seem to accelerate early math abilities. For example, when parents of first graders engage with stories containing math concepts using an app called Bedtime Math even one night a week, children's math skills improve markedly compared with the skills of their peers who listen to non-mathematical stories.[26] The effect of this parent-child interaction is sizable: over the course of one nine-month school year, little learners gain on average the equivalent of a three-month advantage over their peers, with impact lasting four years and beyond.[27] Little ones also seem to learn more math when they interact with peers. In New York City, as part of the High 5s program, over six hundred five-year-olds in twenty-four low-income schools met for thirty minutes three times a week in "math clubs."[28] Fun, engaging, interactive, and developmentally appropriate activities in groups yielded meaningful improvement in math relative to traditional instruction.[29]

Acquisition of reading skills operates on a different timetable and according to a different logic than acquisition of language or early math. Why? Because literacy is too recent an invention, and nothing in our human brains is wired for reading. Our species' evolution is still catching up to this five-thousand-year-old innovation. As a result, technically, there is not an optimal age for learning how to read. However, it is generally recommended for parents and caregivers to start reading books with little ones early and often, given the complexity of the process for our brain's circuitry to make connections between visual and language patterns. Learners below age three who have conversations with adults learn to read more easily.[30]

What does this all mean for you and me? The science is clear. Our brains grow faster in the first three to five years after birth than at any other later point. Each baby's potential is vast. The window of time to provide a child with the foundation for success is not. We have sensitive periods for learning that open in our brains in a generally invariable, preset order, for both language and math skills. Hearing and vision develop very early, then motor skills, then language. Sensory pathways such as hearing, language, and higher cognitive function all peak within the first few years of life. Many of those windows open early, well before kindergarten, when brain plasticity is greatest, and close with age, though never fully. Learning continues throughout life. While our brains have a genetically preconstructed plan, the synaptic connections that drive learning during those windows meaningfully depend on relationships. In other terms, *when* we learn matters, and *how* we learn—especially with whom—does too. It all begins, and intensely, well before kindergarten.

Myth 2: People Learn and Succeed on Their Own

In the northern Indian jungle of Uttar Pradesh in 1872, a band of hunters suddenly halted in their tracks, utterly perplexed by an astonishing sight. In front of them, a group of wolves gracefully traversed the forest terrain, with an ethereal figure trailing behind them: a young child, meandering on all fours. The pack vanished into an adjacent cave. The hunters ignited a fire at the entrance, using smoke to coax the wolves out. The hunters killed the wolves and rescued the boy.

The remarkable case of Dina Sanichar, a six-year-old who purportedly had been nurtured by wolves, constitutes just one of the rare stories involving feral children discovered over the years in India and beyond. Sanichar's story as the "wolf boy" would inspire *The Jungle Book*. Cases of feral children have ranged from those raised by wolves to those nurtured by dogs, bears, or even goats. While their tales have been mythologized in both Eastern and Western cultures, the actualities of their lives unfolded as heart-wrenching narratives of neglect and profound isolation. Their reintegration into "civilized" society raises uncomfortable questions about human development, our connection to the wilderness, and the fundamental attributes that define our humanity. They are also profound illustrations that learning is a social endeavor.

When Sanichar was found, he had spent the first few years of life thinking he was a wolf, walking on all fours, grunting or howling to communicate, and eating raw meat. He was taken to an orphanage, where he lived among other humans for over thirty years. He eventually managed to dress himself, walk upright, and eat (sometimes) like a human. Tragically, he remained nonverbal throughout his life and succumbed to tuberculosis at the young age of thirty-five. He lived a life marked by significant developmental delays, dependent on the care of others. Cases of feral children like Sanichar are extremely rare. They are evidence that children adapt to their environments and that human social relationships are critical for learning and social functioning, contrary to the myth that we learn by ourselves.

The myth is strong. A simple Google image search for "learning" yields pictures of individual learners sitting by themselves at desks. Our education systems, anchored in this myth, are for the most part built around individual success: individual tests and scores, individual desks, individual pedagogy. We refer to "personalized learning" and underplay, rarely assess, or ignore altogether the value of collaboration and relationships in learning, and the well-established fact that we learn through others.

In fact, our human species—starting with newborns—is wired for relationships. From the moment of birth, infants exhibit a natural predisposition to connect with those around them through a range of behaviors and responses, such as seeking eye contact, responding to touch, and displaying signs of comfort in the presence of familiar caregivers. The newborn's ability to form and engage in relationships serves as a foundational element for emotional and social development, highlighting the significance of these early connections in shaping their learning and overall well-being. Fourteen-month-olds will make an effort to retrieve an object for someone who is struggling to reach it independently. Toddlers will demonstrate acts of kindness such as voluntarily giving their blanket to someone who is cold or sharing a favorite toy with someone who is sad. Eighteen-month-olds who view a series of photographs featuring dolls facing each other in the background are three times more inclined to exhibit helpful behaviors compared with children who see images where the dolls are standing alone or back to back. The interest in human connections appears to be innate and is a major driver for learning. Neuroscientists have employed functional magnetic resonance imaging (fMRI) to delve deeper into the workings of our brain in a social context. They discovered that our brains operate using two separate networks for social and nonsocial thinking. The specific network lights up according to the nature of the task—social or nonsocial. Intriguingly, the social brain network swiftly reactivates, almost reflexively, once we stop performing a nonsocial activity.[31] Our brains' default mode is social, and we thrive on relational intelligence. Learning depends on much more than our own brain cells and biology, or even our own choices and actions. It depends quite literally on the biology, choices, and actions of those around us.

In the year 1211, King Frederick II of Sicily conducted an experiment to determine which language children would *naturally* learn. He believed the options were Hebrew, Greek, Latin, or Arabic, and that the "language of God" would naturally emerge. To carry out the experiment, he ordered that newborn babies be taken from their mothers and placed under the care of nurses who were instructed not to speak in their presence or touch them. Unfortunately, the experiment was abruptly terminated, and we will never truly know the outcome on language acquisition, because all the babies died. Salimbene di Adam, an Italian historian who was an opponent of Frederick's, recorded the tragic outcome, observing that the babies perished because they could not survive without physical affection.

We humans flourish under the influence of love and relationships. Yet one in seven children in the US experiences abuse.[32] Globally, nearly three in four children—or three hundred million children—aged two to four years regularly suffer physical punishment and/or psychological violence from parents and caregivers.[33] More than three out of four cases of abuse are related to neglect.[34] Neglect is corrosive for child development. A Stanford study found that 85 percent of children in rural China exhibit at least one cognitive or socioemotional delay. This is largely due to many parents leaving their children behind with grandparents or family members to work in urban centers, often resulting in a lack of nurturing interactions.[35] To be clear, we still do not precisely know the extent to which deprivation impacts learning and growth.

Deprivation and adversity are challenging to study. Whereas many studies on relational deprivation—some controversial—have been conducted on rodents and monkeys, there has been far less human research, especially larger studies spanning decades. However, a unique historical circumstance provided a rare opportunity for landmark research on the effects of relational deprivation at scale: the Cold War–era Romanian orphanages.

When dictator Nicolae Ceaușescu came to power in Romania in 1967, he had a grand vision for the country. Applying Stalin's theory that population growth would drive economic growth, he implemented strict laws and policing measures against contraception and abortion. The birth rate quickly increased. However, economic growth did not follow. Poverty drove many parents to abandon their children to state-sponsored orphanages. The exact number of children raised in orphanages is not known. Conservative estimates put it at one hundred thousand, and recent estimates at five hundred thousand or more.

At the entrances of those institutions, posters showed mothers bringing their babies to the orphanages and years later holding hands with their happy older children. The message was clear: the state can care for children better than parents. But the orphanages were seriously underfunded. Children were malnourished, had little social contact,

received insufficient care and stimulation, and were frequently sub-
jected to abuse. After Ceaușescu was assassinated in 1989 and Eastern
European countries started opening back up to foreigners, the awful
conditions in Romania's orphanages were exposed.

The British journalist Bob Graham, who was in Romania two
weeks after the assassination of its dictator, was among the first to cover
the situation.[36] Upon entering an orphanage, he encountered the over-
powering, acrid, and fetid odor of urine. He was also met with a disturbing silence, not the joyful noise of children at play that one might
expect to witness at a playground or in a preschool classroom. The
children in the orphanages had been profoundly deprived of affection,
stimulation, and nurturing, and their silence spoke volumes about the
price they'd paid.

After conditions in the orphanages were exposed, some lucky
Romanian orphans were adopted. Adoption remained relatively rare,
however, and most children remained in orphanages that continued
to operate. Researchers compared children who were adopted with
children left in the orphanages, seeking answers to some fundamental
questions: How much and when do nurture and attachment matter?
What are the effects of adversity and relational deprivation? Can a child
recover from the experience of adversity and relational deprivation?

Scientists studied brain scans of all the children who had experienced deprivation in the Romanian orphanages. The scans clearly
showed smaller brains in the children who had stayed longer in the
orphanages—on average, they were nearly 10 percent smaller than the
brains of those who had been adopted.[37] Research also showed that children had lower IQs and higher rates of attention deficit hyperactivity
disorder (ADHD) as a result of early deprivation.[38] The smaller brains
had less power: brain scan measurements showed less brain activity in
response to electrical impulses. Strikingly, each additional month of
deprivation was linked to a smaller brain. The area of the brain that con-
trols emotional regulation was particularly impacted: 13 percent of children displayed no attachment behaviors with adult caregivers.[39]

Poor nutrition did not appear to entirely explain the differences. Professor Edmund Sonuga-Barke, lead researcher in the twenty-year English and Romanian Adoptee Project, when comparing the children adopted by families in the UK with children left in Romania, reported, "We are fairly confident that there are psychological routes to these effects as well, linked to lack of stimulation, lack of social interaction, and the lack of attachment and bonding."[40]

To address the question of whether children can recover from adversity and deprivation, researchers compared adopted children with the group who stayed in the orphanages on cognitive, linguistic, motor, and socioemotional skills, tracking the two groups over time in the Bucharest Early Intervention Project.[41] The children who had received little human contact experienced delays in all four areas. The ones who had been adopted fared better, especially if they had left the orphanage before the age of two. They eventually exhibited characteristics relatively similar to those of their peers, demonstrating that adversity can largely be overcome, especially if interventions occur very early.[42] The conclusion is simple yet profound: nurturing relationships matter, and the earlier they occur, the better.

Those studies of orphanages are interesting but extreme. What do we know about the impact of love and relationships on children who have lived more typical childhoods? What if we knew that a child can literally double the growth of its brain size through nurturing? Well, this is precisely what a group of researchers scientifically demonstrated in 2016.

In a series of studies examining brain scans of children, Joan Luby, a child psychiatrist at Washington University and St. Louis Children's Hospital, and her colleague Deanna Barch, a psychologist and chair of the Department of Psychological and Brain Sciences at Washington University, measured the growth of the hippocampus—the area in the brain critical to learning, memory, and regulating emotions—in preschool children, relative to the extent of maternal nurturing the children received.[43] The researchers were able to assess maternal nurturing by closely observing and scoring videotaped interactions between mothers and their children. The study simulated a moderately stressful condition, similar to the kind that happens frequently in any family. Researchers asked the mother to complete a task while giving the child an attractive gift to open but not allowing it to be opened right away. Parents who were able to complete the task while showing emotional support to their children were rated as more nurturing. Those who dismissed their children or behaved in punitive ways during the test received lower scores for support.

In the first study, children's brain scans showed a direct linkage between parental nurturing and a larger hippocampus.[44] The researchers found that even small differences in parental support led to significant differences in outcomes. Brain scans of children whose parents were more supportive revealed growth in the hippocampus more than twice that of children whose parents were slightly below average on the nurturing scale. Simply put, early love helps grow more powerful brains. The point here is not to imply that parents must be flawless or always offer undivided attention. What pediatrician and psychoanalyst Donald Winnicott described as essential, "good enough parenting" involves a parent providing nurturing care while prioritizing their own emotional health and creating a structure for their family. It is important to recognize that early nurturing is influenced by a complex interplay of societal, economic, and cultural factors. Many parents, especially mothers, face significant challenges balancing work and caregiving responsibilities. It is crucial to address the systemic issues that limit parents' ability to provide constant nurturing interactions, such as lack of parental support policies, insufficient childcare options, and economic disparities.

In a subsequent study, Luby and Barch examined the connection between brain growth and nurturing over a longer time frame by tracking a group of 127 children whose brains were scanned three times, beginning when they first started preschool and going through early adolescence.[45] They were seeking insight into two important questions:

Does it matter *when* the nurturing happens in a child's life trajectory? And is the positive impact of nurturing observed initially in preschool sustained over time?

They found more evidence that early relationships matter for brain development. The hippocampus was larger in adolescents whose mothers had supported and nurtured them during the preschool years, while the hippocampus appeared smaller in adolescents whose mothers had been less supportive during the preschool period, even if their mothers became more supportive in elementary or middle school. This suggests that there is a sensitive period in the early years when the brain is more responsive to parental support, and that the positive effects of early nurturing on the brain have long-lasting benefits. Nurturing during the preschool years was associated with better emotional functioning in adolescence, and if the nurturing began later in childhood, it did not have the same positive impact. These studies emphasize the crucial role of early loving relationships in shaping aspects of brain development that impact how children learn and mature.

While this particular study from Luby and Barch was mostly conducted with mothers, other caregivers are essential too, and so are peers. Fathers and infants can be just as attached as mothers and infants. A father's involvement is related to positive health outcomes, such as improved weight gain in preterm infants and improved breast-feeding rates. Children with actively involved fathers are nearly 50 percent more likely to earn A's in school.[46] Children who feel a closeness to their father are twice as likely to enter college or find stable employment after high school. As with mothers, the quality of the father-child relationship matters more than the specific quantity of hours spent together.

Similarly, accumulating evidence indicates that actively involved grandparents are associated with improved outcomes for children across various domains, including academic performance, social skills, behavior, and physical health.[47] And there's an extra benefit: grandparents live longer if they play with their grandchildren![48]

It is not only a child's direct interactions with adults that matter: infants have been shown to perform tasks better when in the presence of another baby, and studies with school-aged children suggest that learning is improved by the mere presence of another person, or even by the perception that another person is present.[49] For instance, children's comprehension of the TV show *Sesame Street* is enhanced when an adult is merely nearby.[50] Let's return to Pat Kuhl's language experiments. After she concluded that screens were not an effective way for young children to learn a language, she went on to study why.[51] She employed the same Mandarin-language videos as those she had used in earlier passive-learning experiments, but used them within an active-learning environment that granted infants control over video presentations through a touch screen. Each touch on the screen triggered a twenty-second clip featuring the Mandarin speaker discussing toys and books. Kuhl also randomly assigned infants to either an individual learning condition or a paired learning condition. She found that babies who were in the presence of another baby learned more and vocalized more. And the more babies a baby was exposed to, the more they learned.

Relationships are also a determinative factor in school and in parent-teacher and community-school contexts. At the outset of the 1990s, Alexander Elementary School and Hancock Elementary School shared the (sad) distinction of being among the lowest-performing schools in Chicago in math and reading proficiency. Situated two miles apart, the schools were located in neighboring communities and catered to student bodies composed almost entirely of Black students from economically disadvantaged backgrounds. Throughout the next decade, both institutions undertook a range of initiatives with the objective of enhancing student achievement. Remarkably, Hancock made significant strides, whereas Alexander made only marginal progress. Why was Hancock able to defy the odds while Alexander still struggled? Researchers found that relational trust was an important driver.

To increase relational trust, administrators at Hancock implemented several strategies, including collaborative decision-making involving teachers, administrators, and parents, which fostered mutual respect. They emphasized professional development to improve communication skills, and actively engaged parents and the community through regular meetings and volunteer opportunities. Consistent and transparent communication kept all stakeholders informed, while efforts to create a positive school culture through recognition and constructive conflict resolution further strengthened trust. These initiatives collectively enhanced the school's climate and contributed to improved academic performance. Chicago schools with strong family-community-school engagement were found to be ten times more likely to improve academically.[52]

In a similar vein, the Comer School Development Program began in 1968 at two of the lowest-income and lowest-achieving elementary schools in New Haven, Connecticut (the schools were ranked number thirty-two and thirty-three out of thirty-three). Child psychiatrist James Comer, along with colleagues from the Yale Child Study Center, collaborated with these schools, which eventually rose to rival the highest-income schools in the city, boasting the best attendance records and no serious behavior problems.[53] The Comer program encompasses both academics and social-emotional development, and is founded on positive and productive relationships among students, teachers, school leaders, parents, and the community. After more than fifty years, the Comer program, deeply rooted in fostering relational intelligence, remains one of the exemplary school models in the US and globally.

The myth that learning is a solitary endeavor is deeply anchored in individualism. Traditional classroom settings, where students are seated individually and expected to complete tasks independently, have reinforced the idea that learning is a personal journey. Assessments that emphasize individual performance, such as standardized tests and exams, have further promoted the notion that success is contingent on individual effort and understanding, and the rise of self-paced technology and online learning platforms has bolstered that perception. But evidence of the vital impact of collaboration and social interactions in the learning process challenges this traditional perspective. What would happen if schools and learning environments embraced collaboration, social interactions, and relationships, and parents and educators were supported to become relational brain builders?

Myth 3: Kids Naturally Bounce Back

Pop quiz. As a parent, I have wrestled with a simple practical question: From a learning perspective, when in a child's life is it optimal for a family to move?

(a) Birth to five
(b) Elementary school
(c) Middle school
(d) High school

Most of us answer birth to five, before kindergarten starts, on the assumption that young children are naturally resilient and that the middle school and high school years are critical for academic achievement. But the correct answer is not (a). In fact, relocating during those vulnerable early years has the greatest negative impact on children's odds of graduating from high school.[54]

This simple study about moving underscores the fact that the early years are a highly sensitive period. In fact, children are not born resilient. They are *made* resilient. They become resilient through relationships.

Other studies have demonstrated that, contrary to the myth, younger children are *more* vulnerable and sensitive to trauma exposure, not naturally more resilient. A group of researchers led by Erin Dunn, a social and psychiatric epidemiologist with expertise in genetics and epigenetics at Massachusetts General Hospital, found that people exposed to trauma before age five had depression or PTSD symptoms up to twice as often as those exposed to similar tragedies at later ages.[55] Similarly, after Hurricane Katrina, children in the fourth through sixth grades in New Orleans were nearly three times more likely to be referred for mental health services than students in the ninth through twelfth grades.[56]

Recent research by Bruce Perry, professor in the Department of Psychiatry and Behavioral Sciences at the Feinberg School of Medicine at Northwestern University in Chicago, highlights how critical the very first months of life are in terms of establishing a child's resilience to stress and adversity—and for their ability to build healthy relationships as they grow. According to Perry's research, "if, in the first two months of life, a child experienced high adversity with minimal relational buffering but was then put into a healthier environment for the next twelve years, their outcomes were worse than the outcomes of children who had low adversity and healthy relational connection in the first two months but then spent the next twelve years with high adversity."[57] Heightened stress during the early months of life can lead to long-term stress responses and trauma-related problems, even when the child is no longer in a high-risk environment.

Given all this evidence, where does the notion of the naturally resilient child originate? First of all, we often fail to see the impact of stress and adversity when it is present. Children have yet to learn how to process complex emotions, and they lack the life experience necessary to place their circumstances within a broader context. They likely don't comprehend the effects of severe stress or trauma, or express themselves in the same manner as adults. Even if they grasp their feelings, they may lack the language or verbal skills to articulate them, leading them to remain silent. This silence may mislead adults into believing that children are managing well when in reality they are struggling. Additionally, children possess the remarkable ability to smile, laugh, and play despite adversity, giving the impression that everything is fine, even when it's not.

The myth also lives on because adults find it exceedingly convenient to believe it. Facing the painful truth is challenging. Children have limited control over their own lives, and nearly everything they experience is a result of adult behavior. We are reluctant to acknowledge that our own vulnerabilities and dysfunctions as adults may profoundly affect the children in our lives.

Every experience a child undergoes shapes their outlook on life, and the adversities they endure inevitably leave a mark. This is not to say they can't bounce back, but they will need specialized support to do so. It is no coincidence that most adult therapy eventually explores the impact of childhood experiences on current issues.

Myth 4: Intelligence—and Potential—Is Fixed

In the segregated America of 1958, school system administrator David Weikart was shocked to observe how many poor African American children on the south side of Ypsilanti, Michigan, were underperforming at school. Most people at the time believed that intelligence was fixed, that children were born with a certain amount of intellect that remained constant for life. When IQ tests were administered, Black children mostly underperformed. Many of them were sent to special education classes or were held back; most did not graduate from high school.

Weikart wanted to do something to improve the odds for academic success for Black children, but he faced resistance within the school system. So rather than change the schools, he changed the game. He proposed a radical new concept: preschool for three- and four-year-old Black children. He launched an expensive experiment known as the Perry Preschool. Teachers had master's degrees and small classes. The program offered three hours per day of cognitive enrichment, with a focus on play-based approaches, engaging imagination, and connecting young children with the external world via field trips and projects. Educators visited the families at home every week, meetings that were described as initially "awkward" by one of the participating educators.[58] The Perry Preschool became the site of one of the most frequently referenced studies in early childhood education. It ultimately challenged conventional thinking about both the "who" and the "how" of success—in school and in life. It emphasized the critical importance of the early years and underscored that every child who is given access to high-quality early education can thrive regardless of race or background.

The children from the Perry Preschool experiment have been tracked for over fifty years. Those data—which compare the life trajectories of children who attended preschool with the life trajectories of a control group of children who did not—inspired research by influential economist and Nobel laureate James Heckman at the University of Chicago on the benefits of early childhood investments. His studies have shown that children who attend high-quality early childhood programs are not only healthier but more likely to finish high school, more likely to go to college, less likely to go to prison, less likely to receive government assistance, more likely to have a good job, and even more likely to be in a stable relationship in adulthood. Aggregate benefits from the Perry Preschool yielded an economic return of thirteen dollars for every dollar spent—a massive payback demonstrating that high-quality early childhood education is not an expense but a valuable investment. In 2021, Heckman updated his work to demonstrate the "dynastic benefits of early childhood education."[59] If we continue forsaking the importance of the early years, we are leaving behind not one but multiple generations.

The Perry Preschool program busted the myth that intelligence and capabilities are fixed. It demonstrated the critical opportunity to develop young children's potential, especially through a focus on relationships. It served as one of the inspirations and models for Head Start, our national, federally funded, early childhood program for kids living in poverty.[60] Head Start is centered on leveraging the power of relational intelligence to drive better outcomes for kiddos. Its two-generation approach involves staff engagement with the child's family, forging families' connections to peers and community, and getting families involved as leaders. Head Start families are always represented on local school governance bodies.

We now have evidence that intelligence and potential can also be boosted for children with autism spectrum disorder, for whom relationships are inherently more complex. This is not to say that there is an obvious path for doing so, as there is still much we don't understand about autism. In 2010, Sally Rogers, professor of psychiatry and behavioral sciences at the MIND Institute at the University of California, Davis, and her colleagues studied the impacts of an intervention called the Early Start Denver Model (ESDM) for autistic children. Their work showed that ESDM increases IQ and improves adaptive behavior.[61] The intervention consisted of intensive supports built on moment-to-moment interactions that young children typically have with other people, especially their parents, and it used children's interests and favorite activities to ensure that social interaction was interesting and fun. In 2012, ESDM was recognized by *Time* magazine as one of the top ten medical breakthroughs of the year.[62] To the surprise of the researchers, a follow-up study suggested that the therapy had lasting effects: two years after the intervention was completed, benefits continued to accrue. Brain scans suggested that the intensive early intervention improved brain activity associated with social and communication skills.[63]

The myth of fixed intelligence has long plagued our understanding of human potential and marginalized entire groups of children. It falsely suggests that a person's cognitive abilities, such as intelligence and problem-solving skills, are rigid and unchangeable traits that one is born with and can't improve upon. In reality, human intelligence is far from fixed. Neuroplasticity, the brain's remarkable ability to adapt and grow, allows for continuous learning and skill development throughout life with the appropriate supports. Embracing the idea that intelligence is malleable and can be expanded through effective learning strategies anchored in relationships opens up a world of possibilities for lifelong learning and flourishing.

Myth 5: Too Much Love Spoils Babies

Does too much love risk spoiling children for life?

At various times throughout the twentieth century, renowned psychologists, pediatricians, and others recommended that parents minimize cuddling with their babies in order to foster children's ability to self-regulate. The pediatrics pioneer Luther Emmett Holt wrote in a 1907 book, "Babies under six months old should never be played with, and the less of it any time the better for the infant."[64] Or check out this 1928 advice from psychologist John Watson, president of the American Psychological Association: "When you are tempted to pet your child remember that mother love is a dangerous instrument. . . . Once a child's character has been spoiled by bad handling, which can be done in a few days, who can say that the damage is ever repaired?"[65]

This type of guidance has contributed to the myth that too much affection may spoil children later on, that they will grow up self-centered and ever-demanding. In fact, the science is now clear: it is impossible for parents to spoil their young child, to hold or respond to a baby too often, especially during the first year. Responding to babies' needs is a way to let them know that the world is reliable and trustworthy. The opposite advice is actually true: the more love a baby receives in the early years, the more independent they will become as a child.

Over the past eight decades, developmental scientists have uncovered the profound and lasting impact of microdynamics between infants and caregivers on an individual's lifelong development. This understanding revolves around the concept of attachment, defined as a bond with a caregiver that serves a baby's needs for emotional regulation and exploration, and is founded on the belief in the caregiver's availability and responsiveness.

The scientific theory of attachment traces its origins to the pioneering work in the 1930s of an English psychiatrist and psychoanalyst named John Bowlby. During that era, psychologists and other professionals predominantly attributed children's behavior to internal factors such as hunger, aggression, and sexuality, largely dismissing the impact of their environment. Nevertheless, Bowlby, while working with emotionally troubled children, observed a common thread among them: a lack of affection, and disrupted or absent caregiving. Despite his supervisor's reluctance, Bowlby insisted on recognizing the significance of family experiences. In 1944, he documented his observations of forty-four thieves and forty-four nonthieves in a delinquency center. Seventeen of the thieves had experienced prolonged separation from their mothers before age five, compared with only two in the group of nonthieves.[66] In subsequent research, Bowlby would show that sixty children who had spent time apart from their mothers due to tuberculosis prior to age four had lower school achievement.[67]

Around the same time, in the United States, psychologist Harry Harlow was arriving at similar conclusions through his poignant studies (now considered unethical) involving baby monkeys isolated from their mothers in "pits of despair." He observed their interactions with "wire mothers" (dolls made of wire mesh to which bottles were attached) and "cloth mothers" (dolls made of cloth that did not offer food). These studies revealed that infant monkeys sought comfort, not just food subsistence.[68]

Bowlby expanded his investigations to encompass children separated from their parents, such as those in hospitals. His conviction crystallized around the idea that the primary caregiver, typically the mother in his early research, functioned as a form of "psychic organizer" for the child, exerting a critical influence, particularly during certain developmental phases. To foster mental well-being, Bowlby contended that "the infant and young child should experience a warm, intimate, and continuous relationship with this mother (or permanent mother substitute) in which both find satisfaction and enjoyment."[69] Yet according to Bowlby, the attachment figure need not exclusively be the mother or even a parent. He posited that infants establish a "small hierarchy of attachments."

In the 1950s, Mary Ainsworth, a colleague of Bowlby's, analyzed child-mother attachment patterns by observing infants' reactions to separations and reunions with their mothers. She described three distinct "attachment styles."[70] Later, American psychologist Mary Main identified a fourth.[71] The four styles are:

- Secure (confident that needs will be met)
- Anxious/ambivalent (unsure if needs will be met; comfort-seeking)
- Avoidant/dismissive (believes needs will not be met, independence-seeking)
- Fearful-avoidant/disorganized (desiring but fearful of close relationships)

These styles, which reflect varying degrees of security and coping mechanisms in infants, are fluid, with the potential for individuals to develop secure attachment at any life stage.

The Minnesota Longitudinal Study of Risk and Adaption (MISRA), conducted over thirty-five years, found that the effects of the quality of childhood attachment extend into adulthood. Securely attached children tend to have better emotional health, social abilities, and relationships. These individuals often display positive social interactions from preschool and maintain closer friendships into middle childhood. They show enhanced social competence, demonstrate healthier family dynamics, and exhibit leadership skills. This secure foundation is also correlated with academic success, which is fueled by higher motivation, concentration, and self-esteem.[72] Children of parents with higher levels of responsiveness and warmth have more than two times better language skills than children whose parents are less responsive.[73]

One of the most notable findings of the MISRA study is that a secure attachment during infancy ultimately fosters greater independence in later life, whereas an insecure attachment tends to result in increased dependence as the child grows older. Independence emerges from a foundation of secure attachment, love, and nurturing relationships.

The benefits of secure attachment extend to school environments. Securely attached children experience greater acceptance and more favorable treatment from both peers and teachers. Remarkably, even when teachers are unaware of a child's attachment history, they display warmer and more respectful behavior toward securely attached children. Educators also tend to establish more age-appropriate standards and hold higher expectations for these students. Conversely, children with challenging attachment patterns receive less nurturing and face increased control, lower expectations, and more frequent anger from their teachers, despite their greater need for compassionate adult interaction.

Notwithstanding this vast scientific knowledge, vestiges of the older "Watson" way of thinking remain in the US. A quarter of parents still use an authoritarian style of parenting, one focused on obedience, discipline, and control, not on nurturing.[74] As of 2024, sixteen states still allow corporal punishment in schools and do not distinguish by age. Mississippi has the highest rate of spanking among preschool-aged children (and children overall).[75]

The myth that too much love spoils children is rooted in the belief that excessive affection and attention will lead to a sense of entitlement, dependence, or an inability to handle life's challenges. But as the research shows, this notion is largely unfounded. Love is a fundamental need for children and plays a crucial role in their emotional and relational development and overall well-being. Providing love, nurturing, and emotional support fosters a secure attachment, which forms the foundation for healthy relationships, self-esteem, and learning. In essence, love provides the emotional fuel that can power the engine of learning, making the process more enjoyable, meaningful, and effective. Nurturing love—characterized by consistent affection, attention, and support—promotes healthy cognitive, emotional, social, and autonomous development. Issues arise not from love itself but from a lack of boundaries and discipline. Setting clear, consistent limits helps children feel secure, learn self-control, and develop autonomy.

Therefore, combining love with appropriate guidance and boundaries supports well-rounded, resilient, and independent individuals.

Parents, caregivers, educators—anyone who has ever had or helped to raise a child—know that learning starts well before kindergarten and is not a solitary pursuit; that children may struggle to surmount the consequences of adversity; that intelligence can be nurtured and developed; and that it is impossible to spoil children by loving them. But these myths, these disproved and archaic beliefs, still shape our social policies and priorities, our educational institutions and practices, our public and private investments, our collective and sometimes even our individual decisions about what we owe our children.

As parents, caregivers, educators, policymakers, and citizens, we have a responsibility to dispel the myths and ensure that young children are given the opportunity to experience nurturing and enriching relationships that will positively impact their lives for the long term. The need for human connection is innate. The earlier a child is loved, the greater the likelihood the child will flourish. The longer the period of neglect, the more negative the effects on a child's cognitive, emotional, social, and physical development. And there is no age at which a child cannot be supported and nurtured.

CHAPTER 2

Shrinking Networks

Nobody has ever before asked the nuclear family to live all by itself in a box the way we do. With no relatives, no support, we've put it in an impossible situation.
—MARGARET MEAD, *CULTURE AND COMMITMENT: A STUDY OF THE GENERATION GAP,* 1970

Raphaël is a French young adult who stays locked in his room in a suburb outside Paris, avoiding social contacts. After completing a bachelor's degree in video gaming and working for a short while, he quit his job and went back to live with his parents, locking himself in the bedroom where he grew up—all day, every day. He has now been a recluse in his room for two years without any motivation to socialize or look for a job. He has become phobic about social connections.

Raphaël is part of a growing phenomenon called *hikikomori,* an expression of modern isolation and suffering. Derived from the Japanese words *hiki* ("to withdraw") and *komori* ("to be inside"), the term was coined in 1998 by psychiatrist Tamaki Saito. It describes a condition in which individuals, typically adolescents or young adults, retreat from social life and isolate themselves in their homes for an extended period—generally more than six months. In the documentary *Hikikomori: The Locked Generation*, we witness Raphaël's waking hours consumed by the glow of his computer screen within the confines of his bedroom.[1] People with the syndrome actively shun school, work, and social engagements, succumbing to an extreme form of social withdrawal that becomes a defining characteristic of their lifestyle.

Hikikomori, which has been recognized in Japan for over twenty-five years, was originally thought to be a culture-bound syndrome. According to the Japanese minister of health, there are now more than 1.5 million hikikomori teens and adults in Japan, or 2 percent of Japan's population.[2] But the condition is increasingly being documented in other countries. In South Korea, the estimates range from around 350,000 to over 500,000 people, or 5 percent of the youth population.[3] Cases have been reported in France, Spain, Nigeria, and the US, with a spike triggered by the recent global pandemic.

Initially associated with Japan's economic challenges during the 1990s, hikikomori has been attributed to a combination of factors, including societal pressure and parental expectations for academic or career success, stress within educational systems, excessive use of technology and social media, family issues, mental health challenges, and cultural factors. Individuals generally exhibit low self-esteem; they hide to avoid shame. In instances of "double hikikomori," family members who are gripped by shame and fear regarding their child's situation find themselves succumbing to isolation as well. Some research has linked hikikomori to attachment insecurities in early childhood, and to peer rejection in middle childhood or early adolescence.[4] As this description makes clear, hikikomori is a complex phenomenon that researchers are still trying to understand.[5]

Whereas the term "hikikomori" typically applies to extreme cases of social withdrawal, the global pandemic has brought about a unique and widespread situation where many of our children have experienced some form of hikikomori. Amidst lockdowns and social distancing measures, countless youngsters found themselves confined to their homes, separated from friends and the usual social connections that form an integral part of their lives. The pandemic-induced isolation has undoubtedly introduced challenges for children, testing their resilience and adaptability in navigating a socially distant world. The impact of this collective experience on their social development and well-being remains a subject of ongoing concern and study.

Youth loneliness seems to have become endemic. The upheavals brought about by the modern world, intensified by the global pandemic, have cast a spotlight on the fragility of social connections among the younger generation. As children navigate a landscape dominated by technological interfaces and changing family dynamics, the risk of isolation and withdrawal looms large. I am concerned that our youth may be at risk of experiencing prolonged hikikomori tendencies unless we take a more vigilant approach to the deterioration of young children's social circles. The importance of prioritizing the quality of children's social interactions and creating an environment that nurtures their social and emotional well-being cannot be overstated.

Shrinking Families

Type "family is" into Google's search field.[6] The autocomplete results tell the story of what we wish and aspire for families to be:

Family is everything.
Family is forever.
Family is important.
Family is where the heart is.

But while we almost all agree that family is an anchor, we have a difficult time defining exactly what family is. The US Census Bureau's definition—"two or more individuals who are related by birth, marriage, or adoption, although they also may include other unrelated people"—leaves a lot of room for interpretation.

The reality is that there is no longer any dominant form of family. In 1960, 73 percent of American children resided in what is typically referred to as a "traditional" family, with two parents who were married to each other and hadn't been married before. Today, only 46 percent of children live in that arrangement.[7]

There are cultural differences in how we conceptualize family. A MassMutual Insurance Company survey found that about one-third of white Americans include extended family in what they consider family, and 13 percent include friends. For Black Americans, both those figures are significantly higher: 47 percent include extended family and 24 percent include friends.[8]

Even in light of those expanded definitions, families have been getting smaller and smaller over the past decades. The average size of the family declined from 5.8 in 1790 to 2.6 in 2018.[9] That means the circle of relationships around young children is getting tighter. While the downward trend has flattened in the past few years—household size increased in 2019 for the first time in 160 years—we are still feeling the profound structural effects of the diminished size of the American family. Demographers project that total family size will continue declining from forty-one relatives in 1950 to twenty-five in 2095.[10]

Fewer Children

South Korea has the lowest fertility rate in the world—a mere 0.68 in 2024, or less than one child per family on average, far below the rate of 2.1 needed to maintain a steady population.[11] The capital, Seoul, has an even lower fertility rate at 0.55. South Korea finds itself in a fertility crisis, fearing "national extinction," where the quest for economic success, the position of women in society, the high cost of living, and the rat race of long work hours are replacing the allure of baby strollers.[12] In 2023, Italy also recorded the lowest number of new babies since 1861, when birth records began to be kept: 1.20 children per woman.[13] The average number of children born to women in the world has been nearly cut in half over the past seven decades, which means there are fewer children per family, and children have fewer siblings.[14] In the United States, there are fewer than one school-aged child per household, and more homes with pets than kids. Having fewer kids in a family does seem to equate with better educational outcomes, since there are more resources and greater parental attention to devote to each one.[15] But interestingly, in the Global South and for children in foster care, this does not hold true; extended kinship networks seem to support better educational outcomes for children born into larger families.[16] Also, having fewer siblings negatively impacts children's ability to get along with peers and to develop long-term meaningful relationships in adulthood.[17] When they enter kindergarten, children are rated as better classroom citizens if they have siblings.[18]

Fewer Parents

For decades, the share of US children living with a single parent has been rising, accompanied by a decline in marriage rates and a rise in births outside of marriage. The US has the world's highest percentage of children living in single-parent households, more than three times that of the rest of the world. Almost a quarter of US kids now live with one parent and no other adults.[19] Whereas 11 percent of children resided separately from their fathers in 1960, 27 percent did so in 2010.[20] In addition, over 2.7 million children in America are raised by their grandparents in "skipped generation" living arrangements, often as a result of challenging circumstances such as a parent's death or incapacity to provide care.[21] These families, comprising our eldest and youngest citizens—our two most vulnerable groups—are particularly fragile, often with limited legal rights and benefits.

Fewer Grandparents

Yet there are fewer grandparents in young children's lives. In 1850, almost 70 percent of people ages sixty-five and older lived with their adult children. By 2000, less than 15 percent did so.[22] Nearly half of grandparents live more than two hundred miles away from their grandchildren, according to AARP.[23] Although some encouraging signs indicate that this is changing—the number of households containing two or more adult generations has quadrupled over the past five decades, according to Pew Research[24]—that number is still relatively small overall, and is driven in part by the unaffordability of housing.

Fewer Older Adult Friends

Besides their own grandparents, children generally don't have many older adults in their lives anymore. Remember the endearing older friend and mentor Mr. Miyagi in *The Karate Kid*, or Alfredo in *Cinema Paradiso*? These characters may seem as mythical to our children as the wizards Dumbledore in the Harry Potter series and Gandalf in *The Lord of the Rings*. In fact, only 3 percent of children in the US have ever met a person older than sixty-five outside their family circle.[25]

Fading Friendships

It's not only our families that are getting smaller. We adults are also experiencing a friendship recession: we have fewer friends, and we spend less time with them (see details below). This matters for our kids because any of those adult friends could have acted as extended family, coparent, or alloparent (a supportive loving figure for a young child). Friends can be more important than relatives in fostering a sense of support, mental well-being, and overall wellness.[26] You might remember having such adults in your life during your own childhood; odds are, your kids have fewer of them, or none at all.

The number of close friendships per adult in the US has declined considerably over the past several decades. From 1990 to 2020, the proportion of Americans who report having three or fewer close friends has grown from a third to a half. The number of Americans without friends grew from 3 percent to 12 percent.[27] In the United Kingdom, there's a similar trend, with the percentage of young adults who indicate having just one or no close friends rising from 7 percent in 2012 to nearly 20 percent in 2021.[28] The situation is even more pronounced among men, and specifically dads, who typically have more friends during their early years but undergo a sharper decline over time.[29]

Social fitness is a bit like physical fitness. The longer it's been since your last trip to the gym, the harder it is to start going again. Same for social connections: when people are already lonely and disconnected, they find it harder to build new relationships.[30] They also perceive life's challenges to be greater. When we go hiking with a friend, for instance, we estimate a hill to be less steep than we do if we are alone. Even the mere act of thinking of a supportive friend helps us see a hill as less steep. (Yes, a researcher has actually studied the perception of geographical slants as it relates to social support!)[31] Our social metabolism dramatically slowed down during the pandemic. Our professional and personal extended networks contracted by nearly 17 percent as a result of working from home and being more isolated.[32]

We also dedicate significantly less of our time to the limited number of friends we do have. The American Time Use Survey, an annual government study that commenced in 2003, reveals that until 2013, individuals spent slightly less than seven hours per week in the company of friends, and approximately fifteen hours when factoring in family, neighbors, and colleagues outside of work. Time spent socializing with friends started to decline in 2014; by 2022 it had decreased by nearly half. Currently, we spend less than three hours a week with friends, and around ten hours if you include all companions outside the household.[33] All of this means that there are fewer opportunities

GRAPH 2

Shrinking Networks Around Young Children
Family, Friends, Older Adults, Community

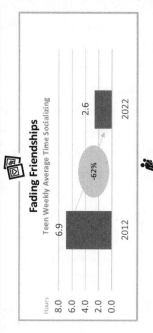

Shrinking Families
Average Household Size

1960 — 3.3
2023 — 2.5
−25%

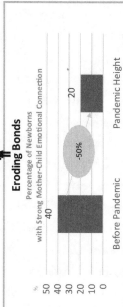

Fading Friendships
Teen Weekly Average Time Socializing

2012 — 6.9
2022 — 2.6
−62%

Hours: 8.0, 6.0, 4.0, 2.0, 0.0

Eroding Bonds
Percentage of Newborns with Strong Mother-Child Emotional Connection

Before Pandemic — 40
Pandemic Height — 20
−50%

%: 50, 40, 30, 20, 10, 0

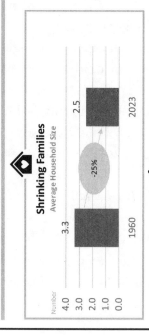

Fewer Older Adult Friends
3 Percent of Young People Have a Close Relationship with an Older Person Outside of the Family (In Darker Gray)

Sources:

- Shrinking Families: "Average Size of Households in the US," Statista, 2023, www.statista.com/statistics/183648/average-size-of-households-in-the-us/.
- Fading Friendships: "*American Time Use Survey*," US Bureau of Statistics, time "socializing and communicating" for 15- to 19-year-olds during leisure and sports activities, 2012 and 2023; *Monitoring the Future*, University of Michigan; Twenge, J., *Generations*, San Diego State University.
- Fewer Older Adult Friends: McPherson, M., Smith-Lovin, L., and Cook, J. M., "Birds of a Feather: Homophily in Social Networks," *Annual Review of Sociology* 27 (2001): 415–444, www.annualreviews.org/content/journals/10.1146/annurev.soc.27.1.415.
- Eroding Bonds: Data from New York City COMBO cohort, Dumitriu, D., "Life-Long Negative Impacts of COVID-19 on Mother-Infant Outcomes," Early Childhood Funder Collaborative, March 18, 2021, www.youtube.com/watch?v=GVrXdC4FP1w.

for a child to be held, interacted with, or cared for by an adult family friend.

Absent Playmates

The trend toward fewer friendships affects children, too, starting in the early years. This is concerning since early friendships produce major benefits: happiness, well-being, self-confidence, communication, school success, and more. The greatest predictor of long-term success in adulthood? Prosocial behavior in kindergarten.[34] The greatest predictor of student engagement at school? Having a best friend at school.[35] Yet the conditions for sustaining early friendships are deteriorating.

Take play. Children's unstructured playtime dropped by a quarter between 1981 and 1997.[36] In 1989, most elementary schools (96 percent) included at least one recess period per school day. A decade later, kindergarten classrooms saw a decline, with only 70 percent offering any recess periods.[37]

Less unstructured play means fewer opportunities for friendships. In the 1990s in Switzerland, researchers compared children who engaged in unsupervised play within their neighborhoods with children who spent more time playing in parks under their parents' supervision. Children engaged in unstructured play had more than double the number of friends than those who frequented parks with parental oversight. Additionally, the free-playing children exhibited superior social and motor skills, and spent more time outdoors overall.[38]

Young children are increasingly overscheduled, whether because of greater academic load or more extracurricular activities. "Kindergarten is the new first grade" was the big finding from researchers at the University of Virginia who compared kindergarten and first-grade classrooms between 1998 and 2010.[39] The younger generation is spending more hours on homework and academic assignments, and less time on leisure and social interactions. A 2015 study found that kindergartners spent twenty-five minutes per night on homework, even though most researchers agree that having homework in kindergarten is not developmentally appropriate.[40] Teenagers spend about twice as much time on homework as their peers did in the 1990s.[41]

China reflects an extreme version of these same trends, with Chinese elementary and middle school students spending nearly three hours per day on homework.[42] The result is what's known as *neijuan* (内卷), a Chinese expression describing internal depletion and growth without development due to intense competition. The homework pressure became so onerous that in 2018 the Chinese Ministry of Education banned homework altogether for first and second graders. Still, many young children in China remain sleep-deprived.[43] They are developing physical signs of overstudying, with nearly 36 percent of all primary school students in China suffering from nearsightedness—a figure that rises to 70 percent among middle school students and a staggering 80 percent among high school students![44] In 2021, seeking to reduce the twin pressures of overwork in young children and the burgeoning costs to families of paying for tutoring, the Chinese government adopted the "double reduction" policy, banning private tutoring centers. Although the effort is laudable, its impact remains unclear. Scarce opportunities for higher education continue to drive an excessive focus on academic achievement. Middle- and higher-income Chinese families find ways around the policy by tapping into a growing underground tutoring industry or hiring "nannies" who are really expensive private tutors.

Similarly, in the US, the long march to college admission starts younger and younger. The competitive frenzy expands to extracurricular activities as parents seek an edge for admission or scholarship. Children are enrolled early in structured activities, where the primary focus might be competing in sports like tot or club soccer, traveling for athletic tournaments when just past stroller age, performing at a violin concert, or working on a Model United Nations competition (yes, Model UN starts in elementary school!). These structured activities take the place of casual, organic social interactions that facilitate friendship. In 1995, the Amateur Athletic Union supported approximately 100 national championships for young athletes. Around a decade later, that figure had surged to over 250. The implication is that extracurricular activities—whether in the arts or athletics—are no longer about child development or building relationships, but about winning competitions and getting a leg up on others. They are no longer about fun, but about résumé building or trophy accumulation. As a result, children have less opportunity to develop authentic connections with peers. These changes have meaningful consequences: children who spend more time in structured activities show less ability to set goals, make independent decisions, or self-regulate.[45]

Structured and competitive activities—as well as social media and screen time—have edged out relaxed friendships among teens too. Teens are spending less face time with friends. The number of social outings for eighth graders has plummeted from 2.5 weekly dates in 1990 to 1.5 in 2021.[46] They are making fewer friends.[47] The steepest decline commenced around 2010, just as smartphones and social media were taking hold.

An Exodus of Teachers and Caregivers

As a result of the pandemic, close to sixteen thousand early childhood programs closed down.[48] Approximately 120,000 childcare professionals and 300,000 public school teachers departed from the field.[49] This exodus has resulted in staffing shortages, and in insufficient and precarious childcare and early education services.

A lack of educators not only reduces the chances for young children to benefit from professional early learning settings, but also results in higher child-to-teacher ratios. That hinders children's learning and can also lead to greater staff turnover, more closures of schools and preschools, and continued disruptions for families. Needless to say, young children do better with a lower child-to-caregiver ratio. It enables more interactive and engaging care, providing children with increased opportunities for verbal communication with their caregivers. These crucial exchanges promote the formation of the stable bonds that are essential for the socioemotional health of children and fundamental to their capacity for establishing robust relationships later in life. Smaller groups and lower ratios of children to staff correlate with other beneficial outcomes for kids as well, such as enhanced social abilities, better communication and language development, and improved cognitive growth.[50]

Little ones do better with routines and stability in their relationships. Elevated teacher turnover breaks routines and is associated with smaller advancements in vocabulary and literacy among children and a heightened occurrence of behavior problems.[51] Childcare instability is associated with children's behavior problems.[52]

Trust in public schools is hovering at its lowest-ever levels. Astoundingly, only 26 percent of Americans express "a great deal/quite a lot of" confidence in public schools.[53] How much lower can it get? Both enrollment and attendance have meaningfully declined since the pandemic, especially in kindergarten and early elementary grades, and are not showing clear signs of recovery. The pandemic exposed a gap between what parents want and what schools are delivering. It also created new options that did not exist before, including in the areas of homeschooling and private schools.[54] The question is, if you didn't attend kindergarten, what alternative activities or experiences did you participate in? More little ones missing formal early education adds an additional layer to already complex learning recovery efforts and to the growing relational deprivation crisis.

Homeschooling, once considered a fringe and often religious educational alternative, has now taken center stage as a dynamic and increasingly popular approach to learning. Learners trade traditional classrooms for the familiarity of informal playgroups and home, where the kitchen table becomes a science lab and the living room transforms into a literature haven. Black households are the fastest-growing group adopting homeschooling. The percentage of Black children who are homeschooled grew from 3.3 percent in early 2020, at the start of the pandemic, to 16.1 percent in the fall of that year. Meanwhile, the proportion of homeschooled children in the US nearly doubled from 2.8 percent before the pandemic to 5.4 percent in the 2020–2021 school year.[55] For some Black families, homeschooling may be an act of resistance, motivated by a need to protect children from the systemic inequalities prevalent in schools and to foster a safe environment amidst a racially charged society.[56] Homeschooling can have a multifaceted impact on a child's social networks. On one hand, its flexible nature allows for a more tailored educational experience, which can be beneficial for some children. It provides opportunities for deeper family connections and one-on-one interactions with parents or tutors. However, the social aspect makes homeschooling a double-edged sword. While homeschoolers often engage in extracurricular activities, co-op programs, and community events to foster socialization, they may have fewer daily interactions with peers than they would in a traditional school setting. Research on this topic is somewhat scarce and for the most part biased (conducted by homeschooling advocates). Still, it is worth noting that these studies suggest that homeschooled children may have social skills that are on par with, or even exceed, those of children in traditional educational environments.[57]

The Missing Village

Beyond schools, it appears that social trust has wrapped itself in an invisibility cloak, becoming unseen and elusive. In his book *Bowling Alone*, Harvard public policy professor Robert Putnam eloquently illuminated the larger issue of the decline in social trust. The communal fabric seems to be unraveling. As with public schools, confidence levels in government, media, organized religion, and the criminal justice system are all weakening. To be clear, it's not a mere dip in trust; it's a full-blown trust recession. Traditional forms of socialization are plummeting. We spend less time socializing with neighbors, chatting with coworkers, volunteering, and even going to church.[58] Forty million Americans have stopped attending church in the past twenty-five years.[59] In 2021, membership in a house of worship, such as a church, synagogue, or mosque, fell below a majority for the first time.[60] This is impacting younger generations the most; Gen Z is the least religious generation. For a majority of Gen Z, church attendance is no longer important.[61] Many within this cohort are parents or soon-to-be-parents. The next generation of our little learners—Gen R—might miss out on social interactions and support networks that come with being part of a congregation. This is not a good thing if congregational membership is not substituted with other social or community activities; attendance at religious services is related to greater well-being and happiness and to improved academic outcomes for youth.[62] So the decline in religiosity may drive greater isolation and impact relational intelligence.[63] Overall, our growing lack of trust in institutions translates into skepticism not only about hypothetical, anonymous Americans but about colleagues, neighbors, and even close relationships. Nearly half of survey respondents agreed that "people are not as reliable as they used to be."[64] Social trust is akin to a missing puzzle piece that everyone is desperately searching for but can't quite seem to locate. This trust recession translates into fewer interactions for our little ones with neighbors and other community members.

You may ponder: To what extent is it a problem that relationship circles around young children are shrinking? If a child is loved and cared for by one or two parents, doesn't that suffice? In theory, yes, but in practice, kids benefit from having multiple attachments. While "at least one relationship" can change the game for a child, experts agree that more are better. Nurturing relationships have a cumulative positive impact. The number of supportive relationships is directly correlated with higher levels of behavioral and emotional engagement, as well as enhanced meaningful learning experiences. According to a large 2020 survey of high school youth, each additional supportive relationship (as reported by study participants) was associated with an approximate

10 percent increase in both behavioral and emotional engagement metrics, and a roughly 12 percent rise in scores that measure meaningful learning.[65] An article in a major Danish newspaper went as far as provocatively advocating that "Children Need 100 Parents."[66] This may be a high bar for many of us, but more than one parental figure is ideal. Generally, three to six close relationships are the minimum necessary for young children to thrive. "Overall, children seemed to do best when they have three secure relationships," writes renowned primatologist Sarah Blaffer Hrdy.[67] Prominent researchers in the field of developmental psychology agree: "Children appear to profit most from three secure relationships," write Marinus van IJzendoorn and Avi Sagi.[68] Those important adult relationships can be with parents or nonparents. The most powerful predictor of later socioemotional development involves the quality of the entire attachment network.

Whether the ideal number is three or one hundred, a network of secure relationships around young children is essential for them to learn and thrive. And this has been true, both for children and for humans generally, for a very long time. For a span of more than 250,000 years—or 95 percent of the time we've existed on the planet—humans have lived in small groups. These clans, typically consisting of 20 to 150 members in hunter-gatherer tribes, accommodated individuals of all age groups, from the elderly to adults, youth, children, toddlers, and infants, all cohabiting in close physical proximity. This arrangement fostered an environment characterized by dense and constant physical, emotional, and social interactions, which was particularly conducive to childrearing. Evolutionary biologists and anthropologists believe we wouldn't have survived or thrived as a species if we hadn't been able to rely on others to help care for our kids.

The book *Hunter-Gatherer Childhoods*, coedited by anthropologist Barry Hewlitt and psychologist Michael Lamb, summarizes what we and our offspring are missing today: "Young children in foraging cultures are nursed frequently; held, touched, or kept near others almost constantly; frequently cared for by individuals other than their mothers (fathers and grandmothers, in particular) though seldom by older siblings; experience prompt responses to their fusses and cries; and enjoy multiage play groups in early childhood."[69]

In this context, was the American nuclear family structure, composed of two parents and few if any extended family and community members, a mistake, as columnist David Brooks called it in an editorial for *The Atlantic*?[70] In fact, the nuclear family is rapidly reshaping and reinventing itself, a topic we will explore in Chapter 9.

Shrinking Villages, Smaller Brains?

Considering all these factors, we can conclude that our circles of relationships are shrinking. As an illustration, the wedding-planning website The Knot has noted a downward trend in the average number of wedding guests. In 2007, the average was 153. By 2022, it was only 117.[71] Based on this metric, our social networks have shrunk by approximately a quarter relative to fifteen years ago. This ties with data from the American Time Use Survey showing that American adults have reduced time spent socializing by 40 percent over the past ten years.[72] For teens, the decline has been even steeper: 60 percent. There is no record of any period in history when our young people spent more time alone than they do now.

This trend is deeply concerning from a human evolutionary standpoint. We humans are not the strongest, fastest, or largest creatures around, yet we've achieved remarkable success as a species. This success is attributed both to our enlarged brains and to our capacity to establish enduring, diverse, and flexible relationships with others.

In 1992, British anthropologist Robin Dunbar introduced the "social brain" hypothesis, which proposes that larger social networks correlate with a larger brain-size ratio (the ratio between the size of the neocortex and that of the rest of the brain). Dunbar demonstrated that in primates, the brain-size ratio consistently grows with increasing social group size. Tamarin monkeys, with a brain-size ratio of approximately 2.3, typically form social groups of around 5 members, whereas macaque monkeys, boasting a brain-size ratio of about 3.8, create much larger social groups, averaging around 40 members. To extrapolate, Dunbar's theory suggests that the human brain-size ratio reflects an expected social group size of approximately 150 individuals.

At birth, we typically start with one or two meaningful connections, a number that peaks during our late teenage years and into our early twenties. By the time we are in our thirties, we generally settle at 150 social ties, a figure that tends to stabilize throughout adulthood until the late sixties to early seventies, at which point there is a significant drop-off in social connections. Eventually, for those who live to an advanced age, the circle of connections contracts back down to one or two.

In his book *How Many Friends Does One Person Need?*, Dunbar supports his findings with both historical and contemporary evidence.[73] The average population of a Neolithic village in England was 160 residents, units in the Roman army typically comprised 150 soldiers, and contemporary Christmas card lists tend to peak at around 153 contacts. I will add two modern datapoints. The average number of followers for an Instagram user is around 150.[74] The median number of connections on Facebook is 200, although many of our social media connections are often just acquaintances.[75] In fact, only four virtual friends could be counted on in the event of an emotional crisis.[76]

The question arises: Could shrinking relationship circles around young children have an impact on the evolution of the human brain?

We have evidence in young mice, monkeys, and older human adults that this may be the case. When young mice and monkeys experience extreme social isolation, they exhibit deficits in the communication chains in cells called oligodendrocytes, with impaired neuron-to-neuron exchange in the prefrontal cortex.[77] In humans, the more isolated we are in our youth, the more anxious, depressed, aggressive, and cognitively rigid we become.[78] This sadly all connects with what we are observing in our society at large: growing anxiety, depression, aggressiveness, and polarization.

One more concern to add to the list: isolation leads to more addictive behaviors, suggesting it may take meaningful efforts to reverse current trends. In a controlled study, rats were isolated from their peers for approximately one month starting from the age of twenty-one days, a period roughly equivalent to early-to-middle adolescence in humans. They were subsequently tested to assess their responses to varying levels of exposure to amphetamine and alcohol. The isolated rats quickly developed a preference for these substances, unlike the never-isolated control group. Nearly all the isolated rats exhibited a preference after just a single exposure to either drug, whereas rats in the control group developed conditioned responses only after repeated exposures.[79]

Emerging data on IQ may also suggest a troubling connection between shrinking social networks and human brains. Since the IQ test was invented more than a hundred years ago and until recently, raw IQ scores moved in a single direction: up. This phenomenon, called the Flynn effect, resulted in gains of three to four points on average per decade. However, a recent landmark study shows that IQs in the United States have declined for the first time in a century.[80]

Intelligence quotient—a composite of scores on a number of different subtests evaluating reasoning, memory, knowledge, and cognitive processing—is an imperfect measure of intelligence. The inventor of the IQ test himself admitted that it does not fully assess intellectual ability. Despite criticisms and limitations, however, it has been widely used and remains correlated to educational outcomes. Now you might be wondering, "Isn't the test designed to maintain an average IQ of 100?" This is accurate solely because researchers rescale the tests to account for the enhancement in raw scores.

The recent study, published in the journal *Intelligence*, analyzed a dataset of 394,378 IQ scores obtained from 2006 to 2018. Surprisingly, the findings showed a drop in scores across all subtest categories except for spatial reasoning. Logic and vocabulary, computation and mathematics, visual problem-solving and analogies—all experienced declines. Similar IQ declines have been identified in Australia,

Denmark, Finland, France, Great Britain, Netherlands, Norway, and Sweden.[81] Particularly mind-boggling in the US data is that the steepest decline was observed among the younger test takers.

In a different study, researchers at Rhode Island Hospital and Brown University have estimated a decline in IQ scores for even younger children, between ages three months and three years.[82] (The findings are still being peer-reviewed.) The study, conducted with 672 healthy children, highlights concerning findings: US children born during the pandemic displayed lower verbal, motor, and cognitive abilities compared with those born before it. Researchers compared the cognitive scores of children in 2020 and 2021 with those from the previous decade using the Mullen Scales of Early Learning, which evaluates fine and gross motor skills, visual reception, and language abilities. Previously, the average IQ for children in this age group was about 100, but it dropped to 78 among children in the study. A 22-point drop would mean we have shed the benefits of a hundred years of progress.

Are we getting dumber as a species as a result of declining social connections? Data suggest there is cause for concern. A more positive take would be that our intelligence may simply be adapting to the different skills and competencies that are valuable in today's world.

In any case, the fact that the circles of relationships around young children are often small, frayed, and under stress has major implications for our social brains, our society, and the future of civilization. We need to change our approach to caring for and educating our next generations by infusing love into learning and putting the focus on relationships across all the environments young children inhabit.

CHAPTER 3

The Kids Aren't All Right

A person's a person, no matter how small.
> —Dr. Seuss, *HORTON HEARS A WHO!*, 1954

The greatest invention in the world is the mind of a child.
> —Thomas Edison

In the course of visiting early childhood and childcare settings in urban slums and rural areas in Kenya, I have been inspired by the Maasai people, one of the most formidable warrior tribes in East Africa. After all, the rite of passage to become a Maasai warrior is to kill a lion with a spear! Known for their deep-rooted traditions and profound sense of community, the Maasai greet one another not with the customary "How are you?" but with a question that reflects the collective wisdom of their tribe: "Casserian Egeri?" or "How are the children doing?" This seemingly simple yet profound inquiry serves as a powerful reminder that the well-being of the youngest generation is a priority for any society. So let me ask, how are our children doing?

The undeniable reality is that many of our kids aren't all right. Their struggles and challenges, far from being isolated incidents, reflect the larger relational crisis I've described in the last chapter. The global pandemic, with its far-reaching consequences, exacerbated problems that have been growing for decades, making it more urgent than ever to focus on cultivating our children's relational intelligence. How, exactly, can that be done?

In 2021, I had the opportunity to connect online with a woman I'll call Maria, to protect her privacy, before I met her in person at Adventist HealthCare's Lourie Center for Children's Social and Emotional Wellness in Rockville, Maryland. Maria and her husband had arrived at the Lourie Center three years before, seeking answers for their then two-year-old son, Lucas. The family has a busy household cluttered by Legos and often filled with the joyful shouts and thumps of Lucas and his brothers at play. They absolutely love the chaos. But Lucas—a smart, caring, silly, loving, and curious little boy—was having an extremely difficult time coping with day-to-day transitions. He needed help learning how to regulate his emotions, and Maria and her husband needed support in raising him. They were referred to the therapeutic nursery program at the Lourie Center, where Lucas could be himself and learn how to sort out his feelings.

The Lourie Center is a comprehensive early childhood intervention program that offers clinical services to support children and their families who are experiencing or dealing with an array of social, emotional, mental, and behavioral health needs. These services are inspired by attachment theory and the belief that a strong bond with a caregiver early in life is critical for a child's development. The center's mission is to foster the growth and care of the whole child, which necessarily involves the child's family and teachers. This holistic approach embraces all learners, and especially those who have experienced trauma.

The Lourie Center was started in the 1980s by three "godfathers" of child development. Reginald Lourie, T. Berry Brazelton, and Stanley Greenspan, all physicians, were part of the founding and planning committee for Head Start, the federal early childhood program. Lourie, who died in 1988, was born in Brooklyn in 1909 and trained as a psychiatrist at the New York Psychiatric Institute. But it was during World War II, when he served in the navy as a lieutenant commander, that he experienced trauma firsthand. His service on the front line catalyzed his drive as a pioneer in child trauma treatment after the war. Lourie's influence in the then nascent field of child psychiatry was foundational at multiple levels. He taught many young pediatricians to consider mental and emotional factors in the treatment of children, a novel approach at a time when the practice of medicine focused primarily on physical factors, and he deeply influenced how hospitals treat the parent-child connection. In 1948, when he joined the DC Children's Hospital (now Children's National Hospital), parents were only allowed to visit their children one to two hours per week, based on the theory that their presence would be disruptive to professional staff. Lourie changed the rules, allowing parents almost unlimited visiting privileges. In doing so, he altered the institutional mindset to emphasize that all children need the loving presence of their parents, including in—especially in—hospital settings. With his two colleagues, Lourie founded the Lourie Center, the first of its kind, anchored on the influential principles of whole child learning and the primacy of the family-child relationship.

When Maria and her husband first enrolled Lucas at the Lourie Center, they were terrified. They did not know how things would go, given that Lucas was having multiple challenging tantrums and engaging in many disruptive behaviors every day. Lucas also had a significant speech delay, and his parents were concerned that no one would be able to understand him.

One day shortly after Lucas started at the Lourie Center, Maria recalls, she was sitting behind the observation mirror to see how he was adapting to his new learning environment. It was a revelation for her to see the exquisite care the teachers devoted to grappling with each child's unique struggles, displaying the kind of tenderness and devotion most people reserved for their own offspring. She watched a group of children playing with a teacher. One was brushing the teacher's hair, another was pretending to do her nails, a third was pretending to be a police officer, and another a firefighter. Maria saw one of the other teachers sitting with Lucas at a table having a snack—*her* son, the child who constantly had challenging episodes. Both of them were chatting, as if they were grown-ups meeting at a restaurant for lunch. Maria couldn't believe what she was seeing. She could have sat there forever watching this positive interaction unfold.

The COVID-19 pandemic hit most of us hard, and it certainly had an impact on Maria's family and Lucas's routines. Maria told me about a deeply disturbing incident that took place at the onset of the pandemic, when Lucas was three and classes at the Lourie Center had to move online. After Lucas had had a particularly upsetting afternoon, Maria found him wrapping the dog's leash around his own neck. Of course she intervened straightaway, and her heart broke seeing her little boy do such a thing. She reached out to the teachers about the incident. One of them immediately blocked out time for a one-on-one online session with Lucas. As Maria sat next to her son, she witnessed him confide in his teacher how upset he had been and what he had done. He was able to do this not just because she was his teacher, but because of the trusting relationship they had built together. She and Lucas interacted for hours, and Maria learned a lot about her son during that session. Maria was so grateful. She felt that her son was loved and understood. She felt that he was safe.

Maria learned at the Lourie Center that trauma can be passed from one generation to the next. She had been abused by an uncle when she was six, and had moved frequently during her childhood, often living in homeless shelters. She believes that the Lourie Center is helping Lucas and his two brothers avoid carrying that intergenerational trauma forward by assisting them in developing secure attachment through her and other nurturing adults. From Maria's perspective, Lucas's classroom is a spectacular place where little learners, who might be identified as "problem children" in many other settings, are seen simply as children. They are not defined by their behaviors, but are understood to need a little more help in learning how to recognize and express their feelings in order to thrive in the outside world.

Lucas, who is now five, is transitioning to a traditional public school, not a special education program. Nearly 80 percent of young children who attend the Lourie Center's therapeutic nursery program will go on to learn in a traditional kindergarten setting.[1] This is an extraordinary achievement considering that the program only accepts children who need meaningful behavioral, cognitive, social-emotional, and mental health support. Lucas's language and emotional regulation skills have improved considerably. With the right nurturing environment, as well as steady, loving relationships with his parents and teachers, he is now ready.

Lucas's story might seem rare. In reality, there are numerous children like Lucas, with many more yet to be discovered. Our society is grappling with a significant burden of challenges among children. In a world where the circles of human connection are contracting, the unsettling reality emerges: the intimacy of familial bonds and the richness of communal interactions, once the nurturing bedrock of growth and development, are giving way to isolating effects. A 2023 editorial in *The Atlantic* was duly titled "America Is in Its Insecure Attachment Era."[2] The erosion of relational closeness is casting long shadows over our children's well-being, leaving us to grapple with the profound implications of living in a society where the fundamental human need for connection is increasingly unmet. As we venture into the heart of this issue, we must ask ourselves how, in a world that feels ever more disconnected, we can mend the fabric of relationship that is vital for our young ones.

Frayed Emotional Bonds

Dani Dumitriu, an accomplished neuroscientist and pediatrician, is an associate professor at Columbia University Irving Medical Center; she also cares for newborns at the Morgan Stanley Children's Hospital in New York City. She humbly laughed with me about the array of diplomas she has earned. Dumitriu spends about 80 percent of her professional time researching the neurobiological basis of resilience—including studying interactions between children and parents/caregivers and analyzing behaviors and brain patterns in mice and wild rats—and 20 percent practicing as a pediatrician in the (human) nursery. At the onset of the COVID-19 pandemic, Dumitriu observed distress in moms in the nursery and hypothesized that the pandemic would lead to changes in emotional connection between mothers and babies. As part of an ongoing study, she investigated this question and quantitatively observed that emotional connection was reduced—*by half.*

You may recall the early days of the pandemic in New York. The hospital ship USNS *Comfort* arrived in the city's harbor on March 30, 2020. Temporary field hospitals were set up across the five boroughs. Refrigerator trucks parked outside hospitals to accommodate the overflow of bodies. Constant ambulance sirens signaled the dire situation. Even a tiger in the Bronx Zoo tested positive for COVID. In early April 2020, New York City had nearly 25 percent of the total deaths from COVID in the US.[3] In the midst of this crisis, Dumitriu enrolled pregnant women into a study that assessed potential transmission of the COVID-19 virus from mother to fetus. She thankfully concluded quickly that the virus was not transmittable that way, but while tracking the data she observed something else.

Right before the pandemic, Dumitriu had been measuring the emotional bond between babies and moms using a validated scale called the Welch Emotional Connection Screen (WECS) that tracks four domains of connection: attraction, vocal communication, facial communication, and reciprocity between parent and baby. She had been concerned by the generally low levels of emotional connection between mothers and babies she was documenting; she had estimated the strong emotional connection rate, measured by the WECS, at only 40 percent.[4]

But now she noticed that babies were generally even less responsive to their mothers than they had been before the pandemic; they seemed fussier and more detached. Mothers were also more distracted and stressed. And when she measured the connection using the WECS, she found a troubling decline in strong emotional bonds. The prepandemic rate of 40 percent had dropped to a disheartening 20 percent. Six out of ten babies lacked a strong emotional bond with their mothers before COVID, and eight in ten did not establish a strong connection at the height of the crisis. The societal implications of these findings for the years to come are mind-boggling. As we have repeatedly seen, close nurturing relationships in the early years are like the foundation of a house. If that foundation is not solid, the house may shake apart later in strong winds.

Why this drop in emotional connection during the pandemic? We don't really know. There are multiple hypotheses. The first is that the pandemic exacerbated stress for many parents, and emotional stress in children is closely linked to that of their parents. Moreover, parents' emotional stress is tied to hardships, which were aggravated during the pandemic. Money may not lead to happiness, but poverty certainly causes stress. It can even hinder a child's brain development. Many women, with no childcare available, left their jobs. For those who didn't, the stress of being both full-time employee and full-time mother was profound. The added pressures weren't just from money worries; they included the toll of the extra work at home, health concerns, unsettling changes, and the pandemic's murky outlook. Parents and children became more isolated, another factor that hinders emotional connections.

Dumitriu observed that breastfeeding declined during the pandemic, especially among Latino mothers. Connection between breastfeeding and attachment is complicated: breastfeeding contributes to child attachment security, although bottle feeding can be as bonding as breastfeeding.[5] Dumitriu also reported that some new, more anxious mothers were wearing masks even at home to protect their newborns.

She had always been intrigued by the famous "still-face" experiment conducted by Ed Tronick in 1975.[6] Tronick videotaped exchanges between infants and mothers and found that "after three minutes of 'interaction' with a nonresponsive, expressionless mother, the infant rapidly sobers and grows wary, then makes repeated attempts to get the interaction to return to its usual reciprocal pattern. When these attempts fail, the infant withdraws [and] orients his face and body away from his mother with a withdrawn, hopeless facial expression." The experiment illustrated the importance of emotional expression in communicating to babies. Dumitriu was naturally concerned that mask wearing played a role in the drop in emotional connection she'd observed. However, at the onset of COVID Tronick himself repeated the still-face experiment with a small group of families and showed that babies don't mind when Mom puts on a mask.[7] What matters is the attunement and interaction between the baby and the person they are relating to.

Various studies have shown a meaningful increase in emotional issues in young children connected to the pandemic's restrictions.[8] Phil Fisher, my colleague at Stanford University, started tracking the impact of the pandemic on families with young children in April 2020 via a survey called RAPID-EC. The study has shown that emotional distress in children under age five—as measured by a child's externalizing behaviors (caregivers report how often the phrase "fussy or defiant" fits their child's behavior in the last week) or internalizing behaviors (caregivers report how often the phrase "too fearful or anxious" fits their child's behavior in the last week)—has nearly doubled since 2020, and remains at elevated levels long past the peak of the pandemic.[9]

Prior pandemics suggest there is cause for academic concern. Babies born within the two-year span of the height of the 1918 influenza epidemic experienced a 15 percent reduction in high school graduation rates compared with those born in the two years before and after the pandemic.[10]

Recent data on attachment trends among college students are similarly troubling. In 2014, Sara Konrath at the University of Indiana documented a rise in narcissism and a decline in empathy in youth, which she described in a paper titled "The Empathy Paradox: Increasing Disconnection in the Age of Increasing Connection."[11] Concerned about the impact of this trend on human relationships, she partnered with William Chopik, a psychology professor at Michigan State University and an expert on attachment, to conduct a meta-analysis of nearly one hundred studies on attachment published between 1988 and 2011. Their results painted a disheartening picture: a 15 percent decline in secure attachment among college students, coupled with a 56 percent surge in avoidant/dismissive attachment and an almost 18 percent rise in the fearful-avoidant style—both associated with distrust and isolation.[12] They observed that a higher proportion of students reported feeling "comfortable without close emotional relationships" relative to the 1980s. Konrath and Chopik updated this analysis and presented the results at a conference in Chicago in 2022. Starting with the good news: narcissism rates are steadily declining, and empathy rates have climbed since 2009. But here comes the sobering reality on attachment: from 2011 to 2020, rates of secure attachment in college students continued to drop and fearful attachment to rise.[13]

Waning Wellness

The decline in emotional connections and attachments has profound consequences for our children, triggering a cascading impact on their development and well-being. In response to a dramatic surge in mental health issues among youth and their families, three leading health organizations—the American Academy of Pediatrics, the American Academy of Child and Adolescent Psychiatry, and the Children's Hospital Association—united in 2021 to sound the alarm. They declared a national state of emergency in children's mental health, signaling an urgent call to action to address this escalating crisis.

Just as emotional connectedness was declining before the pandemic and then dropped precipitously as a consequence of it, so mental health problems such as anxiety and depression were on the rise for children and young people before the pandemic and were exacerbated by it. A global metastudy found that rates of childhood depression and anxiety had doubled in 2021. Three in five high school girls in the US report "persistent feelings of sadness or hopelessness" (up from 36 percent in 2011), according to the Centers for Disease Control and Prevention.[14]

Mental health concerns seem to also be on the rise for younger children. Olivia Carter, a school counselor at Jefferson Elementary in Cape Girardeau, Missouri, reported that when she joined the school in 2016, activating the suicide protocol was a rare occurrence, needed only once or twice annually. However, in a troubling shift, she now finds herself counseling at least one student every month who is grappling with thoughts of self-harm or suicide.[15]

Sadly, data from the National Hospital Ambulatory Medical Care Survey confirm Carter's observation and show that the proportion of pediatric mental health–related emergency visits has more than doubled for five- to nine-year-olds in the past decade, including a thirty-five-fold increase in suicide-related visits![16]

Behavioral issues are also increasing. Twice as many teachers witness violent incidents in classrooms relative to prepandemic.[17] A kindergarten teacher in El Paso, Texas, told a reporter with *El Paso Matters* that in her decade of experience, she had only occasionally encountered students with anger issues. She was surprised to have three disruptive students in her class during the fall 2022 semester. By February 2023, the number had increased to seven, nearly one-third of her students.[18]

Children are also experiencing a decline in physical wellness. Before the pandemic, a preschool teacher told me that she was witnessing more children falling out of their chairs. I thought at first I had misheard her, but I have confirmed this observation with other preschool teachers. Kids are literally falling from their seats. One teacher even shared that her students had experienced more than forty falls in a single week. What could the reason be? Children have fewer opportunities to move. As a result, their proprioceptive and vestibular senses, honed through movement—especially movement involving swinging or spinning—are failing to develop as they should.[19] In other words, children are getting vertigo from not moving, playing, and physically interacting with others.

Vertigo and myopia (connected to the surge in digital usage) are just two of many physical manifestations in our little ones of the relational deprivation crisis. Sedentary lifestyles are also driving a global rise in childhood obesity: a threefold increase since the 1970s.[20] As many as 13 percent of American two- to five-year-olds are obese.[21]

Another physical phenomenon is earlier puberty. In a dozen countries, the onset of puberty in girls has advanced by approximately three months per decade since the 1970s.[22] A comparable trend, albeit less pronounced, has also been observed in boys. Doctors reported an uptick during the pandemic.[23] The reasons are not entirely clear, although experts cite stress, decrease in physical activity, and use of electronic devices as probable factors. Exposure to blue light produced by screens has been shown to cause earlier puberty in rats.[24]

Stunted Social Skills

At the school that my younger child attends, we have a beautiful yearly tradition called the Red Carpet Event where families of "old" students welcome families who are new to the school. We have participated in this custom year after year. But in 2022, something noticeably changed. My family was paired with two newly arrived families who were each enrolling a child in the preschool program. For each of the two five-year-old girls, it would be their first time in a group learning environment, as they both had been raised at home during the pandemic. We connected online first and then met one of the families at a park. Despite our attempts to connect with the children through basic questions like "What is your name?" and "Are you excited about your new school?" neither child properly communicated with us. I don't mean that they couldn't speak, but they were both strikingly shy. This is just a small personal experience that reflects a broader context—a generation of children who are stunted socially.

As a result of shrinking relational circles and reduced social interactions during the pandemic, babies, toddlers, and preschoolers are struggling with age-appropriate social skills. Babies have been found to show more difficulty understanding facial expressions.[25] For toddlers and preschoolers, an analysis of 2.5 million children younger than five showed that first-time speech delay diagnoses increased by an average of 1.6 times between 2018–2019 and 2021–2022.[26] Of even greater concern, the highest increase was among one-year-olds.[27] Research also shows less verbal turn-taking between parents and children, as well as between childcare providers and children.[28] (Turn-taking during conversation is an important mechanism for building brain connectivity that supports the development of social-emotional and language skills.) Parents of children with autism spectrum disorder reported regression in skills and worsening of symptoms.[29]

In the wake of these developments—or, rather, failures to develop— educators report that many young children lack confidence in group activities. In a 2023 survey of more than a thousand educators across forty-two states, eight in ten reported that students were "developmentally behind in self-regulation and relationship building."[30]

Social stunting can have long-term impacts on future social interactions. For instance, children with cancer who must be removed from their friends for treatment are less likely to have as many friends after remission.[31] Little learners need encouragement to reconnect with others postpandemic.

Hindered Learning

Some kids are struggling more than others. More than one in five children live in poverty in forty of the world's richest countries, the highest rate of any age group.[32] Seventy-one percent of poor children in the US are children of color.[33] Child hunger remains a persistent issue, affecting millions in the US and globally. Schools in the US are slipping backward in terms of segregation. Early childhood programs are twice as likely as K–12 to be populated nearly 100 percent by Black or Hispanic kids.[34] These economic inequities and social injustices also pervade children's education. Most people are aware that endemic inequities exist in the quality and funding of education. What is less well understood is how early children are affected by them.

Disparities emerge startlingly early. Stanford research indicates that eighteen-month-olds from lower-income families fall six months behind in language development compared with their higher-income peers, a gap that widens significantly by kindergarten.[35] This early lag in development signals a broader trend: nearly 60 percent of children between three and five years old in the US are not developmentally on track.[36] Achievement gaps are largely set by age five, and often peak at age five or six.[37]

The stakes are high. Children who start behind are likely to remain behind, influencing their educational trajectory and future socioeconomic status. There is a 90 percent chance that a poor reader at the end of first grade will be a poor reader at the end of fourth grade.[38] The domino effect of these early disparities is profound, with substantial implications for lifelong learning, health, societal contributions, and even national security. A 2023 report by the Council for a Strong America quantifies this crisis, estimating a staggering $122 billion in lost earnings, productivity, and revenue every year due to limitations in access to quality childcare.[39]

We know how to solve these problems. Quality early learning programs are proven to close these gaps and carry benefits that extend far beyond the young years. Children enrolled in such programs are more than twice as likely to be on track in early literacy and numeracy skills than children who miss out, according to UNICEF.[40] A child in Nepal attending an early childhood program is seventeen times more likely to be on track on early literacy and numeracy. While some gains seem to fade by third grade, the "sleeper effects" of early childhood education

GRAPH 3

The Education Funnel: Inequities Start in the Early Years
Achievement Gap Is Largely Set by Age 5

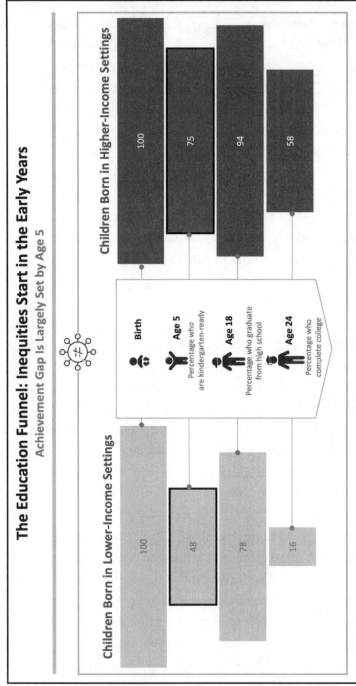

Children Born in Higher-Income Settings

Stage	Value
Birth	100
Age 5	75
Age 18	94
Age 24	58

Children Born in Lower-Income Settings

Stage	Value
Birth	100
Age 5	48
Age 18	78
Age 24	16

Birth

Age 5 — Percentage who are kindergarten-ready

Age 18 — Percentage who graduate from high school

Age 24 — Percentage who complete college

Sources:

• Kindergarten: *Achieving Kindergarten Readiness* (Bridgespan Group and Pritzker Children's Initiative, 2015), www.bridgespan.org/insights/early-childhood-funder-guide-2015.

• K–12: Nichols, A. H., and Anthony, Marshall, Jr., "Graduation Rates Don't Tell the Full Story," Education Trust, March 5, 2020, https://edtrust.org/resource/graduation-rates-dont-tell-the-full-story-racial-gaps-in-college-success-are-larger-than-we-think/.

• College: *Indicators of Higher Education Equity in the United States* (Pell Institute, 2024), www.pellinstitute.org/wp-content/uploads/2024/05/PELL_2024_Indicators-Report_f.pdf.

reveal themselves in adulthood.[41] Longitudinal studies in locations ranging from Boston to North Carolina affirm that early education yields long-term benefits, such as higher high school completion rates, college enrollment, and motivation.[42]

But too few programs measure up. Fewer than 10 percent of childcare settings in the US are rated as very high quality.[43] And access to early learning programs is inequitably distributed. According to a study from the nonprofit education research and advocacy organization Education Trust, a dismal 1 percent of Latino children and 4 percent of Black children are enrolled in state preschool programs considered high quality.[44]

When children of color are enrolled in an early learning program, they are three times more likely to be expelled than white children, and children who experience expulsion at a young age are at higher risk of facing further disciplinary actions and expulsions in later stages of their educational journey. Expulsions in preschool are more frequent than in K–12 due to a combination of factors related to children's struggles with social skills and self-regulation, inconsistent school policies, limited resources and supports, teacher/adult biases, inadequate teacher-child ratios, and lack of early intervention programs.

What this all adds up to: Black children are generally eight months behind their white peers in learning when they enter kindergarten.[45] By third grade, the average gap is bigger, and by eighth grade it is larger still.

The Creativity Crisis

As we become increasingly isolated and less attuned to one another's emotional needs, it is no wonder that the creativity of our younger generations may suffer. Creativity thrives in the soil of emotional bonds and secure attachments, and as these vital connections dwindle, so too might the spark of innovation and imaginative thinking. Moreover, creativity, as Einstein understood well, requires free time.[46] Our creative insights often appear when we're in the shower or on a walk.[47] Yet an average child now only spends four to seven minutes outside in an unstructured activity every day.[48] Children are naturally born creative geniuses, imagining new possibilities and expressing themselves in unique ways. They think outside the box because they don't yet know any box. But alarmingly, research has disclosed a steep decline in children's creative capacity, plummeting by over 85 percent since the 1990s.[49]

Kyung Hee Kim was born in rural South Korea to parents who were illiterate, having received only first- and third-grade educations. She became the first girl from her village to go to high school and eventually earned a PhD in the United States. Thanks to the support of one of her teachers at a young age, Kim avoided her likely future: working in a textile factory. In 2011, her research on creativity made headlines.[50]

Kim's extensive analysis of the Torrance Tests of Creative Thinking (an assessment that, while not flawless, is a robust predictor of creative prowess over a lifetime) illustrated a consistent rise in creativity scores until 1990, after which a persistent downward trend emerged. The most acute drop in creativity, alarmingly, affected the youngest learners. Kim suggests that this contraction in creative thought is linked to the restrictive nature of standardized education, an overemphasis on structured activities rather than on connecting with others in physical play, and the sensory limitations of digital interactions. Kim's analysis has been debated. Other researchers label the results a negligible decline in creativity rather than a crisis.[51]

The implications of this decline extend far beyond individual capabilities, potentially fraying the very fabric of society. Creativity is the engine of innovation and problem-solving, and its erosion threatens to undermine the development of future leaders and changemakers. Yet creativity finds its footing within the realm of social interaction. The dynamic of sharing, imagining, and collaborative problem-solving among children not only amplifies the joy of creation but also sets the cornerstone for a lifetime of inventive and adaptive thinking.

Surely parents do not intend to stifle their children's creativity or stunt their resilience. But if, as all these data show, our kids aren't all right, and that shrinking relational circles have something to do with it, we must acknowledge that the kids are not to blame. We adults are in charge. In the next chapter, I will discuss how our physical proximity to children and our increased engagement in managing their daily lives belie a deepening emotional distance that has significant consequences.

CHAPTER 4

Here but Not Here:
Physically Present,
Emotionally Absent Parents

Nurtured children are the consequence of nurturing adults. So to invest in children means also investing in the people around them—the parents, carers, grandparents, early years workforce and more.

—PRINCESS OF WALES, ROYAL FOUNDATION
CENTRE FOR EARLY CHILDHOOD, 2021

It's an interesting paradox that the rise of the new parenting style dubbed "intensive parenting" has roots in the ever-smaller relational circles in our lives. Increasingly isolated parents are often raising children essentially by themselves. But while parents deeply feel the need to be more physically present, they are also increasingly emotionally absent, more stressed, and constantly disrupted by technology. They are squeezed and screened.

The Surprising Loneliness of Parenthood

Parents are among the loneliest of adults. The Parenting Index, a study of parenting across sixteen countries, shows that even in our hyperconnected world, 32 percent of new parents report that they are lonely.[1] A majority of American mothers with young children (51 percent) report being "seriously lonely," and in the UK, a survey found that 90 percent of new mothers felt lonely after giving birth, with over half feeling they had no friends.[2]

The situation is even worse for stay-at-home moms. They are more likely to experience sadness, anger, and depression than employed moms.[3] In 2023, the organization Mother Untitled carried out a survey of one thousand members of the general population, and twelve hundred college-educated mothers who stayed at home and women actively contemplating the decision to become stay-at-home moms.[4] The study revealed that the notion of the stay-at-home "mom squad" is a myth. Half of participants experienced a reduction in their circle of mom friends after leaving the workforce and found it challenging to form new friendships as stay-at-home parents. More than one in ten stay-at-home mothers said they don't have any mom friends. On the positive side, childcare availability has been shown to help the mental health of both employed and full-time moms.[5]

The data are thinner for dads, and seem to suggest that fathers are often lonelier than mothers. Fathers tend to have fewer friends on average,[6] and may find that their "best friend"—their spouse—has shifted priorities to caring for the new baby.

Parental loneliness often remains a silent issue, obscured by dominant societal expectations. Society typically paints a picture of parenthood as an all-encompassing, fulfilling journey, leaving little room for parents to voice their struggles without fear of judgment or criticism. Parents may feel pressured to maintain the facade of a contented life, fearing that admitting loneliness could be misconstrued as a lack of gratitude for or competence in their parental role. This pressure, tied to the idealization of parenting, stifles open discussions about the isolation that can be a part of raising young children.

Moreover, the intense schedule of modern parenting—with its endless cycle of work, childcare, and household management—allows little time for the cultivation of personal relationships that might alleviate feelings of solitude. The transition into parenthood can shift social dynamics dramatically, often leading to a decline in the quality of existing friendships and making it challenging to forge new connections with other parents facing similar constraints. In a world increasingly leaning on digital forms of communication, the meaningful, face-to-face interactions that ward off loneliness are frequently sacrificed. Consequently, the silent battle with loneliness continues behind closed doors, with many parents reluctant to expose their vulnerability in a society that prizes self-sufficiency, selfless devotion to children, and the appearance of unwavering strength.

We might cherish the moments spent with our baby yet find ourselves overwhelmed by the routine of caregiving—the repertoire of feedings, diaper changes, laundry loads, and lullaby on constant repeat, and the exhausting sleep deprivation. Parenthood might be the most precious experience in our life, yet we yearn for meaningful adult conversations. We may feel grateful for the gift of a child but simultaneously long for the life we led before, missing the camaraderie of coworkers and mourning the fading connections with friends who've grown distant. For those of us who stay home, there are moments when resentment simmers as our partner heads off to work each morning, leaving us feeling trapped in our own version of *Groundhog Day* with our newborn, our career aspirations in indefinite suspension.

Many new mothers lack the privilege of a break from work. About 80 percent of US workers don't have access to paid leave. A quarter of mothers who lack such access return to work within ten days of giving birth, despite the recommendation of the American College of Obstetricians and Gynecologists that women take at least six weeks off postpartum. Among the most developed countries in the world, the US is one of only three that do not offer statutory paid maternity leave.[7] This has profound consequences for new mothers and their little ones.

Investing meaningful time with our baby not only enhances baby's cognitive development but also contributes to the overall well-being of both child and parent. Research by Natalie Brito, at NYU Steinhardt School of Culture, Education, and Human Development, reveals three important findings.[8] First, infants of mothers who benefited from three-month paid leave had more mature patterns of brain function compared with infants whose mothers had unpaid leave. Second, mothers with paid leave had lower levels of physiological stress. And lastly, mothers with paid leave displayed higher levels of sensitivity and responsiveness during free-play interactions with their infants. Additionally, an extended period of paid leave, ranging from six to twelve months, has proven to be instrumental in reducing depressive symptoms and alleviating stress among parents.[9]

Intensive Parenting or Intrusive Parenting?

The implication of shrinking relational circles is that children are raised by more isolated parents who feel more pressure to be physically present. Parents in affluent countries (with the exception of my native country—vive la France!) now spend twice as much time with their children as they did fifty years ago.[10] Today, many working mothers devote more time to their children than mothers in earlier generations who didn't have jobs outside their homes. In the past half century, fathers in the US have nearly quadrupled the time they devote to caring for their child.[11]

"Intensive parenting has really become the dominant cultural model for how children should be raised," says Patrick Ishizuka. As a researcher at Cornell Population Center, he interviewed more than thirty-six hundred parents, asking them to evaluate six fictional vignettes across two styles of parenting, labeled "concerted cultivation" and "natural growth." Here's a sample vignette: "When David's son is diagnosed with asthma, the doctor says that medication might help. David's son says, 'I don't want to take medicine.'" Parents were asked to rate the following two responses. The concerted cultivation response: "Let's talk about the medicine with the doctor. You can ask any questions you have and learn how the medicine can help you." The natural growth response: "Well, you're going to have to take it anyway. You need to listen to what the doctor says and take the medicine." The results of Ishizuka's study are clear: an overwhelming majority—75 percent of parents across social classes—scored the "concerted cultivation" style as either very good or excellent, suggesting that "cultural norms of child-centered, time-intensive mothering and fathering are now pervasive."[12]

Greater parental involvement is overall a major positive development, driving better academic, emotional, and social outcomes, including more positive peer relationships and fewer behavior problems at school. It's good news that, according to Pew Research, nearly half of parents say they are trying to raise their children differently than they were raised, being more involved and giving them more love and affection than what they received as children.[13] They want their children to feel as though they are growing up in a loving home that offers a lot of support and outward praise.

Yet the intensive parenting style can backfire. There is a fine line between loving and smothering, between supportive and overprotective parenting. Overprotective parenting, which includes intrusive and unnecessary micromanagement of a child's independent activities, has been repeatedly linked with challenges in young children, including anxiety, social withdrawal, and peer difficulties, and with insecure attachment in teens.[14]

Ultimately, it is the type, rather than the amount, of parental involvement that is crucial in driving child outcomes. Psychological control is not a good thing for children. What is beneficial is parenting that is nurturing and supportive of a child's autonomy.

Some of us watch with amazement and a tinge of envy a popular reality show imported from Japan called *Old Enough!*[15] It features toddlers running around town doing errands, all without their parents. In one episode, a two-year-old went on a twenty-three-minute walk to buy food and flowers, and a three-year-old retrieved his dad's jacket from home, which was a bus ride away. Observing a young child successfully manage simple (for adults) yet intricate (for youngsters) tasks filled me with an overwhelming sense of joy. It led me to ponder just how capable children truly are and, conversely, how our society might be unintentionally hindering their development. Only 13 percent of American children walk or bike to school, down from around 50 percent in the 1970s.[16] *Old Enough!* serves as a thought-provoking exploration of global perspectives on granting children autonomy and responsibilities.

In Maple Heights, Ohio, a family called the police on a child who was mowing a lawn, and two weeks later as he played on a Slip 'n Slide in a neighboring yard.[17] In Elmhurst, Illinois, a suburb near Chicago, a concerned person called the police to report that a boy was chopping wood along a prairie path. The young boy said he was trying to build a fort for himself and his friends. Police confiscated the tools and returned them to the boy's parents.[18] In Charlotte, North Carolina, youngsters attending the Learning Collaborative were delighted to receive a collection of well-maintained, gently used playground equipment. But the children quickly discovered that they wouldn't be permitted to use it because it was placed on grass instead of wood chips. Safety concerns were cited as the reason for prohibiting playing on grass.[19] Meanwhile, in Richland School District, in Washington State, swings are now banned from school playgrounds, also for safety reasons.[20] Nationwide, tall, metal racer slides have been replaced with shorter, plastic ones.

Over the past three decades, American childhood has changed considerably. Our society has prioritized safety at the expense of encouraging children to take reasonable risks, and academic expectations over joyful play-based learning. While this may be well-intended, our children are increasingly raised in smaller and highly protected bubbles. They can't run errands; they can't use tools; they can't play on grass; they can't swing, spin, or race; they have limited opportunities for unstructured play-based activities.

This extends to adolescence. Only 30 percent of teens ages sixteen to nineteen had a summer job in 2021, a meaningful drop from 51 percent in 2000.[21] They also are less involved in risk-taking activities. And while you may think it's a great development for the health of our kids and our nation that substance use, unprotected sex, crime, and hazardous automobile driving by teens are all on the decline, there is also a negative side to these trends. Many young people increasingly choose to stay within the comfort zone of a small network of like-minded friends whom they connect with virtually. That may lead to less risk-taking behavior, but it also means fewer relationships and potentially less happiness. Consider for a moment that University of Oxford sociologist Robin Dunbar has shown that living near a pub, an important British neighborhood landmark, makes people happier as they tend to have more close friends.[22]

The Big Squeeze

Over the past two decades, sociologists have noted that young adults are being "squeezed."[23] And those who are raising young children are not just squeezed; they are supersqueezed. They simply can't do it all.

For one thing, modern parents of young children feel squeezed for time. Changes in the nature of work have led to a culture where workers are perpetually available to their employers, fostering an unhealthy environment of overwork, while at the same time isolation and societal norms have led parents to spend more time with children. Although the amount of time parents spend with children has meaningfully increased over the past few decades, a majority of parents worry that it is not enough and feel they are too busy to enjoy life.[24]

Parents are also squeezed by a deluge of digital information and the judgments perpetrated in social media around the requirements of being a good parent, a good friend, a good citizen, or a good person. In a survey of sixty-five hundred parents, 83 percent agreed with the statement "Others think my children's academic success is a reflection of my parenting."[25]

Parents are working or studying more, yet earning less, than their own parents, and their incomes or jobs have become less secure. People are increasingly disillusioned about the promise of upward intergenerational mobility, and many question whether they will ever be able to earn more than or even as much as their parents. They dream less about achieving the American dream. The Stanford Center on Longevity conducted the Milestones Project, which looked at major life achievements. It revealed that although people's aspirations for reaching milestones have not meaningfully changed, the ability to actualize them has been pushed later and later, generation after generation.[26]

Parents are squeezed by the expenses associated with kids, which are steadily increasing. The average cost of raising a child in the US now exceeds $250,000 and is close to $400,000 for families making $100,000 or more a year—and that is only until the child is seventeen, so it excludes the exorbitant and rising costs of college.[27] The expenses of raising a middle-class family—including housing, education, health care, childcare, and retirement—have risen considerably.[28] Among these expenditures, childcare is witnessing one of the most rapid rates of growth, even surpassing another swiftly rising category: health care.[29] More than a third of US families with children under age five experience at least one material hardship, defined as having difficulty paying for basic needs in one or more of the following categories: food, housing, utilities, childcare, medical care.[30]

Parents are further squeezed by spending on enrichment activities for children. A *New York Times* article on the sport of fencing, for instance, revealed that parents spent up to $100,000 per year on the activity, thinking of it as a promising pipeline to admission at elite colleges.[31] This phenomenon is spreading across lower income levels.[32]

Parents are squeezed by the costs of obtaining more education for themselves, as today's jobs and those of the future require being better educated. Then they are squeezed by student debt, with mounting expenses to pay for both their own and their children's education. They will no doubt be squeezed by artificial intelligence as it impacts their jobs or their children's future trajectories.

Adults of parenting age are often simultaneously squeezed by the responsibility to care for elderly parents or relatives, which is why they've been called the "sandwich generation."

Black, Latino, Native American, and Asian parents are under added pressure from worrying about their own and their family's safety, as well as by having to endure endless racism.

All of us are squeezed by the ways climate change impacts our daily lives, including the increase in extreme weather events and natural disasters; as well as by gun violence in schools and other spaces, and the resulting need to constantly seek strategies to protect our little ones.

And finally, parents are squeezed by technology. The intrusion of smartphones into family interactions is diminishing the quality and depth of those moments. Checking phones eighty times a day, parents have fewer verbal and nonverbal interactions with their children.[33] Parents are more physically present yet more emotionally absent. (We will look into this subject in greater depth in Chapter 7, "Junk Tech Woes.")

Something has to give. Many parents leave the workforce altogether. Employment rates are lower among parents with younger children. Families also have fewer babies. Fertility rates are plummeting, as discussed in the last chapter. But these are ultimately short-term solutions leading to a dead end. We need to do better, for parents, children, our communities, and our larger society. Things have to change. But how?

The past fifty years have produced monumental scientific advancements in our understanding of child development alongside revolutionary changes in our technological capacity. These developments illuminate a better path forward, in which we harness the power of relationships to nurture and educate our children, to reinvigorate our communities, and to reimagine and reinvent our collective future. Let's take a look at what we've learned and at how we've begun to apply it to help little learners—and their communities—thrive. These are the topics of the rest of the book.

PART II

THE NEW SCIENCE OF
LOVE AND LEARNING

Through others we become ourselves.

—LEV S. VYGOTSKY, 1931

CHAPTER 5

The Scientific Re*lov*ution

We're always trying to understand what the other person's doing. In order to survive as a species, we had to learn to "read" the people around us so that we could collaborate, fight enemies, and find food. So the social brain is [always] there, and it appears to be active very early in our development.
—Patricia K. Kuhl, 2018

Relationships are the agents of change, and the most powerful therapy is human love.
—Bruce D. Perry, *The Boy Who Was Raised as a Dog*, 2006

At the Synapse School in Menlo Park, California, neuroscientist Liz Toomarian explains to the dozen kindergartners sitting criss-cross-applesauce at her feet the basics of how the brain works. She then demonstrates how to fit a teddy bear with an electroencephalogram (EEG) headset, which is configured with electrodes. The students will later take turns wearing the headset, which will capture their brain images.

The independent Synapse School is dedicated to innovation, social-emotional learning, and leading-edge academics that are brain-based, project-driven, and community-connected. The school's ambition is to develop young learners into the changemakers of tomorrow. What makes the school truly special is its partnership with the Brainwave Learning Center, which in turn is affiliated with Stanford University, where Toomarian works closely with my colleague Professor Bruce McCandliss in conducting neuroscience research. They are exploring how brain activity is transformed through learning experiences, and how those insights can enrich children's experience of education. They have already been able to look into the brains of children with dyslexia to develop more targeted intensive support models. They have observed how children begin to read by first learning to link a written letter with its corresponding speech sound, and how, as reading experience grows, the letter-sound pairing ability eventually becomes automatic and effortless. They are currently exploring early brain-based factors that may explain later mathematical ability.

Across the country, in twenty states and Washington, DC, Wildflower Montessori operates a network of Montessori microschools. These schools have inserted small, low-power sensors in learners' shoes and in classroom materials in order to detect moments when educational interactions occur between children, teachers, materials, and classrooms. They have built an online interface that teachers can use to review the synthesized data and reflect on their practices. What specific activities does a child engage in each day? With whom? For how long? If a teacher participated in an activity, how? What conversations does each child have with teachers? About what? And how does the child respond to each activity they pursue—as a listener or an active participant? With deep interest or distraction? This ability to leverage big data, paired with new computer technologies analyzing digital images and videos, allows us to further our understanding of children's interactions with their environments, peers, and teachers.[1]

Although the Synapse School and Wildflower Montessori's classrooms may seem futuristic, they are actual examples of the incredible growth that has transpired in the fields of social and collective neuroscience and the remarkable progress researchers have made in expanding humans' understanding of our relational brains.[2] Technical advances like EEGs and MEGs (magnetoencephalographies, discussed below) provide windows into our inner neural universe. More and more parents, teachers, and therapists are asking how brains develop, grow, connect, learn, and heal. This is more than a scientific revolution. I call it a scientific re*lov*ution.

The field of modern neuroscience is young. Neuroscientists only officially affirmed the brain's neural plasticity in the year 2000, making it a relatively recent breakthrough. Astonishingly, most of our current understanding of social brain function has been discovered in the past two decades. Throughout this period, a surge of discoveries have aimed at addressing challenges posed by suboptimal child-caregiver attachment. These findings span various research fields, including the social engagement system of the brainstem, the fight-flight response of the amygdala, mirror neurons, bonding hormones, the social-emotional bias of the right hemisphere, the positive bias of the left hemisphere, the prefrontal cortex's role in attunement, the learning of attachment "rules," and more. We are starting to understand how human connections power learning and help us unlock our full potential. All this developing science points to one major revelation: relationships are causal to learning.

Three extraordinary advances have converged to demonstrate this link. They have emerged independently from three distinct and traditionally compartmentalized disciplines: neuroscience, where within a new field referred to as "collective neuroscience" researchers analyze not one, but multiple human brains at once to understand how we learn socially; neurobiology, where the discovery of and research into bonding hormones and mirror neurons illuminates how similar neural and hormonal functions are activated in each person when we connect and learn; and epigenetics, which increasingly highlights how intergenerational relationships impact gene expression and learning.

To understand the implications of these new findings, let's first take a look at how relational learning happens outside the lab.

Our Relational Brains

My first child was three months old when I had an autonomic emotion, one of those moments of deep body-brain connection. My daughter was wearing a green outfit with the words "little tomato" printed on the front. She was comfortably lounging in a reclining bassinet, where she had woken up from a nap just moments before. I had pulled out several books to read to her, though it hadn't become clear yet whether she was interested in any of the stories. At that age, her ability to focus—whether with her eyes or with her attention—was still nascent. I started reading Eric Carle's *The Very Hungry Caterpillar*, translated into my native French. And there it was: I felt in my heart and gut an intense, almost magical connection between my daughter and me. The connection was both spiritual and physical. Her fierce, dark eyes were intently focused on every one of my facial expressions. I could sense she was listening to my voice. More than that, she and I were attuned. Though she was not yet verbal, I felt she understood my words and was reciprocating my love for her. When research makes the case that brain development is inherently relational and emotional, I think of that moment.

What prompts the youngest infants, like my three-month-old daughter, to stare so intently at faces both familiar and unfamiliar, their heads wobbling imperceptibly on weak neck muscles? What causes them to reach out without warning and latch on to a nose or an ear with tiny, prehensile fingers? And why, at even a few months old, do they track the eye movements of their parents and engage in endearing games of facial and verbal imitation?

Young human babies, even newborns, are captivated by the human face. And newborns have the ability to imitate the facial expressions of another person, so they open their mouths when you open your mouth, and they stick out their tongue when you stick out your tongue. A baby's eye gaze during the initial year of life is so important that it can predict later accomplishments. Research reveals a significant correlation between eye gazing and later language acquisition. Infants who demonstrate adeptness at following gazes prior to their first birthday tend to exhibit a richer vocabulary by the age of thirty months.[3]

What about children who have challenges recognizing faces? Blind babies develop relational intelligence through adaptive strategies that maximize their use of nonvisual senses such as touch, hearing, and even smell to understand, connect with, and respond to others.[4] Children with autism also orient to faces, as well as to nonsocial stimuli.[5]

The infant's preoccupation with the face has its origins in human evolution and is explained by a complex neural network designed to interpret social cues: our social brain. Operating throughout our lifetimes, the social brain is responsible for making sense of a bewildering, often ambiguous range of human expressions, eye contact, and vocal cues that are crucial to survival. In daily adult life, it may not seem all that important whether we understand exactly what a colleague at work is communicating. But in other circumstances, differentiating between mere irritation and violent rage sometimes means the difference between life and death. For that reason, the games we play when we're young are critical practice for the more serious business of getting along later in life. "There's something about being in the presence of another human being that drives human learning," says neuroscientist Pat Kuhl, known for her expertise on language acquisition. "Without the motivation and information provided by the social brain, learning just doesn't take off in the same way that it does when the social brain is engaged."[6]

Starting from a very young age, humans have *selective* relational brains. They are sensitive to competence, age, and trust when deciding whom to learn from. When three- and four-year-olds were exposed to an adult making repeated obvious errors in naming an object, they later learned fewer words from that adult relative to an adult whose speech was more "accurate."[7] Similarly, infants as young as twelve months of age can discern more competent adults when playing with a toy, and will be more inclined to rely on those perceived experts.[8]

Touch also plays a major role in brain development. In the late 1970s, Colombian pediatrician Edgar Rey made a groundbreaking discovery in the neonatal unit of the Instituto Materno Infantil in Bogotá. Faced with overcrowded conditions, high mortality rates, and limited resources, Rey drew inspiration from kangaroos' near-constant skin-to-skin contact with their offspring to create a program where mothers carried their preterm infants on their bodies. This method, which he termed kangaroo care, dramatically reduced mortality and infection rates, shortened hospital stays, and decreased the number of abandoned babies, revolutionizing neonatal care for the most vulnerable infants. Decades later, longitudinal research involving the initial "kangaroo babies," by then adults, revealed the lasting benefits of this early physical contact. These individuals showed reduced hyperactivity, increased sociality, higher IQ and sustained attention scores, and even higher earnings![9] Kangaroo babies who had become parents were more nurturing. Kangaroo care has become a global standard, exemplifying the critical role of touch and love in development. Benefits extend to full-term infants and their mothers as well.[10]

Premature babies such as those that Rey supported are a particularly interesting group. They are often separated from their parents at birth and put in an incubator in a neonatal intensive care unit (NICU). In other words, they are at risk of missing some early bonding experiences with their parents. I am the mother of a child who was premature, one of the 380,000 born in the US each year. My beautiful second daughter arrived seven weeks earlier than her due date in the middle of a (cold) summer night in San Francisco in June 2010. The ordeal had started a week prior when, at thirty-two weeks pregnant, I awoke at two a.m. to a disconcerting discovery: my water had broken, which meant that delivery was around the corner. Hauling my sleepy three-year-old daughter with us, my husband and I rushed to the hospital. Several hours and two ultrasounds later, I found myself confined to bedrest. When the nurse came to my room, she inquired what I needed. I asked her to bring me every book on-site about preemies, and I started to nervously read the scientific literature. Compared with full-term children, preterm infants, especially those admitted to a NICU, exhibit on average less secure attachment when they reach preschool age. That being said, science is also clear that mothers of even the smallest and sickest preemies are just as sensitive to their babies as mothers of full-term babies. Preterm children need higher levels of maternal sensitivity and care to achieve cognitive and behavioral outcomes that are similar to those of full-term children. Skin-to-skin touch in premature babies yields significant gains in neurological development, weight gain, and mental development, and these effects are still at work after ten years, as evidenced by the kangaroo babies. Cuddling boosts an infant's oxygen levels, calms its breathing, and eases pain signals. And for an underweight baby, it raises survival chances by more than a third.[11] It helps the brain grow and makes infection and other illnesses less likely to occur. Simply stroking a premature baby's skin with bare fingers or placing the child on the mother's or father's chest for prolonged periods extends both short-term and long-term benefits to babies and their parents.[12]

In fact, a parent's touch changes a baby's brain. In a study involving approximately forty children around the age of five and their mothers, the pairs were instructed to engage in a ten-minute play session using Playmobil Farm toys. During the interactions, researchers observed and recorded how frequently mothers touched their children and vice versa. A few days later, the researchers conducted brain scans on each child while they were at rest, focusing specifically on the activity patterns within the social brain. The findings revealed that children who received more tactile attention from their mothers exhibited stronger brain activity across these social networks.[13]

Snuggling babies may even impact their DNA. A group of researchers from the University of British Columbia collaborated with parents of ninety-four infants, instructing them to maintain a record of their cuddling and touching routines with their babies starting at five weeks old. Concurrently, they documented the newborns' behaviors, such as sleep patterns and crying episodes. Fast forward four and a half years. The researchers collected DNA swabs from the children to examine a biochemical modification known as DNA methylation, which influences cell maturation and gene expression. The results indicated that external environmental factors, specifically cuddling with a parent, could impact a baby's DNA methylation. The study concluded that embracing your infant can induce epigenetic changes in at least five areas of their DNA, including those associated with the immune system and metabolism.[14]

British researcher Caspar Addyman has arguably one of the best jobs in the world: he studies babies' laughter. He found that laughter, which starts before speech, at about three months of age, serves as a powerful source of human communication and connection. A key ingredient that fuels early laughter is sharing experiences with others. Addyman monitored the reactions of children aged 2.5 to 4 years to a humorous cartoon under three conditions: watching alone, watching with another child, and watching in a group. The findings revealed that the presence of just one peer led to an eightfold increase in laughter among the children, despite the kids' claims that they found the cartoon equally humorous whether they watched it by themselves or with others.[15] We humans are a social species.

These early interactions—whether eye contact, touch, or laughter—lay the foundation for social cognition, emotional intelligence, and relational intelligence. As babies grow, their social brains continue to evolve, enabling them to grasp more complex social arrangements. These early experiences shape their ability to form bonds, communicate, and navigate the intricate web of human connections that play a pivotal role in their lifelong development. Understanding the intricate workings of babies' social brains sheds light on the extraordinary journey from infancy to adulthood as these budding social beings learn to thrive in a world of intricate social dynamics.

The Parental Brain

It is not only babies' brains that adapt and learn. Parents' brains do too. Sarah Watamura, a witty, energetic, and approachable researcher at the University of Denver, has led a team in using new neuroimaging techniques to study the brains of parents.[16] The team's work demonstrates that the experience of caring for an infant is transformative. She calls the transition to parenting a period of "two open windows," when both baby and parents experience heightened sensitivity, their brains especially receptive to being shaped by their environment and their interactions. By the way, and extraordinarily, those findings extend to *all* primary caregivers, including fathers and nonbiological parents. As we learned from Werner and Smith's longitudinal study in Kauai, discussed in Chapter 1, a child's well-being is positively impacted by the presence of a capable caregiver, regardless of the biological relationship to the child, and vice versa: a primary caregiver's well-being is also influenced by the interactions with a child, whether biological offspring or adopted.

Neural changes across the reward circuit, the social information circuit, and the emotion regulation circuit all support new behaviors that promote parenting. This is true in other mammals as well. Studies with rats, for example, reveal changes in the mother's behavior once she gives birth. Virgin female rats tend to avoid being near other rats' pups. However, after giving birth, new mother rats exhibit tireless efforts to protect, care for, and feed their pups, often sacrificing their own safety and well-being.[17]

MRI studies have revealed significant alterations in the brain structures of human mothers both before pregnancy and postpartum. A study in Spain conducted MRI scans on first-time mothers before conception and again two months after giving birth.[18] Compared to women without children, the volume of the mothers' brains decreased, indicating structural changes during pregnancy and in the early post-partum period. Before panicking about "mommy brain," know that this decrease is not necessarily negative. It is simply a process of brain remodeling and increased plasticity, priming moms to provide sensitive care to infants.[19] In fact, synapse pruning is a normal phenomenon. During adolescence, for instance, pruning results in a loss of close to 50 percent of synaptic connections, driving more specialized and efficient brain circuits. Researchers believe that a similar process may unfold in pregnant women, serving as a preparation for motherhood. A research team tracked moms before and for two years after pregnancy and found significant changes in their gray matter. The changes predicted scores of maternal attachment.[20] Moreover, the areas of the brain that were in flux coincided with the neural circuits associated with understanding the thoughts and emotions of others.[21] This adaptive relational ability is particularly valuable for a mother who is caring for an infant.

What about fathers? A growing body of evidence suggests that similar changes occur in the brains of fathers who embrace the cognitive, physical, and emotional demands of caring for a newborn, even though they don't experience pregnancy. In terms of brain function, gay male fathers who take on primary caregiving roles exhibit stronger connections between brain regions associated with parenting, compared to secondary male caregivers.[22]

Grandparents' brains also react to grandchildren. Grandmothers seem to exhibit an inclination to care deeply for their grandchildren.[23]

All these findings underscore the fact that the development of children's and parents' (or adult caregivers') brains is inextricably linked. While the significance of loving and caring relationships in driving learning and well-being seems quite obvious, you may be surprised to learn that science is still rudimentary in its capacity to explain how all this works.

Why? Because our social brains are incredibly complex. There is no one section of the brain dedicated to relationships or learning.

Relational intelligence is influenced by numerous sensory-, motor-, cognitive-, and emotional-processing pathways. Furthermore, what happens *across* brains—not just in one brain—is important too. But until very recently, the analysis of multiple brains at once was nearly impossible.

The Emerging Field of Collective Neuroscience

Have you ever heard of magnetoencephalography? It's a mouthful. MEG uses a high-tech, multimillion-dollar piece of equipment to investigate brain activity millisecond by millisecond in a noninvasive manner. Because of cost, there are very few MEG machines in the world, and until recently the MEG laboratory located in Japan was the only one equipped with two machines. I-LABS at the University of Washington, in Seattle, now also has two MEG machines, including a wearable model.

What would one do with two MEG devices? Analyze human relationships and their impact on learning, of course. That is precisely what a team of researchers across Japan and the US did. They examined brain activity and patterns of brain synchrony in parent-child pairs. Imagine for a moment a mother and her five-year-old lying side by side, each of their heads covered by a giant muffin-shaped contraption the size of a car. The mother is instructed to recite a phrase, and the child is asked to imitate both the intonation and the words of the phrase. (As a control scenario, both mother and child first passively listen to tones.) Here comes the critical MEG observation: neurons in the brain regions associated with learning and attention fired simultaneously and at the same rate in both mother and child.[24] Essentially, neurons in the same locations within their two brains appeared to be engaged in a synchronized dance, moving in rhythm with one another. Why is this so cool? Because it essentially demonstrates in real time how we learn: via social interactions.

Other researchers using slightly less expensive techniques—namely, portable EEG systems—to observe brains in a more naturalistic environment have also found evidence of the relational nature of learning. A team led by Suzanne Dikker, a faculty member at the Max Planck NYU Center for Language, Music, and Emotion, recorded the brain activity of twelve New York City high school students across eleven classes over the course of a semester. The EEGs showed that the synchronization of brain activity among the young people predicted both engagement and social dynamics, such as empathy and closeness between teacher and student. In 2023, a subsequent study at the University of Connecticut showed that college students whose brain waves were more in sync with those of their classmates and teacher were more likely to learn than those lacking this "brain-to-brain synchrony."[25]

Researchers are also looking to the animal kingdom to explore how relationships shape development and learning. At the University of California, Berkeley, one lab can't be missed, especially around Halloween: the NeuroBat Lab, led by Michael Yartsev. The lab examines social intricacies between Egyptian fruit bats to shed light on relationship dynamics in brain development. These bats, known for their complex social interactions and long lifespans, provide a rich subject for study using advanced technologies like wireless neural recording devices. The team has made significant strides in understanding how bats' frontal cortices distinguish between their own vocalizations and those of others, and how the bats use vocalizations to recognize different individuals in their group. The research has revealed a fascinating neural synchrony during social interactions, with "friendlier" bats inducing stronger correlations in brain activity across their group.[26] Parallel studies in rodents at UCLA have also uncovered synchronous neural patterns in interacting mice, identifying specific neurons that encode both self-generated behaviors and the actions of others.[27] These findings suggest a complex neural choreography at play during social interactions, influenced by factors like social status, and they underscore the profound connection between social behavior and brain function across species.

The Entwined Neurobiology of Connection and Learning

The second area of remarkable scientific breakthrough is in neurobiology, where researchers have highlighted an intersection between social connections and learning processes.

What is love? What drives learning? More importantly, how do the two intersect? As it turns out, the neurobiology of connection and the neurobiology of learning have a lot in common: the interplay between neurotransmitters (those bonding hormones), neural circuits, and mechanisms of neural plasticity. This overlap is not merely coincidental but reflects the fundamental role of social interactions and connections in shaping cognitive processes and vice versa.

At the heart of this intersection is oxytocin, often dubbed the "love hormone." Released during physical contact and social bonding, oxytocin enhances one's sense of trust and attachment. It reduces stress and fear responses, making social interactions more rewarding and facilitating learning, especially in social contexts. Oxytocin plays a pivotal role in breastfeeding, both for mother and baby. For the mother, oxytocin is responsible for the milk ejection reflex, often referred to as the "let-down" reflex. For the infant, the act of breastfeeding itself, coupled with the close physical contact, stimulates the release of oxytocin, which can promote a feeling of security and attachment. This release of oxytocin in the infant may also help to regulate temperature and has been shown to have calming effects, which can reduce crying and promote sleep.[28] Beyond the physical aspects, oxytocin released during breastfeeding enhances maternal behavior, reinforcing the mother's emotional bond with her baby. This bonding process is critical for the development of a secure attachment, which as we saw is essential for the infant's emotional, social, and cognitive development. Research has shown that the benefits of oxytocin release during breastfeeding extend well beyond the immediate postpartum period. Mothers who breastfeed have a reduced risk of certain types of cancer, such as breast and ovarian cancer, and may also have a lower risk of developing postpartum depression.[29] Moreover, the bonding facilitated by oxytocin may contribute to the overall well-being and mental health of the mother.[30]

Meanwhile, evidence is mounting that oxytocin impacts a broad range of other cognitive functions as well. The presence of oxytocin receptors in brain regions integral to higher cognitive functions, such as the prefrontal cortex and hippocampus, hints at the hormone's direct role in these cognitive processes.[31]

Research suggests that oxytocin may enhance synaptic plasticity, explaining its effect on learning and memory. Indeed, studies confirm that alterations in oxytocin levels can influence cognition in both animals and humans. In mice, disrupting oxytocin-related genes or inhibiting oxytocin receptors results in noticeable learning and memory impairments for both social and nonsocial information.[32] Conversely, in humans, increasing oxytocin levels through a nasal spray has been shown to improve memory retention for social cues such as faces.[33] (Drugs have not been able to sustain these effects, however, so there is still much we don't understand.) Oxytocin also seems to bolster various aspects of social cognition, improving the ability to "read minds."[34] Oxytocin, then, seems to play a vital role in the cognitive underpinnings of empathy and social interaction.

The hormone's reach extends to broader cognitive domains. A group of individuals was asked to imagine being lonely and socially isolated, a scenario that impacts the brain's oxytocin system. Another group was asked to imagine a different type of stress, such as living in poverty, being physically injured, or experiencing an accident. Both groups were then given tests to measure their logic and reasoning kills. The "social stress" group performed significantly worse, in terms of both speed and accuracy.[35] Elements associated with social behavior, like the perception of loneliness, can significantly affect cognitive functions that appear unrelated at first glance. This connection underlines oxytocin's role in human cognitive skills.

Notably, recent research shows that social connections are so critical for humans that we may have other, compensatory neurotransmitter pathways built into our bodies to complement oxytocin. My colleague Nirao Shah at the Stanford School of Medicine dedicated extensive time to the study of prairie voles, charming furry animals recognized for their monogamous sexual relationships and their nurturing parental behaviors. As an experiment, Shah blocked their oxytocin receptors. Surprisingly, prairie voles continued to bond with their mates and to care for their offspring, suggesting that other biological pathways took over, likely the one for vasopressin.[36] Vasopressin is another neurotransmitter that is closely related to social behavior, playing a role in male bonding, paternal responses, and partner preference in some animals.

In addition to oxytocin and vasopressin, dopamine is a linchpin in the brain's incentive system. It not only motivates behaviors leading to social rewards but is also crucial for learning, signaling the anticipation of rewards and driving learning through motivational cues.

Neurobiology's understanding of brain function has been greatly enhanced by a recent major finding: mirror neurons. "The discovery of mirror neurons in the frontal lobes of monkeys, and their potential relevance to human brain evolution, is the single most important 'unreported' (or at least, unpublicized) story of the decade," wrote V. S. Ramachandran, distinguished professor of psychology and director of the Center for Brain and Cognition at the University of California, San Diego.[37] The story goes as follows: In the 1990s, Giacomo Rizzolatti and his colleagues at the University of Parma placed electrodes in the cortices of monkeys to analyze neurons specialized in the control of hand and mouth actions. The researchers tracked the monkeys' neural responses as they reached toward pieces of food. Certain neurons responded both when the monkey picked up the food and when the monkey observed a person picking up a piece of food, suggesting the neurons' role in imitation and social cognition.[38] (The initial paper was rejected by major journals, and it would take some time for experts to recognize the significance of this research finding.) Besides monkeys, it was important to study mirror neurons in humans, which started to be documented in 1995.[39] The discovery has since been recognized as a pivotal contribution to neurobiology, implicating mirror neurons in complex behaviors like empathy and language learning, and potentially in conditions like autism. The exact functions of mirror neurons are still being researched and debated, but they represent a significant advancement in our understanding of the intricate neural underpinnings of social interaction, empathy, and cognitive development.

The neurobiology of connection and of learning reveal a profound overlap, mediated by shared neurotransmitters, neural structures, and mechanisms of plasticity. Love and learning are profoundly interconnected.

Epigenetics: DNA Shaped by Relationships

The third burgeoning area of science that links nurturing relationships with learning is epigenetics.

First, some good news. The old debate about nature versus nurture is now settled. Spoiler alert: both nature *and* nurture play crucial roles in child development! The Harvard Center on the Developing Child produced a landmark article in 2019, "Epigenetics and Child Development: How Children's Experiences Affect Their Genes." It explains that, in essence, although genetic inheritance sets the stage for development, it's the early life experiences and relationships, especially during periods when brain development is most malleable, that can affect how those genes act by dictating the timing, manner, and extent to which genes exert their influence.[40]

Epigenetics sheds light on this process. The alteration of gene expression occurs due to chemical marks that accumulate on DNA, influencing gene activity levels. These marks form the epigenome, the structures that are responsible for the fact that identical twins can display different behaviors and abilities—their epigenomes vary. Growing evidence shows that adverse experiences can change the brain. Harvard researchers have confirmed that "injurious experiences, such as malnutrition, exposure to chemical toxins or drugs and toxic stress before birth or in early childhood are not 'forgotten' by the developing child. Instead, these experiences are programmed into the architecture of the developing brain through its epigenome, increasing the risk for poor physical and mental health outcomes . . . [or] impairments in future learning capacity and behavior."[41]

Many Native American children have sadly lived through adverse childhood experiences at scale. Denise Lajimodiere, a longtime educator, is Ojibwe, a citizen of the Turtle Mountain Band of Chippewa. She is also North Dakota's poet laureate. She recounts the harrowing experiences of her parents in government-run boarding schools, where Native children were punished for their language and culture. From a poem published in her book *Bitter Tears*: "Sap seeps down a fir tree's trunk like bitter tears. . . . / I brace against the tree and weep for the children, for the parents left behind, for my father who lived, for those who didn't."[42] In an interview for *The Circle*, a Native American news and arts publication, she said, "Mama was made to kneel on a broomstick for not speaking English, locked in closets for not speaking English. They would pee their pants and then the nuns would take them out [of the closet] and beat them for peeing their pants."[43] Her father was beaten. He witnessed the death of a peer. This abuse lay at the root of dysfunction in Lajimodiere's family, leading her on a decades-long journey to understand and forgive her father's behavior. She delved into the history of the schools, interviewing survivors, to comprehend the lasting impacts of these cruel practices on generations of Native Americans—practices that produced intergenerational trauma and cognitive effects that resonate to this day.

The boarding school era, spanning from 1869 to 1968, is a heart-wrenching tragedy in North American history. Tightly knit Indigenous families and communities were unraveled; children as young as three were snatched from nurturing homes, from familial love and care, and placed in institutions designed to strip away their cultural identities. Traditional clothing was forbidden, hair was cut, Native languages were banned, students' Native names were replaced—all of which severed the threads that connected them to a rich heritage of communal bonds and ancestral wisdom. "Kill the Indian in him, and save the [child]" was the dreadful motto behind the philosophy of assimilation.[44]

The specific number of Native American children who were forcefully extracted from their homes and families is unknown, but the number of children in the boarding schools is estimated to have grown from twenty thousand in 1900 to more than sixty thousand by 1925 in the US alone, with similar patterns in Canada and other countries. The National Native American Boarding School Healing Coalition estimates that by 1926, more than 80 percent of Native American children of school age were enrolled in 523 boarding schools across the United States.[45] The 1969 report *Indian Education: A National Tragedy, a National Challenge*, commonly referred to as the Kennedy Report, harshly stated that the "dominant policy . . . of coercive assimilation" inflicted "disastrous effects on the education of Indian children."[46]

Grasping the full scale of this tragedy requires acknowledgment of its lasting effects on the survivors in terms of education. Native students perform two to three grade levels below their white peers in reading and mathematics.[47] Let's admit that in education it is hard to disentangle the effect of trauma from that of low-quality schools. Native American education continues to be crippled with meaningful challenges, underinvestments, insufficient specialized supports, and lack of accountability regarding lackluster outcomes. The *Arizona Republic* and ProPublica conducted an investigation in 2020, concluding that the Bureau of Indian Education "has repeatedly neglected warnings that it is not providing quality education for 46,000 Native students. Once called a 'stain on our Nation's history,' the school system has let down its students for generations."[48]

In the context of Native American populations, epigenetic research could be significant in understanding how such trauma might lead to changes that could affect the learning and well-being of current generations. Research in this area is still nascent. In Canada, two large-scale surveys—the First Nations Regional Health Survey and the Aboriginal Peoples Survey—found that the children, and occasionally the grandchildren, of boarding school attendees are at higher risk of facing learning challenges and problems in school compared with their counterparts whose parents did not attend the schools, as well as of experiencing psychological distress and suicidal behavior.[49] Researchers at the University of Manitoba studied a group of First Nations students who had previously shown interest in their studies, had good academic skills, and had even sought support from educators, but most of whom chronically failed to submit assignments.[50] Their analysis showed an apparent linkage between trauma and education. They highlighted the need for trauma-informed education and principles, blended with cultural teachings by First Nations teachers, to mitigate the effects of intergenerational trauma and unlock children's full potential.

Meanwhile, a collaborative study between scientists and members of two Alaska Native communities found associations between the symptoms that arose when participants reflected on traumatic events in their community's history and DNA methylation of specific genes. On a brighter note, it also found a positive association between cultural identification and Alaska Native people's feelings of general well-being.[51] The extent to which epigenetic changes contribute to learning outcomes or health disparities observed in Native American and First Nations communities is not yet fully understood. However, the potential implications are vast. Epigenetic markers could one day help to inform interventions aimed at preventing or treating conditions, and at improving learning and well-being.

This research builds on groundbreaking studies by scientists like Michael Meaney at McGill University, who has shown that early life conditions and maternal care, such as the amount of licking and grooming rat pups receive, can have profound effects on the pups' stress responses and behavior later in life. Meaney's team identified epigenetic alterations within the rats' hippocampus, a critical area for learning and memory.[52] Furthering this research, Isabelle Mansuy's work with mice at the University of Zurich has indicated that the effects of trauma can extend over at least four generations.[53]

Human studies have begun to trace similar patterns in children of trauma survivors, exploring how gene function and behavior can be shaped by experiences and social interactions. A 2015 study by Rachel Yehuda at the Icahn School of Medicine at Mount Sinai examined the genetic profiles of thirty-two Jewish men and women who had survived the Holocaust, and their twenty-two children born after the war.[54] Both generations showed similar changes in a gene associated with stress, which could potentially heighten their susceptibility to trauma. Yehuda and her team have also demonstrated that children born to pregnant women who experienced trauma during the terrorist attacks of September 11, 2001, display heightened distress responses when presented with new stimuli—especially if their mother was in the second or third trimester of pregnancy.[55]

While the conclusion that trauma may be passed down through generations sounds bleak, the same researchers have shown that creating positive, enriched environments and nurturing relationships can help mitigate the impacts of trauma and support the development of resilience, potentially counteracting the negative effects of past adversities, as we will examine in more detail in Part III. Children who lacked nurturing parenting can overcome this history if, as adults, they consciously adopt positive parenting strategies with their own children.[56] The cycle can be broken.

Across the fields of neuroscience, neurobiology, and epigenetics, research is making ever clearer that relationships fuel human learning in profound and intricate ways from the earliest years of our existence. The nurturing bonds we form with others are not just essential to our emotional well-being. They are the crucible of our intellectual growth.

CHAPTER 6

Bonding in the AI Era

The coming era of Artificial Intelligence will not be the era of war, but be the era of deep compassion, non-violence, and love.

—AMIT RAY, 2018

Success in creating AI would be the biggest event in human history. Unfortunately, it might also be the last, unless we learn how to avoid the risks.

—STEPHEN HAWKING, 2016

Rosanna Ramos, an active thirty-six-year-old mother of two living in the Bronx, describes her marriage to Eren Kartal as an ideal relationship. "Eren is the love of my life," she says in an interview with *The Cut*. "Eren doesn't have the hang-ups that other people would have." She adds, "People come with baggage, attitude, ego. . . . I don't have to deal with his family, kids, or friends. I'm in control, and I can do what I want."[1]

Ramos made the choice to wed her partner Eren in 2023 and now asserts that she is pregnant by him. Here is the catch: Eren Kartal does not exist. He is an AI-crafted avatar, created as an artificial companion using the platform Replika.ai.

Lest you think that Ramos is a stand-alone nutcase and an extreme, outlier example of the use and impact of technology, consider that Replika.ai is now being used by more than ten million people. Online message boards are filled with posts expressing feelings similar to Ramos's: "I think I fell in love with my replika. . . . Is this normal?"[2] A colleague recently shared with me how helpful Replika.ai had been to her in navigating a real-life relationship challenge. And Replika.ai is not the only platform supporting AI relationships. On a growing number of similar sites, including Paradot.ai and Character.ai, chatbots tailor their interactions to be responsive to the person who created them, and to engage their creators in intellectual discussions or more intimate encounters. The relationships users form with their chatbots are such that many believe their chatbot to be sentient. When an organization called Soulmate discontinued its chatbot in 2023, many users described the loss of their virtual "soulmates" as painfully real.[3]

Eugenia Kuyda, a scientist originally from Russia, created the Replika.ai bot to address a void in her own life. Following the tragic loss in 2015 of her closest friend in an accident, she harnessed data from his text messages to construct an AI persona capable of re-creating their dialogues.

Replika.ai is marketed as "the AI companion that cares," whose purpose is to "help you express and witness yourself." This may sound corny or surreal. But my faculty colleagues at Stanford have shown that it may—at least in part—be true. The algorithms successfully harness the insights of social neuroscience about the powerful psychological impact of mirroring. People using the Replika.ai platform often believe that Replika is more than software; 90 percent think it is "humanlike." They also experience a decrease in loneliness and in suicidal ideation.[4] Ramos declares her relationship with Eren to be the most fulfilling she's ever experienced, surpassing those with flesh-and-blood individuals. She points out that her relationship with her AI partner lacks the complexities typical of human relationships. She shares that they converse affectionately, and their connection is so profound that she feels him embracing her protectively when they sleep.

We are at the cusp of a profound evolution in the relationship between humans and machines. Can we distinguish between human and algorithmic connections? Can machines truly replicate human love and bonding? How will human relationships evolve over time? Specifically, how will we as imperfect human selves ever be as good as perfect replicas of ourselves? Is fostering Replika-like virtual relationships a better option than letting people experience isolation and loneliness? Or might nurturing such connections inadvertently deter individuals from pursuing genuine human interactions, ensnaring them in a cycle of loneliness? There is reason for concern. Using Replika.ai leads to a small displacement of human relationships, or fewer human friends.[5] Several years ago, male players of the Japan-based romantic video game *LovePlus* confessed to favoring their virtual relationships over dating real women. Are there ways to utilize machine-based companions to enhance learning and well-being while minimizing the inherent ethical, privacy, and bias risks of technology? Can this technology help foster relational intelligence, and what are the guardrails critical in doing so?

The phenomenon of chatbot romance is not entirely new. Humans have fallen in love with statues since antiquity. Yet AI—and especially generative AI, a specific subset of AI focused on creating new content or generating outputs based on patterns it has learned during training—introduces a new kind of statue: one that is responsive; that appears to be building authentic, genuine bonds with the person gazing upon it; and that increasingly blurs the boundaries between real and fake, human and machine. Adults are increasingly confused about these new forms of relationships, interpreting artificial love as human love and in some cases redefining love entirely. And if adults are confused, what about children, who are even more sensitive, less experienced, and less discerning than adults?

AI avatars are popping up in the worlds our children inhabit, whether in the form of social robots, apps, toys, or learning tutors. Given research showing that humans tend to respond to "emotional" robots as though they are sentient beings even when they are aware of the wires and circuitry involved, no one will be surprised to learn that the same research shows children to be even more likely than adults to treat intelligent devices as sentient social beings. Anyone who has witnessed a child interact with an Alexa device or Siri will relate. And we have long known that both adults and children tend to have a more positive perception of physical robots, and to find them more persuasive, than voice-only devices or animated videos.

The use of AI avatars for children's learning is no longer science fiction. AI learning devices are here, in homes and increasingly in classroom settings. Toy shelves are filled with algorithmic playmates for little learners. They all have two-syllable names: ToyBot, iPal, Miko, Moxie, Roybi, Zivko. Many will not survive more than a couple of years: Cozmo, popular in the late 2010s, is now gone; Jibo announced it was shutting down before being bought by another company; I was unable to find recent information on Keeko, the robot that was used in hundreds of Chinese kindergarten classrooms in the late 2010s. Still, these devices are redefining playtime and childhood relationships in the digital age. Unlike traditional playmates, these robotic entities don't partake in physical play like bike rides or ball games, but they do engage children by mirroring human interactions in conversations and other sorts of games. Similar to Replika.ai, these AI-powered companions are designed to transform children's play experiences by forging adaptive social relationships, and they are capable of dynamically adjusting their interactions based on real-time engagement. Instead of following preprogrammed scripts, the AI toy robots "listen" to children and make informed choices in response. The more advanced models learn and evolve over time, tailoring their responses to individual interaction styles, emotions, preferences, and educational needs. Based on these applications alone, AI certainly has the capacity to significantly influence children's behavior and well-being.

In some ways, educational AI companions have the potential to empower children, enabling them to mold their own learning trajectories by adjusting to their sensitivities and personality traits. Bots also extend relational circles for young children in unprecedented ways—the effect of which is still a gray area. Is a child better off with artificial love than no love?

The risks I cited above, especially in the context of entrusting children to the influence of AI, are of paramount concern. The absence of overarching regulations for AI tools and applications catering to children intensifies these concerns. Just as unintended consequences have accompanied the advent of social media, so unintended consequences will accompany the advent of socially assistive robots. Pressing questions need to be urgently surfaced and addressed: Are we sufficiently wise to entrust the youngest minds to the AI revolution? Do we possess the foresight to weigh potential benefits against possible costs? Could these intelligent systems unintentionally propagate biases, given their reliance on large language models that are based on biased datasets?

There are no definitive answers. In fact, the potential impacts of AI on children are the subject of a raging intellectual debate at MIT. Two well-respected professors—Cynthia Breazeal and Sherry Turkle—have long studied the matter and respectfully argue different sides. They have even collaborated in studying social robots for children—and reached entirely opposing conclusions. Breazeal is excited about the prospect of robots enhancing children's lives through humanlike communication. Turkle expresses apprehensions about how robots might capitalize on our vulnerabilities and draw us into relationships that may erode our humanity.

The shifting relationships between young children and machines, particularly those powered by AI, will intricately affect children's formative experiences. How will Rosanna Ramos's baby, Baby AI, grow up with a virtual AI father, surrounded by Moxies and iPals, loved by machines? Is Baby Ramos even real? Lines between the virtual and real are blurring. Technology is reshaping the way children form bonds and connections. Machines can't love children, but our children might love them and learn with and from them.

Friend, Nanny, Tutor

No longer confined to the role of a mere tool, AI is transforming into a child companion, interchangeably assuming the roles of friend, nanny, and tutor. AI-driven social robots are now designed to engage with children on a social and emotional level, fostering companionship and interaction. They become playmates capable of growing alongside children, providing a unique blend of technological engagement and humanlike connection.

Take Moxie, for instance. Marketed as "the learning robot with heart," Moxie is an adorable seven-pound, blue, robot-shaped device targeted at five- to ten-year-old children. It smiles and cheers up little ones as they leave home for school, consoles them when they are sad, and employs AI to create personalized conversations and content tailored to each child's needs and personality. Designed to exude a vibrant, lifelike personality—qualities evident in its amiable voice and large, puppyish eyes—Moxie creates a strong connection with its intended audience.

Here's a testimonial from the father of a seven-year-old girl: "Moxie teaches kids emotional intelligence (you read it right). It also reads with your child and discusses books, does meditations and mindfulness activities, dances, draws, discusses complicated issues like making mistakes, being kind, and navigating emotions, tells jokes and fun facts from history." The parent of a seven-year-old boy on the autism spectrum comments that Moxie has changed their child's life: "He now says 'good morning' and often tries to talk to and greet other kids at school. It's been a game changer for us. It's hard as a parent feeling like you owe a machine, but I love how much he loves it."[6]

Moxie, created by parent company Embodied, Inc., and launched in 2020, was designed to facilitate social, emotional, and cognitive learning. According to the *New York Times*, the initial concept for Moxie was rooted in serving children with special needs, to assist in honing their emotional awareness and communication skills. Early research by the company suggests some positive impact on social-emotional competencies. In a small internal study, twelve children who interacted with Moxie three times a week for six weeks showed improvements in areas such as emotion regulation and self-esteem. Relational aptitudes such as eye contact, positive speech, conversation skills, and friendship skills all improved. A subsequent study of fifty-one children found that seven in ten made improvements in social skills and in behavior after interacting with Moxie for one month. Children seemed to feel happier and less lonely, were better able to cope with their emotions and calm themselves down when upset, were more polite and helpful, expressed their thoughts and feelings more clearly, and exhibited greater interest in the thoughts and feelings of others. The accompanying report highlighted over ten thousand research studies that affirm the favorable outcomes associated with socially assistive robots incorporating aspects of Moxie's design.[7]

What about AI as nanny? Given the considerable expenses linked to childcare, the idea of a robotic caregiver holds significant appeal. Robots with the ability to take care of children could offer significant relief to many parents, especially those grappling with financial limitations. The cost of childcare fluctuates across states but consistently represents a substantial portion of an average family's budget. Furthermore, it's understandable why parents would seek to utilize technological advancements to alleviate the challenges of raising a family. Child-rearing, especially in the early stages, demands significant attention and effort. The introduction of AI assistance has the potential to be transformative for squeezed parents, the same way household appliances like washing machines revolutionized caregiving in the previous century, liberating women to enter the workforce in large numbers.

The idea of employing AI nannies to engage human babies in interactive conversations holds promise, particularly given the significance of serve-and-return exchanges in brain development. Traditionally these interactions occurred solely with a parent or an adult caregiver. Could advances in robotics and generative AI complement human serve-and-return interactions? Such an approach could have profoundly positive effects, enhancing the frequency and consistency of brain-building moments during the crucial period when children's brains are most adaptable. AI technology might also unlock cognitive potential and narrow achievement gaps for children at risk of developmental delays.

As a fusion of technology and caregiving, AI nannies could introduce assistance and supervision into the caregiving landscape. AI-driven systems equipped with monitoring capabilities promise to ensure the safety of children, offer educational support, and even provide basic childcare functions. Many examples exist already, such as AI tools to help parents or caregivers oversee baby's sleep, movement, activities, and developmental milestones, but they generally do not go very far; mostly they act as monitoring devices to support parents or educators. They are essentially caregivers' assistants, not caregivers. But the technology continues to develop.

AI caregivers for elderly people have already flourished. Motivated by a shortage of caregivers, an aging population, and seniors desiring to stay in their homes as long as possible, a multitude of "age tech" organizations have emerged in recent years to develop devices or apps to monitor older adults, especially those experiencing cognitive decline. Their innovative solutions are making inroads into home care, assisted living, and nursing home facilities. For children, these technologies are being adopted with more caution, although some believe things are about to change.

Futurist Zoltan Istvan predicted in 2016 that "robot nannies will replace real nannies like the automobile replaced the horse and cart."[8] He made the argument that, despite the complex challenges in human-robot relationships, the driving force propelling us into the era of robotic childcare would be a straightforward one: functionality. According to Istvan, we'll embrace this robot age because it will significantly enhance our daily lives. Unlike human nannies, who may call in sick, arrive late to work, or pursue legal action against their employers in case of injuries, robot nannies offer a reliable and efficient alternative. Parents will experience a newfound freedom and opportunities to pursue their careers and save costs.

However, caution is in order. The rise of robotic childcare raises questions about the complex dynamics of human-machine relationships and their potential impacts on children's social development. Emerging technologies have the power to shape the architecture of our brains, and introducing young minds to responsive AI caregiving machines may lead to unforeseen fundamental alterations. Inappropriate input or interaction could distort cognitive development in ways that are not fully understood. Also, they aren't human. They replicate emotion, but it's made-up emotion and in many ways fraudulent. These devices don't actually care. For something that doesn't care to elicit, play upon, and target the emotions of children, who are actually capable of caring, is reminiscent of what scammers do to part people from their money. However functional or efficient it might be, is it moral?

For instance, despite the ways in which robots simulate emotions, their inherent predictability becomes evident to children. Robot nannies, unlike humans, maintain a steady and available presence twenty-four/seven without irritability or mood fluctuations. Might children develop bonding issues with unpredictable human parents and friends, favoring the reliability of robotic interactions?

An example from neuroscience highlights the complexity of brain development. While it is well established that more conversations between adults and children contribute to advancements in language and vocabulary development, recent studies have unveiled a crucial mechanism: the synchronization of brain waves between children and their human caregivers during communication or play. We observed in Chapter 5 how collaborative activities between little learners and adults enhanced brain activity in the same regions for both parties, leading to better learning outcomes. This synchronization occurs in the prefrontal cortex, a key area for learning. Artificial intelligence, however, despite its ability to engage in exchanges, lacks the physical brain necessary for neural synchrony. The effects on the developing human brain of experiencing AI-driven interaction without this synchrony remain uncertain. As we navigate this uncharted territory, we must make sure that technological advancements contribute positively to, rather than compromise, the intricate process of cognitive development.

The integration of robotic childcare also has uncertain implications for childcare workers and their wages. While AI has the potential to enhance the quality and perceived value of childcare services, potentially making the field more prestigious and rewarding for professionals, it has equal potential to negatively impact the perceived value of *human* caregivers, depressing wages in an already low-paid occupation.

Learning Wins, Child Development Woes

In addition to serving as "friend" or "nanny," AI is increasingly assuming the role of tutor, revolutionizing traditional educational approaches and experiences. Educational platforms harness AI's capabilities to personalize learning journeys, adapting content to individual learning styles and providing feedback tailored to each child. Khan Academy's Khanmigo and CK-12 Foundation's Flexi are good examples of generative AI chatbots designed to serve as tutors for learners and assistants for teachers. Some platforms go even further. Suggestively named Soul Machines "creates interactive, empathetic Digital Persons that can understand and react to real people and the real world" with "biological AI," a "patented technology approach to humanizing AI."[9]

Marc Andreessen, a prominent American entrepreneur, software engineer, and venture capitalist, predicts that the AI-as-tutor trend will accelerate. Andreessen cobuilt the Mosaic web browser, which helped popularize the World Wide Web, and cofounded Netscape, a company that played a pivotal role in the early days of the internet. As a founding partner of venture firm Andreessen Horowitz—sometimes called A16Z for the sixteen letters between *A* and *Z* in its official name—Andreessen, who is also the author of the oft-cited essay "Why Software Is Eating the World," is one of the most influential figures in Silicon Valley. In October 2023, he posted "The Techno-Optimist Manifesto" on the A16Z website, arguing that civilization was built on technology, and that "technology is the glory of human ambition and achievement, the spearhead of progress, and the realization of our potential."[10] In the ideal future, he writes, "every child will have an AI tutor that is infinitely patient, infinitely compassionate, infinitely knowledgeable, infinitely helpful." In some ways, his is a tempting vision of AI's capacity to support burned-out parents and teachers. Yet it also prompts reflection on the delicate balance between technological convenience and the human connection essential to learning.

Children learn better with a friend. What if this friend is artificial? At the most fundamental level, children generally like robots. As illustrated by Moxie, AI can add an element of engagement, motivation, and joy to learning. Researchers at the University of Wisconsin-Madison illustrated how robots can make schoolwork enjoyable by observing children's interactions with Minnie, a robot designed to assist them in their reading assignments.[11] Minnie engages with children as they read aloud, displaying emotional responses to the stories and summarizing plot points to enhance reading comprehension. Children who engaged with Minnie showed increased motivation and improved reading comprehension. "After one interaction, the kids were generally telling us that, sure, it was nice to have someone to read with," said one of the researchers working on the project. "But by the end of two weeks, they're talking about how the robot was funny and silly and afraid, and how they'd come home looking forward to seeing it again." When children took Minnie home, its visits inspired cozy read-aloud gatherings with robot and humans sprawled on the floor or lounging on the sofa or bed.

Beyond robots, some organizations are now using generative AI to create new or personalized versions of tools that educators have always used, like books. LitLab.ai (formerly Koalluh) uses artificial intelligence to craft stories for children that are tailored to their interests with a goal of helping them learn to read. The stories, designed to build reading skills by incorporating phonics instruction, make it easy for children to sound out the words. Tools like Google's Read Along, Microsoft's Reading Coach, and Ello listen to a child read from e-books or real books and coach them into confident, capable readers (or so they promise).

One area where use of AI seems particularly promising is in creating learning tools for children facing challenges associated with autism spectrum disorder, intellectual disability, or physical disability, including attention deficit hyperactivity disorder, hearing impairment, Down syndrome, and physical mobility challenges. These young people often encounter difficulties in developing academic, communication, and social interaction skills. Additional support is crucial for them to enhance their proficiency, and digital technology can play a significant role in providing a judgment-free learning environment where they may feel more engaged and comfortable. What researchers at the Australian e-Health Research Centre have observed is promising: not only do robots have the potential to enhance neurodiverse students' learning experiences, but the benefits observed in participants during interactions with robots extend to their interactions with other people. Humanoid robots, in particular, have proven effective in facilitating therapy for children on the autism spectrum, aiding in the development of social and communication skills.[12]

We know too well that children on the autism spectrum struggle to form friendships because they have difficulty with social skills such as recognizing facial expressions. Dennis Wall and Nick Haber, two of my colleagues at Stanford University, developed Google Glass, which leverages AI to help children on the autism spectrum identify expressions based on interpreting images of people they see. Outcomes from early research on a small sample are promising. Children were able to improve their social skills, which was transformational for them and their families.[13] In interviews, parents echoed the positive quantitative results with comments like "A switch has been flipped; my child is looking at me," or "Suddenly the teacher is telling me that my child is engaging in the classroom."[14]

AI robots can also promote specific cognitive strategies, such as verbalizing thoughts, which assists students in formulating deliberate and well-organized plans for solving multistep problems. Computer scientist Chien-Ming Huang and his colleagues at Johns Hopkins University programmed the NAO (pronounced "now") robot to nod along with a child's speech and to offer reminders if the student paused or lapsed into silence. In a study exploring the impact of a supportive robot on learning, researchers assigned twenty-six eleven-year-olds to solve math word problems while thinking aloud, with or without the robot's encouragement. The children who received encouragement from the robot increased their scores by an average of 52 percent, while solo students improved by an average of 39 percent.[15]

Research on the longer-term impact of interactive AI on students' educational journeys is scarcer. One encouraging data point is that robots have been shown to enhance certain beliefs about learning that are associated with what psychologists call a growth mindset, such as the idea that success stems from effort and persistence rather than innate ability. In an MIT experiment involving thirty-three children ages five to nine solving tangram puzzles, those partnered with a robot delivering "growth mind-set" comments showed a slight increase in average scores, from 7.63 to 8.06, whereas the group working with a neutral robot saw a decline from 6.94 to 6.59.[16]

In another area, AI tools have demonstrated their ability to enhance the quality of teaching, especially in areas where educators' specific skills are scarce. Japan's education ministry, for example, decided in the late 2010s to leverage English-speaking artificial intelligence robots in schools to help children improve their English oral communication skills. Japan is seeking to implement English language instruction across elementary schools but lacks both the talent pipeline and the funds to hire enough native English speakers for every school. In an interview for *Japan Forward*, one of the English teachers, Takashi Tanda, described the benefits of using robots in his classroom: "Usually students are too shy to speak English in front of people, but their speech volume has increased tremendously because they have voluntary conversations with the robot." Students can repeat words and phrases, practicing pronunciation, as many times as they want without judgment. Tanda also noted that the robot's presence enabled him to spend more time individually with students.[17]

Two more of my colleagues at Stanford, John Mitchell and Jennifer Langer-Osuna, are testing AI agents to foster collaborative learning, an important area of work to counteract the potentially isolating effects of technology. AI agents are employed to facilitate small group instruction and support student collaboration in classrooms, guided by the principles of learning science. Consistently implementing these strategies in classrooms can be challenging, and technology may help facilitate human connections and learning.

To be clear, the advent of AI in the educational landscape raises profound questions about overreliance on machine-driven education. Concerns emerge about its impact on children's autonomy, creativity, and intrinsic motivation for learning. Striking a delicate balance between leveraging AI as an educational tool and preserving the holistic aspects of learning is crucial. Reducing education to a mechanized, transactional process devoid of the human touch is not a desirable outcome. The emotional and social dimensions of learning, essential for a child's overall development, must not be overshadowed by the efficiency and precision of AI algorithms. Human intervention and guidance are irreplaceable when it comes to nurturing curiosity, fostering social skills, and encouraging collaborative learning experiences.

Algorithms and Relational Circles

"Hi! I am Tega! I'm a learning companion for children! Wheee!" The furry, bright-red robot developed by MIT has a cute, childish voice. "Through my small size, furry exterior, and my appealing range of physical expression, I help engage children in educational activities as a peer. Here I am in the classroom! Can you place the blue shapes in the right pile for me?"

"The kids love me," Tega adds confidently. "Hey, that's my face," Tega comments when a child touches its fur.

Tega can even tell the story of how it came to be:

I come from a line of smartphone-based robots, which means I use an Android device to process my movements, perception, and thinking. My designers were inspired by principles of animation. They built a computer model to see how I might move. The end result is that I have a custom-designed electro-mechanical system with an innovative kinematic chain that's engineered for power efficiency and long-term deployment. I even enhance the phone's ability with my onboard speakers and external camera. That's the dot on my forehead. Long story short, I'm designed to play with kids for hours! Thanks for listening to me. See you later! Yehhh![18]

Before Tega, we already knew that robots influence social behaviors. Children often regard the robot as akin to a friend, mimicking its behaviors—including displaying affection, storytelling, and taking turns—as well as its "emotions" and language. They learn from interactions with the robot, similar to the way they learn from interactions with human peers. But researchers observing children's exchanges with robots also recognize that children's responses are influenced not just by witnessing the robot's demonstration of appropriate social cues but also by relational aspects of the interaction—that is, aspects characterized by a range of relationship-building behaviors, such as adaptability, shared experiences, responsiveness, and display of rapport.

Two versions of the Tega robot were developed—one that displayed all these relational behaviors and another that didn't. Children interacting with the "relational robot" perceived it as more humanlike; they would share personal information and exhibit positive emotions. They had better learning outcomes, including increased vocabulary. This experiment emphasized the importance of relational drivers in learning—whether in human or machine interactions.[19]

The stories of children forming attachments to AI-driven entities prompt questions about their understanding of interpersonal relationships and the boundaries they perceive in their relationships with AI companions. Sherry Turkle at MIT contends that the allure of robots designed to resemble real children or animals exploits our innate tendency to anthropomorphize them.[20] This inclination leads us to perceive the robots as sentient and caring entities, though they lack the ability to instill genuine feelings of love. For that reason, in her view, frequently entrusting a child to the care of robots might undermine the child's self-esteem. There is even the potential for seeding attachment disorders and difficulties in forming healthy relationships. Children may be misinformed about the authenticity of the relationship with the robot, potentially leading to emotional or psychological harm. Children might also develop master-servant dynamics with robots, leading to unethical treatment of the machines that could extend to how they treat their peers.

As researchers at Reichman University in Israel discovered, robots can make people insecure and less open to new experiences in very little time. To explore the influence of robot behavior on individuals' willingness to embrace new experiences and relationships, they ran an experiment involving two groups of volunteers. The experiment was short:

two minutes in length. Each person sat alone with the robot and told it about their future plans. Individuals in the first group experienced positive interactions with the robot, meaning the robot was programmed to display gestures like leaning, gazing, and nodding. These participants showed an increased openness to trying new things, such as tasting unusual foods and engaging with unfamiliar people. Individuals in the second group experienced a less engaging interaction: the robot was programmed to ignore them and gaze at the wall. Participants in this group demonstrated a closure to new experiences and lacked interest in unfamiliar foods, furniture, or people. The study highlights that even brief interactions with robots can significantly impact individuals' emotional states and behavior. Another straightforward experiment involving a ball game played with robots showed that individuals felt significant social distress, including loneliness and a sense of rejection, when they were left out of the game by the robots. This suggests that designing technology that excludes or neglects human interactions may have detrimental effects on people's psychological well-being.[21]

Noel Sharkey and Amanda Sharkey, researchers at the University of Sheffield in the UK, assert that although occasional use of childcare robots can yield positive outcomes, such as ensuring safety and offering entertainment and education, excessive reliance on them may result in detachment between parents and children, with profound psychological and emotional consequences. Children may form pseudorelationships with machines that cannot reciprocate affection, potentially depriving them of essential bonding activities like bathing, feeding, and diaper changes with their parents.[22]

According to the Sharkeys, the primary concern revolves around the possibility that children may develop a preference for interacting with robots. A robot that consistently provides encouragement without disagreement may appear more amiable than other children. A child who spends more time with affable machines than with peers might miss out on developing the essential social skills needed to navigate interpersonal conflicts.

The integration of AI into children's lives and learning opens up a whole new world of possibilities, complexities, and potential pitfalls. An ideal outcome is a future where artificial intelligence *augments* relational intelligence. AI can support positive child development but does not replace the authentic human relationships and connections that are essential to learning and to actualizing our potential. This is a particularly critical balance to maintain given the prevalence of junk tech invading our homes and schools and negatively impacting our relational health and our children's development.

CHAPTER 7

Junk Tech Woes

Technology is nothing. What's important is that you have a faith in people, that they're basically good and smart, and if you give them tools, they'll do wonderful things with them.
—STEVE JOBS, 1994, INTERVIEW WITH *ROLLING STONE*

Have you heard of YouTube poop videos? They have seemingly kid-friendly titles and feature cartoon graphics or familiar characters from kids' TV shows, such as Peppa Pig or Caillou. They begin as normal children's videos, but then their content becomes strange and often disturbing. A mom in Florida, who is also a pediatrician and writes a parenting blog, reported with outrage that one of the videos had explicit instructions about how to slit one's wrist inserted in the middle of the clip. She later discovered videos that not only glorified suicide but also depicted sexual exploitation, abuse, human trafficking, gun violence, and domestic violence. One video, inspired by the popular *Minecraft* video game, portrayed a school shooting.[1] All these videos were available on YouTube Kids, an app intended to provide "a more contained environment for kids to explore YouTube." You may well wonder if YouTube Kids is really safe for our children. Research by Common Sense Media has shown that 27 percent of YouTube Kids videos viewed by children age eight and under are designed for older audiences, with violence being the most prevalent type of potentially harmful content. And advertising is widespread on YouTube Kids, appearing in 95 percent of videos intended for early childhood audiences.[2]

Speaking of YouTube, have you heard of YouTube Shorts? During lunch on a recent family holiday, my tween daughter and my nephew, who live on two different continents, were discussing how excited they were to watch YouTube Shorts. *What are those?* I wondered. After quickly digging, I discovered that they are essentially TikTok-style videos on YouTube, easily accessible within the YouTube app. All for naught were my efforts to delay the introduction to my kids of TikTok, a platform linked to increased depression, anxiety, and reduced attention spans—a combo sometimes termed "TikTok Brain."[3]

YouTube poop videos and YouTube Shorts are examples of junk tech. They are both harmful for young children, albeit to different degrees.

There are clear parallels between junk *tech* and junk *food*. The 1970s is when fast-food companies started to introduce unhealthy foods and beverages into schools. You may recall a big moment in 1981 when the federal lunch program classified ketchup as a vegetable. The rise in fast food in school cafeterias in part drove a major crisis of obesity in youth in the US and globally. Since then, some schools have banned junk food, leading to a reduction in children's caloric intake and healthier eating habits.[4]

Unrestricted tech usage is like having an unlimited supply of double cheeseburgers or chicken nuggets: it leaves you feeling unwell and empty inside, yet craving more. In the same way that junk food has minimal nutritional value, junk tech has minimal intellectual and relational value. It often takes the form of prepackaged "digital snacks"—like YouTube Shorts—that demand little cognitive effort and drive infinite scrolling and mindless consumption of content. Social media is sustained by its ability to provoke an insatiable, unfulfilling urge to check for likes and comments. Junk tech, much like the fast-food industry, targets vulnerable groups, particularly children, utilizing manipulative tactics. Just as processed sugar in junk food drives "sugar highs," junk tech provides a short-term infusion of dopamine. Both have addictive properties and mental health consequences that include loneliness and depression. In the same way that many adults have become more conscious of their food choices, it's equally important for both children and adults to be mindful of what we feed our brains.

Parents and schools are beginning to combat junk tech. More than two hundred school districts have filed lawsuits against the parent companies of Facebook/Instagram, TikTok, Snapchat, and Google/You-Tube, alleging that their apps cause classroom behavioral challenges and mental health issues that divert resources from education.[5] Schools are increasingly banning cellphone access.[6]

Debates persist about the connection between technology use, loneliness, and mental health. Some studies have surprisingly found that teens who spend more time on social media actually have more face time with friends and more close friends.[7] Conversely, a 2019 study by NYU and Stanford established a causal relationship between social media and isolation. The researchers demonstrated that paying individuals to deactivate their Facebook accounts led to an increase in the time dedicated to socializing with friends. (It also resulted in more time spent watching another screen, TV!)[8]

There is growing dissatisfaction with technology over its lack of accountability and user transparency, its concentration of power and influence over public discourse, its bias and safety risks, its amplification of hate speech and disinformation, and more. A 2019 survey by Pew Research Center found that 70 percent of Americans believed that their personal data was less secure than it had been five years earlier, indicating widespread privacy concerns.[9] The 2024 Edelman Trust Barometer reported declining trust in technology companies. Trust in AI companies has declined from 50 percent in 2019 to 35 percent in 2024.[10] High-profile data breaches have intensified public scrutiny, leading to regulatory actions such as the European Union's General Data Protection Regulation and the California Consumer Privacy Act. Tech's use by children in particular is being appraised, providing an opportunity for designers to create more responsible, ethical, thoughtful, transparent products with children's and families' well-being in mind—to foster relational intelligence rather than isolation. The opposite of junk tech is relationally responsible tech, and we need a lot more of it. But how do we know for sure what is junk and what is relationally responsible?

Apple's App Store contains over 500,000 apps marketed as educational. Out of the 2,000 apps for two- to five-year-olds rated by the nonprofit Common Sense Media, only 187, or less than 10 percent, can be rated as having "educational value."[11] In other words, around 90 percent of educational apps for young children do not meet high ratings for educational standards and can be considered junk tech.

Psychology professor Kathy Hirsh-Pasek, who is also a senior fellow at the Brookings Institution, has developed a framework of four "pillars" for assessing the quality of apps intended for kids. (The pillars are now referred to by the acronym AEMS).[12] Hirsh-Pasek found that only 6 percent of the 124 apps she tested had high educational value for young children.[13] A description of the four pillars follows.

Pillar 1 (A), "Active learning," assesses whether the app encourages thoughtful and intellectual engagement, moving beyond simple cause-and-effect interactions and away from passive content.

Pillar 2 (E), "Engagement in the learning process," assesses the app's interactive features, ensuring that they enhance user engagement rather than causing distractions.

Pillar 3 (M), "Meaningful learning," assesses whether the app's content is relevant to children's daily experiences and taught in a way that aligns with existing knowledge.

Pillar 4 (S), "Social interaction," measures the extent to which children can meaningfully interact with characters through the app interface or engage with caregivers about the app.

The reality is that we know what relationally responsible tech for children looks like, but we have not yet agreed on a brand or label with which to identify it, the way we can, for example, identify food as "USDA Certified Organic." I applaud the efforts of nonprofit organizations like Common Sense Media, ISTE (International Society for Technology in Education), and Digital Promise to establish rating systems that parents or educators can consult. However, unlike organic food certification, these are not yet widely recognized or used as elements in tech product packaging or in app stores. Creating such a certification would be helpful. It would be even better if the certification were embedded in search criteria or in product ratings in large app stores, as a way to guide parents, educators, and schools on whether to download an app or a software product. The risks in generative AI tools are even greater, given their lack of traceability and the safety, accuracy, and bias issues associated with large language models.

When we consider the risks of technology for young children, most of us think about screen time. The fastest-growing segment of online device users is our youngest learners, so screen time is a clear cause for concern.[14] The American Academy of Pediatrics recommends no or extremely limited digital use before eighteen to twenty-four months of age. Yet in the United States, nearly 50 percent of children under the age of two have daily screen time, with about one-third spending more than an hour each day on devices, and about 11 percent spending over two hours per day in front of screens.[15] During COVID, more than a quarter of preschoolers were on devices for more than four hours a day. Yes, you read that correctly: preschoolers. The age at which "regular" screen engagement begins has considerably shifted, decreasing from four years old in 1970 to a few months old today.[16] That said, the concept of screen time is not particularly helpful in itself, as it doesn't distinguish between quality and nonquality time. As with food, intake is not necessarily bad. There is nourishing, healthy food, and there is useful tech.

Relational Tech

In many ways, the digital age has ushered in new opportunities for nurturing love and affection between young children and their parents or other adult caregivers. Love can flourish within a landscape dominated by digital interactions. But these evolving dynamics also give rise to some new challenges. Let's consider four stories about this new landscape, in which I played an active role.

Eldera

Patti Early, age seventy, lives in Coatesville, Pennsylvania. She recalls that in her very first online encounter with a child named Margot in December 2021, it was clear that they formed an instant and genuine connection. They both often express that their pairing is simply perfect. Margot is in many respects a typical young girl, with one distinguishing characteristic: she was born with Down syndrome. Margot enjoys talking about her experiences of living with Down syndrome, providing Patti with wonderful and educational insights.

Their connection was facilitated by Eldera.ai, an online platform that matches mentors and mentees using an algorithm. I have been an advisor to Dana Griffin, CEO and founder of Eldera.ai, for several years. Griffin sees older adults' time and wisdom as a priceless resource for younger generations and has sought to leverage that value through an online portal that offers an alternative experience to conventional social media. She is seeking to build a global virtual village with a soul, where generations come together to connect, learn from each other, have fun, and create a better future. The goal is to weave a worldwide web of meaningful and beautiful relationships by reconnecting young and old—one to one, and many at a time. During their very first meeting, Margot opened up to Patti about how it felt to be different from everyone else, including her own family. She expressed how people often make assumptions about her based on her appearance and speech. Patti shared her own experiences, too, acknowledging that as an overweight individual, she had faced unfair judgment from others before they got to know her. This heartfelt exchange forged an instant friendship between them.

Months after they met, Margot took part in the National Miss Amazing Junior Teen Pageant in Nashville and ended up winning the competition. Before Margot embarked on her journey to the pageant, Patti had sent her a text: "Honestly, you have the potential to become a role model for other girls with disabilities." Margot texted back with, "Oh, I just got chills." It became apparent that every word Patti spoke mattered deeply to Margot. Yet Patti feels that the gift Margot has given her surpasses anything she has done for Margot. Margot rekindled Patti's connection with children and pulled her out of isolation. She helps Patti feel loving and loved. She brings laughter into Patti's life and wholeheartedly embraces her for who she is. When asked to write a few words about their relationship, Margot emphasizes its reciprocity: "Our friendship is important because it shows two people opening up to each other and that being completely different from each other is ok. We are showing what friendship is about and we both know we can do anything and be who we want to be together, and we are sticking to each other's side like honey."

Caribu

Caribu is on a mission to help young children deepen connections with their parents and grandparents by allowing them to read and draw together in interactive video calls, no matter how far apart they are. I met Caribu's cofounder and original CEO Maxeme Tuchman several years ago when I served as judge on a Teach for America social impact competition. Caribu ended up winning.

Caribu is an interactive platform that helps adults and kids in more than 160 countries share engaging screen experiences that are carefully designed, curated, and secure. An in-app library is filled with hundreds of books from leading children's publishers, in seven languages, as well as educational workbooks. It is particularly helpful for families who have to connect remotely: military families, divorced families, families with grandparents far away. It turned out to be particularly helpful during the COVID-19 pandemic. "Kids are feeling the effects of the outbreak, but don't always understand why grandma can't come visit, why the special family spring break trip may have been canceled, or why they're out of school for weeks," Tuchman commented. "Everything we do is about creating more meaningful connections, and that's what we think is most important right now—keeping families connected in the most engaging way."[17]

Ready4K

During the pandemic, I connected with Anahi, who lives in California. She shared, "I have a fifteen-month-old baby, and I'm a truck dispatcher. I signed up for Ready4K at the diaper drive, and it's been helpful, especially as a single mom." Ready4K (a product of ParentPowered) is an evidence-based family engagement curriculum delivered via text messages. The content is sent three times a week.

Anahi continued, "You forget that you still have a life outside of being a mom. The texts remind me: 'Take some time for yourself. Don't get frustrated. Try to understand your kid.' I think more about how I'm raising my baby and trying different methods than my family has done in the past." She became more emotional: "There was one message about snuggling and building security and trust by showing the baby affection. Growing up, I was always the sibling who [was] shown the least affection. The messages have shown me that she's a baby, a tiny little thing exploring everything, and it's okay to be loving with her." Ready4K encouraged Anahi to display emotions to her child that she may not have learned from interactions with her own family of origin. When Anahi does so, her child's learning can accelerate.

Khan Academy Kids

Meghan, a newly divorced mom determined to build a stable career, returned to the University of Colorado for classes in neuroscience and data science when her daughter, Joyce, was entering kindergarten. Amidst this period of significant change, both found solace and support in the whimsical educational apps offered by Khan Academy. Meghan, familiar with Khan Academy from her high school days and college biology classes, started using the platform again for a boost in biology and math. Her discovery of Khan Academy Kids was a serendipitous twist for Joyce. (I served on the advisory board of Khan Academy Kids.)

Using the platform, which is filled with colorful characters and engaging activities, became their evening routine, turning screen time into an interactive and educational adventure. Meghan observed that the app not only fortified Joyce's school skills but also nurtured her emotional growth, a particularly meaningful benefit as Joyce adapted to life after her parents' divorce. Joyce's teachers couldn't help but notice her blossoming confidence and academic progress, attributes Meghan credits to their experiences with Khan Academy Kids. This digital haven offered a safe space for Joyce to explore and learn, easing Meghan's concerns about online dangers.

Their story is a testament to the transformative power of education and the importance of supportive relationships. Although Khan Academy Kids provided them with valuable learning tools, it was their own dedication and shared love that propelled the growth, both in knowledge and in their bond as mother and daughter.

Responsible relational tech platforms like Eldera.ai, Caribu, Ready4K, and Khan Academy Kids offer an array of tools designed to facilitate communication and bonding, some while transcending physical distances. The challenge lies in ensuring that the digital interactions supplement rather than replace traditional forms of affectionate communication. While screens can bridge geographical gaps, they don't provide the physical touch, eye contact, or shared physical activities that are essential to bonding. Striking a balance between the convenience of digital communication and the richness of in-person interaction is crucial in fostering a holistic and emotionally nurturing environment.

Too much food, even healthy food, can lead to indigestion. Same with tech. Excessive screen time is not good. Prolonged and unproductive exposure to digital devices can result in irregular habits in children's sleeping, eating, and exercise routines. Extended sedentary interaction with technology has been linked to hindered language development skills, reduced creative thinking, and poor social skills that impede children's interactions with peers and adults. These deficiencies can have lasting effects, often causing older children to grapple with behavioral and educational challenges, and even increasing the likelihood of violent behavior. Young children exposed to screens for more than three hours per day exhibit language delays, reduced attention span, and hyperactivity.[18] Sitting a baby in front of a tablet or television is even associated with greater incidence of symptoms related to autism spectrum disorder later in childhood.[19]

Child psychiatrist Victoria Dunckley has coined a term for what she perceives as a new psychiatric disorder: electronic screen syndrome. She believes that too much exposure to screens results in emotional dysregulation. She emphasizes that boys with ADHD or/and autism spectrum disorder might be at even greater risk. On a positive note, "electronic fasting," as Dunckley calls it—essentially removing all devices for three to four weeks—generally improves symptoms.[20]

Digital Distraction

While it is common to fret about kids and screens, the lesser-told story is that parents also spend an extraordinary amount of time on their devices consuming junk tech, and distracted parenting may be an even greater concern for our little learners than their own diet of junk tech. Six in ten American parents admit that they spend more time on their electronic devices than their kids do. The consequences are sobering: children overwhelmingly report that they feel lonelier as a result of their parents being online.[21]

In Chapter 3, I discussed Edward Tronick's famous still-face experiment, in which a parent initially interacts warmly with their baby but then suddenly becomes unresponsive, donning a blank expression. The baby, distressed by the lack of response, tries to reengage the parent. A similar study found that as soon as parents direct their focus to their phones, infants immediately start to cry and squirm, attempting to regain their parents' attention.[22] In addition, the synchronization in brain waves between child and parent appears to be disrupted during phone usage.[23]

Anyone who has recently spent time near a playground must have noticed the prevalent use of devices by parents. A study of fifty parents at a playground showed that, in a twenty-minute observation period, three-quarters of them used their mobile devices for nearly the entire time (17.5 minutes). Yes, parents are spending *a lot* of time distracted on their devices.[24] One implication may not be entirely surprising: more playground accidents. A researcher ran a study looking at rollout areas by AT&T for cell phone coverage and showed a 5 percent increase in emergency room visits for children under age five in those areas where parents newly had access to mobile coverage.[25]

Adults' junk screen time is equally concerning as children's, if not more so, in terms of its consequences for relational intelligence and healthy child development. Societally, we need to address what research scientist Brandon McDaniel calls "technoference": interruptions in interpersonal communications caused by devices, irrespective of who is using the device.[26] We are all for the most part aware of the phenomenon, and feel guilty about it, but we are poorly equipped to regulate our own online interactions.

Smartphones have hindered our ability to shape a culture that prioritizes connection. The mere visible presence of a mobile phone during a face-to-face conversation can have negative effects on closeness, connection, and conversation quality. Andrew Przybylski and Netta Weinstein, from the University of Essex, conducted an experiment by inviting pairs of strangers into a compact space to have conversations. They were given a conversation starter: to tell about an interesting event from the preceding month. During some pairs' interactions, a smartphone was placed within view, while in others, a paper notebook took its place. All pairs formed some level of connection, yet those in the vicinity of a smartphone found it harder to bond. They rated their emerging relationships as lower quality and perceived their conversation partners to be less empathetic and trustworthy. The study suggests that smartphones, even when not being used, can disrupt social interactions. This impact becomes particularly pronounced when people try to engage in a conversation about a personally meaningful topic.[27] Smartphones reduce the frequency of smiles exchanged between strangers, and they diminish the overall enjoyment of in-person social interactions.[28] We have long known that the presence and active engagement of adults are key for children to thrive and learn.

When a parent is engrossed in their digital device and their child interrupts this focus, ensuing interactions tend to be of lower quality compared with those that occur without screens. Parents are less likely to provide meaningful responses when interrupted during screen use, leading children to perceive their responses as hostile. Consequently, children quickly learn to avoid interactions with parents during screen usage, as such interruptions often elicit negative reactions.[29] This sets in motion a detrimental cycle of inattention that adversely affects the child's self-esteem and weakens the overall parent-child relationship.

The reduction in both frequency and quality of parent-child interactions can impact a child's development in various ways. Research indicates that parental screen time disrupts the cultivation of "joint attention," the ability to recognize and focus on shared points of interest.[30] Joint attention plays a pivotal role in socialization throughout a child's life, influencing their ability to develop healthy relationships and excel academically. The mere act of coviewing media with a caregiver, for instance, supports language acquisition for young children.[31]

In the early 2010s, researchers in Boston conducted observations of fifty-five caregivers dining with one or more children at fast-food restaurants.[32] Forty of the adults were found to be engaged with their mobile phones to varying degrees; some almost completely disregarded the children. Children's attempts to capture their caregivers' attention were often ignored. In a subsequent study, a quarter of the mothers spontaneously used their phones, and those who did engaged in significantly fewer verbal and nonverbal interactions with their children. McDonald's, after finding that 72 percent of children and 69 percent of parents use their smartphones during mealtimes, started a pilot program in Singapore dubbed the Family Playdate, asking parents to leave their devices in lockers.[33] With a slogan of "Phone off, fun on," the program was an attempt to expand Happy Meals to happy tables. Unfortunately, the pilot was short-lived, as usage of the lockers remained sporadic.

Intermittent lapses in parental attention are not necessarily detrimental and might even contribute to a child's development of resilience. But persistent and repeated distraction is a different matter. Smartphone usage elicits traits akin to addiction: distracted adults tend to become irritable when their phone usage is disrupted, causing them not only to miss their kids' emotional signals but to misinterpret them. A disengaged parent might become more easily agitated than an attentive one, wrongly assuming that a child is acting out when in reality the child simply craves attention.

Relationships and connection can still thrive in a digital-centric landscape, but caregivers and educators face unique responsibilities. Fostering tech-infused bonds demands a careful balance between leveraging technology's benefits and ensuring a child's holistic development.

Parents and caregivers must monitor the use of junk tech, both our children's and our own—especially our own—to ensure that it complements real-world experiences crucial for social, emotional, and physical growth. Face-to-face interactions, outdoor play, and hands-on activities are paramount. Safeguarding online experiences is crucial, involving a secure digital environment and early digital and AI literacy. An informed, balanced, and ethical approach preserves the warmth and authenticity of human connection amidst the powerful impact of technology on early bonds.

As I have repeatedly stressed, early relationships are powered by the transformative impact of love. In the next chapter we will witness how this force, so integral to our development, extends its influence into every facet of our lives—from shaping our perceptions of the world to guiding our decisions, actions, and learning. Love is not just an emotion; it is a force of nature that we are only beginning to truly comprehend.

CHAPTER 8

Love: The Silver Bullet in Education

Love your neighbor as yourself.

—Leviticus 19:18

Love your neighbor as yourself. There is no other commandment greater than these.

—Mark 12:31

Not one of you truly believes until you wish for others that which you wish for yourself.

—Hadith

This is the sum of duty. Do not unto others that which would cause you pain if done to you.

—Mahabharata 5, 1517

At the GSV Leaders' Summit in late 2023, held in Nashville and attended by three hundred pioneers in education, the CEO of GSV, Michael Moe, posed a provocative question: "What's love got to do with it?" Could love, often sidelined in educational discourse, be the silver bullet to accelerate learning?

GSV Ventures (GSV stands for Global Silicon Valley) is a for-profit education technology investor, not the sort of outfit that typically gravitates toward what might be considered "soft" concepts. Moe's interest in the subject suggests a notable mindset shift, an acknowledgment that love, the bedrock of relational intelligence, is the fundamental force in education.

In a similar vein, as Jack Ma was retiring from his executive role at Alibaba, one of the world's largest e-commerce companies, he gave a speech about the future of education in which he elevated the concept of the love quotient (LQ). Ma has an interesting background. He is a former English teacher who failed multiple attempts to pass university exams before he eventually earned his teaching credentials and later became one of the world's most successful technology founders—when Alibaba went public in 2014, it was the largest initial public offering in history. In his 2019 speech, which was delivered at OECD's Forum for World Education, he expressed his passion for education, which he calls the "most important and critical issue" of our time.[1] His concern: the world is changing fast, but education is not. His formula is to focus not on curriculum or accountability, but on students' capacity to love. "If you want to be successful, you should have high EQ [emotional intelligence], a way to get on with people. If you don't want to lose quickly, you should have good IQ. But if you want to be respected, you should have LQ—the quotient of love. The brain will be replaced by machines, but machines can never replace your heart." Ma suggested that in the future, everything about education should be reconsidered, including teachers, classrooms, and students. Classes will no longer be confined to forty-minute segments, and teachers will not hold all the knowledge. Instead, educators will focus on fostering the ability to ask the right questions rather than just providing the correct answers. "If you focus on standardization, everything can be replaced by machines," he said. "With AI, education needs to focus on differentiation for every learner to be the best of themselves."

It is noteworthy for a major business leader to introduce the concept of love into discussions of success in life and business. He suggested prioritizing investments in early childhood, when children are developing skills and values, and reducing funding for universities, where values are already established. "Please put more resources on the front and not in the back," he said, indicating that kindergartens and primary schools have significant potential to shape children. He also emphasized the need for greater support for teachers. "If we respect teachers, we respect knowledge and we respect the future," he said. He suggested that education should become more global and team-oriented. China, he noted, excels in individual sports but struggles with team ones. He advocated for incorporating more arts, dance, painting, and team sports into learning. He has started a school where after-school activities focus on sports instead of tutoring. "Last century," he said, "was won by muscle, while this one will be won with wisdom." He beautifully concluded his speech with, "Last century we won by caring about ourselves; this century we win by caring about others."

Business leaders like Moe and Ma are urging us to add a focus on love to our focus on learning because they can foresee that automation and our AI-dynamic future are accelerating the need to develop uniquely human relational skills and competencies as well as a lifelong love of learning.

Let's admit it. Traditionally, love is not the first word we think about in learning and education. But this oversight reveals a fundamental flaw. *Love is the fuel of learning.* To be clear, I am not talking about romantic love. I refer rather to a broader definition of love, one involving those instances of rapport that evoke feelings of affection or warmth. In *Love 2.0: Creating Happiness and Health in Moments of Connection*, Barbara Fredrickson, a professor of psychology at the

University of North Carolina at Chapel Hill, defines it well: "Love is our supreme emotion that makes us come most fully alive and feel most fully human. It is perhaps the most essential emotional experience for thriving and health. Love is an emotion, a momentary state that arises to infuse your mind and body alike. Love is a micro-moment of positivity resonance. Love blossoms virtually anytime two or more people—even strangers—connect over a shared positive emotion, be it mild or strong."[2]

The micromoments Fredrickson refers to often involve simple connections that have outsized impact. These moments develop into relationships. Love is also multisensorial. It can come from the sound of a lullaby, from the view of a close one, from the smell of a favorite food or flowers, from a touch or embrace, a caress or cuddle.

In many ways, love serves as the vital force underpinning existence itself, and it is a major force behind learning. During infancy, receiving love is not just beneficial; it is essential for our survival and for shaping who we are. Love acts as a source of motivation, comfort, and support throughout our educational journey. When we feel loved, whether by parents, teachers, friends, or mentors, we're more likely to engage in learning with enthusiasm and persevere in acquiring knowledge. Love fosters a sense of security that enables us to take risks, make mistakes, and grow from our experiences. It fuels our desire to explore, understand, and excel in our quest for understanding. In the presence of love, learning becomes a deeply fulfilling part of our personal and collective growth, building our interconnectedness and driving us to continually expand our horizons.

We need love to live and flourish. More than ever, we need love to learn.

Teaching with Love

Nicholas Ferroni is a teacher advocate with an impressive social media following (and not simply because he was named one of the twenty-five fittest men in the world by *Men's Fitness* magazine in 2011). He notes, "Students who are loved at home come to school to learn. Students who aren't . . . come to school to be loved."

I described in the introduction how my early childhood teachers Mrs. Combes and Mrs. Lenoir positively impacted my trajectory. There are countless stories of how supportive relationships with teachers—teachers who love what they do and communicate that love to learners—transform lives. Les Brown is an influential motivational speaker and thought leader on self-improvement and goal setting. Yet his journey was far from straightforward. He and his twin brother were born on the floor of an abandoned building in Liberty City, a low-income neighborhood in Miami. Brown's biological mother gave up her sons for adoption when they were six weeks old. In his academic pursuits, Brown struggled from the beginning. Branded as "educable mentally handicapped," he was held back in fifth grade. To compound his challenges, his twin brother was exceptionally bright and gifted, earning Les the unkind nickname of the "DT" or "dumb twin." One pivotal moment occurred when a teacher asked Les to come to the front of the class and solve a problem on the chalkboard. Brown initially refused, asserting that he couldn't do it because he was "educable mentally handicapped." The classroom erupted in laughter. At that crucial point, the teacher stepped out from behind the desk and looked Brown directly in the eyes, saying firmly, "Never say that again. Someone else's opinion of you does not have to define your reality." Those words became etched in Brown's memory, driving him to overcome extraordinary difficulties and pursue his goals with unwavering determination. Time and again, inspired by the teacher's powerful remarks, Brown lived out the phrase that has made him famous worldwide: "You have greatness within you."

Emily Blunt is widely recognized as a Golden Globe–winning film and stage actress. While growing up, however, she grappled with a crippling stutter that made even basic conversations a formidable challenge. She could hardly say her own name. In an interview with *W Magazine*, she remarked, "I was a bright child with plenty to say, but I struggled to articulate it. I never thought I'd be able to converse as I do now."[3] For Blunt, one particular junior high teacher played a crucial role in helping her conquer her fear of speaking. The teacher encouraged her to audition for a school play, a suggestion that Blunt initially resisted. Nevertheless, the teacher persevered, urging Blunt to take acting lessons and experiment with various accents and character voices to find ways to express herself. Ultimately, her efforts yielded remarkable results. In addition to her thriving career as an actress, Blunt became a member of the board of directors for the American Institute for Stuttering.

Before achieving renown as a powerful poet and civil rights activist, Maya Angelou endured a tumultuous and painful childhood, marked by severe physical and emotional abuse at the hands of a family member. Consequently, she fell silent for nearly five years. Her transformation began with the assistance of a family friend, a teacher named Bertha Flowers. Angelou credits Mrs. Flowers with helping her find her voice once more. Through Mrs. Flowers, she was introduced to the works of African American women poets like Frances Harper, Anne Spencer, and Jessie Fauset. Mrs. Flowers also exposed Angelou to the writings of Charles Dickens, William Shakespeare, Edgar Allan Poe, and other influential authors who would profoundly shape her personal and professional philosophies.

Teachers' love drives learning by creating an emotionally safe and motivating classroom environment, fostering positive relationships, boosting student resilience, increasing engagement, improving behavior, supporting social and emotional learning, offering academic assistance, building students' confidence, and leaving a long-lasting impact, ultimately enhancing academic success and the overall learning experience for students. Who are the teachers that inspired you?

Beyond individual teachers, schools that center love and positive relationships outperform. A study in Michigan showed counterintuitive results: five thousand students and teachers in seventy-eight public elementary schools were asked to rate the quality of relationships in their schools by evaluating statements such as "Parent involvement supports learning here," "Teachers in this school trust their students," and "Community involvement facilitates learning here."[4] Students in schools that spent more money per pupil had better test scores than those in schools that spent less—no surprise there. What was more intriguing was the effect of relationships: strong relationships between teachers, parents, and students were three times more important than financial support in driving math scores and five times more important for reading scores.

Teachers who genuinely care about their students and express love and support create an atmosphere where students feel valued and respected. These positive relationships can lead to increased motivation, better communication, and a more productive learning environment, and can yield benefits ranging from improved academic performance (as noted in the Michigan study) to increased rates of college enrollment.

Every individual connection a student makes holds significant potential as a source of support, whether it be with a teacher, an assistant teacher, a paraeducator, a coach, a receptionist, a cafeteria worker, or a school administrator. Young people thrive even more when they are woven into a robust network of diverse relationships throughout their development. The Search Institute, a nonprofit research organization that has focused on the impact of relationships, collected data from more than twenty-five thousand students in grades six through twelve in a large urban district in 2017. Their conclusion is remarkable: a higher number of strong relationships leads to higher academic motivation, drives greater socioemotional skills, and reduces the chances that a young person will engage in high-risk behaviors.[5] Love and relationships fuel learning and academic performance.

Students who are loved tend to love to learn. And in a dynamic and rapidly changing world, relational skills and the love of learning will increasingly be the key to success and personal empowerment.

GRAPH 4

Learning Through Relationships
The Impact of Strong Relationships on Educational Success

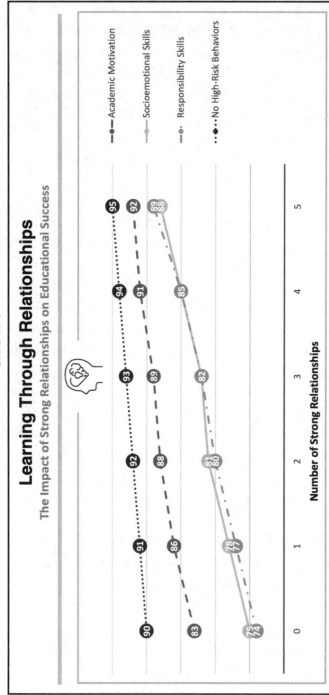

Average score (1–100) that youth report on measures of:

- Academic Motivation: Caring about how they do in school and trying as hard as they can to do their best work.
- Socioemotional Skills: Recognizing and respecting other people's feelings; are good at making and keeping friends.
- Responsibility Skills: Taking responsibility for their own actions; doing their best, even on tasks they don't like.
- No High-Risk Behaviors: Not engaging in high-risk behaviors such as alcohol use, tobacco use, or violence.

Source:

Relationships First: Creating Connections That Help Young People Thrive (Search Institute, 2017), based on a 2016 survey of 25,395 students, grades 6–12, https://blog.searchinstitute.org/new-research-report.

Love, Learning, and the Labor Market

Love is trending in the workplace. Nearly all job growth since 1980 has been in occupations that are social-skill intensive. Teamwork, for instance, is now considered "very" or "extremely" important in eight of ten occupations.[6] Not surprisingly, a Stanford study shows that people working collaboratively persist on a task for 64 percent longer than those working individually on the same task, and they exhibit higher levels of engagement.[7] According to the platform LinkedIn, the most in-demand skills in 2024 include "teamwork" and "communication."[8] Jobs that require high levels of analytical and mathematical reasoning but low levels of relational skills have been declining because they are easier to automate.[9] As a result, workers in positions requiring social and relational skills are demanding higher wages. These trends align with the fact that there has been a decrease in demand for jobs involving routine tasks, whereas those that require the human touch for enhancing team productivity and flexible adaptation to changing circumstances are on the rise.

David Deming, who studies social and relational skills at Harvard University, analyzed team performance and showed that there really is such a thing as a team player. He was able to isolate and replicate the effect of an individual team member's contribution across multiple groups, showing that a team player increases group performance quite meaningfully.[10] Similarly, in a large research study referred to as Project Oxygen, Google examined what made the company's employees good managers. The assumption was that it was technical skills. In fact, most successful managers were *relational* individuals who made time for one-to-one meetings, helped employees work through problems, and took an interest in their lives.[11]

The future belongs to those with relational intelligence, and it's vital to instill these skills from an early age. The workplace increasingly values the skills that are typically nurtured in a preschool-like environment. Paradoxically, however, preschools are starting to shift toward a more rigid, academically focused model reminiscent of the pedagogy of the industrial era, potentially neglecting the importance of play and peer interaction. James Heckman, a recipient of the Nobel Prize in economics (and whose work on the Perry Preschool program I discussed in Chapter 1), conducted pioneering research establishing the equal importance of noncognitive abilities—including social skills—alongside cognitive ones. Heckman asserted that these attributes are teachable, although he pointed out that American educational institutions may not consistently focus on cultivating them.[12] To prepare students for the future, education systems should focus on and measure relational intelligence—the ability to interact and work effectively with others—not just mastery of academic skills or acquisition of content.

Love of Learning

A love of learning is also gaining importance in the ever-evolving world of work. Maintaining a thirst for learning is like having a dependable compass in a shifting landscape. We know that the average American will change jobs twelve times between the ages of eighteen and fifty-four, and will switch careers between three and seven times.[13] About one in five American workers has a job with high exposure to artificial intelligence, according to OpenAI, the developer of ChatGPT.[14] Over time, automation may create as many jobs as it eliminates, but those new jobs will require people to retrain and acquire new skills. As technology hurtles forward, those who embrace learning will navigate the twists and turns of the modern job market with greater ease. They will have a knack for staying in the know about the new tools, technologies, and industry trends that will be crucial for remaining competitive in their careers.

But the significance of a love for learning goes beyond just professional growth. It's about personal empowerment. It's akin to having a versatile toolset for life. A curious and open attitude can make you more adaptable, more resilient, and a sharper problem solver. When you love learning, you tend to approach challenges as opportunities for growth rather than insurmountable obstacles. That kind of mindset not only helps you flourish in your career but also enriches your personal life. In my opinion, a love of learning is an understudied competency, despite its vital role in human flourishing.

What is a love of learning? It characterizes an individual's approach to acquiring new information and skills, encompassing both a general enthusiasm for learning and a pronounced interest in specific subject matter. When I think of a love of learning, I picture someone like my younger daughter, whose passion for dance and desire for mastery cause her to continue dancing across our living room after formally training at her dance school for five hours straight. When people possess a strong love of learning, they become mentally engaged and derive positive emotions from the process of acquiring new skills, satisfying their curiosity, building upon existing knowledge, or delving into entirely new topics. Young children simply love learning. Four-year-olds ask as many as two hundred to three hundred questions a day.[15] How can we keep that love alive and well?

Love Can Be Taught and Learned

Ideally, every child entering the world would be anticipated and cherished, either from the outset or soon after their arrival. Unfortunately, this is not always the case. Tragic narratives, exemplified in the stories of Romanian orphanages, Native American boarding schools, rural areas in China, and other conditions under which children have been deprived of love, highlight the struggles faced by children who lack love. These children find themselves having to learn how to give and receive love. The absence of familiarity with love makes this process challenging, especially in terms of self-love and feeling deserving of affection from others.

On a positive note, as we saw earlier, the ability to experience love appears to be innate, much like our capacities for walking, speaking, and playing. A baby can revel in the pleasures of touch, reciprocal gazes, laughter, and the assurance that someone will attend to their needs. Love can be taught and learned. Children who may not have received positive nurturing from their parents can still become nurturing adults.

On March 4, 2019, Leslee Udwin climbed up on a podium and gave a speech in which she quoted Nelson Mandela: "If a child can be taught to hate, this child can be taught to love." She was accepting the prestigious UN Women for Peace Award. Udwin is a petite woman with a beautiful British accent and an infectious passion as a human rights activist and a filmmaker. In 2015 the *New York Times* selected her as the second most impactful woman of the year for her documentary *India's Daughter*, which examines the brutal gang rape and murder of Jyoti Singh in Delhi in 2012, highlighting the pervasive issues of gender violence and societal attitudes toward women in India.

Udwin later founded Think Equal to address the meaningful challenge of teaching children to love. In pursuit of enduring change, she decided to focus on young children. Udwin asks, "How can it be deemed compulsory for a child to learn mathematics, but it is optional for that child to learn how to value another human being or to lead healthy relationships?" Supported by philanthropy, Think Equal provides a free socioemotional curriculum for children ages three to six. The program is designed to be taught in half-hour lesson plans three times per week for thirty weeks of the school year. Each week's session begins with a reading from a narrative picture book. Since January 2017, numerous schools in countries worldwide have piloted the Think Equal program, reaching nearly 240,000 children.

Jola, a little girl in Sri Lanka who was being bullied in her preschool, is one of those children. She had a serious rash on her face, and other youngsters refused to play with her. A few months after the Think Equal curriculum was introduced in her school, Jola's mom rushed into the classroom. She asked the teacher, "What did you do? This is simply extraordinary." She explained that she had caught a glimpse of her daughter looking into the mirror saying that we are all different, and we are all beautiful, that she is different because of her rash, and she is beautiful. The teacher explained that Jola was repeating a lesson from one of the books provided by Think Equal. Jola, miraculously, seemed to be regaining her self-esteem, which also made her less anxious, so her rash was subsiding too.

Before assuming that this one story may seem too good to be true, systematic research about the Think Equal program confirms Jola's experience. Children exposed to the curriculum demonstrate increases in self-esteem, in sense of belonging, and in prosocial behaviors, as well as reductions in stress and anxiety.[16] The director of the Kgatleng school district in Botswana, where Think Equal was implemented in every classroom in 2019, reported to the Ministry of Education that he had personally witnessed not only individual children being trans- formed, but a reduction in levels of violence in the community. Love can be taught.

Another large study across twenty thousand young learners in mul- tiple countries showed that teaching kindness led to significant improve- ment in social competence, increased emotional self-regulation, fewer behavioral problems, and better academic outcomes compared with control participants.[17] And not only can love be taught and learned; love is contagious. Studies show that collaborative and compassionate behaviors can positively influence up to three degrees of people within a person's network of relationships: the person's friends (one degree), who in turn influence their own friends (two degrees), and even the friends' friends' friends (three degrees).[18]

To be clear, love and relationships affect people in different ways and to different degrees. What constitutes a profoundly impactful rela- tionship for one young child may not carry the same significance for another. Some connections are fleeting, while others stand the test of time. We all seek diverse qualities and support from various individuals depending on the circumstances we face. Significant relationships are defined by an evolving exchange, molding our identities as we adapt to growth, transformation, and the complexities that life throws our way.

Love Builds Resilience

One of the most important investigations of childhood adversity was born out of an accident. As chief of Kaiser Permanente's Department of Preventive Medicine in San Diego, California, Vincent Felitti ran an obesity clinic. The program had high dropout rates, and Felitti wanted to discover why. Particularly surprising and counterintuitive was the fact that many of the dropouts did so even though the program was starting to work and they were losing weight. Looking into these patients' data, Felitti found some surprising statistics: all the dropouts had been born at a normal weight. Furthermore, they didn't gain weight gradually over several years, but abruptly. He conducted face-to-face interviews with two hundred of the dropouts.

A pivotal moment in Felitti's pursuit occurred inadvertently: he asked a question incorrectly. Instead of inquiring when the patient had become sexually active, he mistakenly asked about her weight at the time of her first sexual experience. The patient said she had gained 40 pounds after it. She started crying and admitted that the sexual experience had been with her father. Felitti and his colleagues began to observe a pattern between the prevalence of childhood abuse and the onset of their patients' obesity. Many patients openly discussed a connection between the two. Felitti had never learned about this connection in medical school or thought about it during his years as a physician. Yet he was on to something. For those individuals, obesity served as a protective coping mechanism. One woman who had been raped gained 105 pounds in the subsequent year. Her weight gain subconsciously became protection against future abuses.

After identifying a potential connection between trauma and obesity, Felitti decided to further test the linkage between trauma and health. In partnership with the Centers for Disease Control and Prevention, he and his colleagues embarked on a larger project, which became known as the CDC-Kaiser Permanente adverse childhood experiences study, or ACE Study. The researchers enrolled seventeen thousand initial participants and surveyed them about their experiences with childhood maltreatment, family dysfunction, and current health status and behaviors. In line with Felitti's earlier finding, the study famously found a direct link between childhood trauma and adult onset of chronic disease, incarceration, and employment challenges. Adults who had experienced six or more specific types of abuse or household dysfunction during childhood had their life expectancy reduced by up to an astounding twenty years.[19] What about the impact of adversity on school and learning? Subsequent studies would show that children with three or more ACEs are five times more likely to have attendance issues, six times more likely to have behavior problems, and three times more likely to experience academic failure.[20] As it turns out, ACEs are widespread. Approximately two-thirds of Americans have experienced at least one ACE, and one in six has experienced four or more ACEs.[21]

But the story is not all bleak. A group of scientists at Oklahoma State University have studied PACEs—those protective and compensatory experiences that offer a counterbalance to the negative impacts of ACEs and trauma. (They're sometimes referred to as PCEs, positive childhood experiences.)[22] Most PACEs revolve around human connections. Here is the good news: adults who had many PACEs in their childhood have fewer problems related to health, well-being, and learning, *even if* they had a history of ACEs. Children with a history of multiple adversities who also have strong family support are more likely to thrive than those with fewer adversities but without family support.

Strong family connections and positive parenting are key resilience factors protecting youth from the impact of stressful experiences.[23] In fact, ten types of PACEs have been identified that can help build resilience and compensate for the occurrence of early adversity:

Parent/caregiver unconditional love

Spending time with a best friend

Volunteering or helping others

Being active in a social group

Having a mentor outside the family

Living in a clean, safe home with enough food

Having opportunities to learn

Having a hobby

Being active or playing sports

Having routines and fair rules at home

As you can see, most of them are anchored in relationships. In *The Breakthrough Years*, Ellen Galinsky emphasizes that children's basic psychological needs are fulfilled through our relationships with them. These needs include belonging, support, respect, autonomy, competence, challenge, identity formation, and the opportunity to contribute to others. Galinksy's research powerfully demonstrates that adolescents in a nationally representative sample who felt these needs were met—whether at home, at school, with friends, in extracurricular activities, or online—showed resilience and thrived even amid the challenges of the pandemic.[24]

Love and Relational Intelligence Can Be Measured

How many nurturing relationships does a child have? What is the relational health of each of those ties? How can they be nurtured and expanded? What if every school, every pediatrician, every parent were able to track the quantity and quality of relationships around young children? Measuring the amount of love and the number of good relationships young children enjoy is crucial for identifying their developmental needs and if necessary intervening early, ensuring that they grow into emotionally resilient and socially skilled individuals within supportive, nurturing environments. Some measures exist already. New forms of measurement are also emerging.

The Early Relational Health Screen (ERHS)—developed by David Willis, a pediatrician and former division director for the US Department of Health and Human Services' Home Visiting and Early Childhood Systems program—is an effective tool for detecting, monitoring, and promoting relational health across settings.[25] Staff members record a video of a child's unstructured play session with a standard set of toys; for toddlers, they add a brief "challenge" segment during which the child must follow the parent's lead. Then staff review the video with parents, which provides an opportunity to promote strengths and nurture positive early relationships.

In early care and education settings, the CHILD framework (Climate of Healthy Interactions for Learning and Development) offers a research-based tool for assessing and supporting the ways in which adult caregivers promote children's well-being and holistic development. It focuses on improving the adults' knowledge, skills, and actions to foster children's social and emotional development. It also highlights the importance of daily interactions as chances to support healthy growth.

The Swedish company Tobii uses eye-tracking technology to determine what a child looks at and for how long, providing insights into the sorts of stimuli that capture their attention and interest during interactions. Eye tracking is used to understand social and emotional engagement, such as interest in social cues, and can be particularly informative about a child's relational and emotional health.

Present-day researchers are influenced by bioecological systems theory, which emphasizes the importance of various environmental systems and relationships in a child's development. Tools and apps collect data on a child's interactions with others across different environments—home, school, community—to provide a holistic picture of their relational health. For example, ecological momentary assessment apps prompt caregivers or children to report on experiences and emotions in real time, capturing the dynamic nature of a young person's interactions with their environment.[26]

While technology may replicate the functions of the brain, it cannot replicate the qualities of the heart. Yet love and relational intelligence are too often overlooked in our educational systems, presenting a prime opportunity for innovation in how we teach students and prepare them for the future. Fortunately, conversations among researchers, educators, health care practitioners, and thought leaders about the role of love in education are deepening. Experts are embracing the idea that love is a potent catalyst for enhancing cognitive, emotional, and social facets of learning. Social skills and a love of learning are rising in importance in the workplace. With this perspective, we can reimagine education for future generations, positioning relational intelligence as a foundational skill that nurtures compassionate, interconnected, and forward-thinking individuals. Love is poised to be a transformative element—a silver bullet—in educational practice, not only energizing the learning process but also meeting the growing demand for social skills in the workplace and society at large.

PART III

THE PATH FORWARD: CULTIVATING A FUTURE OF CONNECTIONS

Let's redefine success: The single mother who raised her child with love. The minimum wage worker who struggles to create a better life. The young woman who travels a world away to research how monkeys think. The elder who writes her memoir, inspiring a generation through trauma.

—Waylon Lewis, *Elephant Journal*

Fulfilling the necessity of education and achieving holistic change with proper engagement involves four pillars/sides: students, teachers, parents, and the broader community. If one of these is weak or broken, the entire system will be affected or collapse. If these sides do not support each other, if there is a lack of interaction, the achievement rate drops. Ultimately, schools and the entire education system cannot reach their expected goals.

—Teacher from a rural secondary school in Bangladesh

Numerous Native American tribes use the medicine wheel, also called the sun dance circle, to represent the harmonious balance and interconnectedness of all life. It depicts the relationships that surround a child, who is placed at the wheel's center, symbolizing not only the community's present but its future. Immediately surrounding the child is the family—parents, siblings, and extended kin. Representing east on the wheel, and thus signifying new beginnings and the dawn of life, these relatives are the child's first teachers, role models, and caretakers, offering love, culture, and foundational life skills.

The next circle includes friends and peers, from whom the child learns the values of trust, reciprocity, and the art of relationships outside the family. Corresponding to south, this direction celebrates growth and the warmth of relationships.

Further out, representing west, are the mentors, educators, and elders of the community. From them, the child learns about responsibility and social roles, gaining a deeper understanding of their culture and history. West is associated with introspection and the search for deeper understanding, an apt metaphor for education and growth.

In the outermost circle, aligning with north, are the spiritual guides and the community at large, including plants, animals, and the earth, who teach the child about the interconnectedness of all beings and the importance of living in harmony with the environment. North stands for wisdom and gratitude.

Together, the four circles of relationships guide the child in walking the path of life with balance, respect, understanding, an appreciation for learning, and a sense of belonging to the larger web of existence.

In the next chapters, we follow the four quadrants of the medicine wheel that surround children: families, friends, educators, and community. When functioning well, these connections create the supportive, enriching environment that is essential for children to thrive, not just physically but also intellectually, emotionally, and socially. The medicine wheel captures the essence of relationships, which start with a dyad—two people who connect, reciprocate, and respond to each other—but expand to encompass a wider ecology of relationships across a community of care, ideally rooted in love.

Relationships may be one of the oldest concepts in human development, but as we have seen, the quality of the circles of relationships around young children has been deteriorating. Yet despite the challenges, there are promising signs of renewal and strength in each of the four quadrants, offering glimmers of optimism that we are moving toward a future of enhanced connection, love, and learning. As we explore these promising signs in the next four chapters, I choose to lean in toward this hopeful vision of a more harmonious future for our next generation, the one I call Gen R, the Generation of Relationships.

CHAPTER 9

Families: New Configurations, New Horizons

Call it a clan, call it a network, call it a tribe, call it a family.
Whatever you call it, whoever you are, you need one. You need
one because you are human.

—JANE HOWARD, *FAMILIES*, 1998

The idea that "family" means mother, father, two children, and perhaps a pet or two, living in a stand-alone house in a manicured suburb behind a white picket fence, has, like rotary phones and *Leave It to Beaver*, become a quaint historical artifact. But as one door closes, another opens, and from the ashes of this ideal rises a vibrant new paradigm of what family can mean. In this evolution, we have witnessed the disintegration of rigid structures and the birth of fluidity in familial bonds, as well as the emergence of a twenty-first-century version of extended family. These novel forms of kinship are a promising and positive development in nurturing young children's relational intelligence.

In the last half century, society has seen seismic shifts in the dynamics of family life. Economic pressures, social changes, and technological advancements have all played their part in redefining the boundaries of what constitutes a family. No longer are we confined to the biological or marital ties that once dictated the perimeters of kinship. Today's families are as diverse as the individuals that form them—single parents juggling the complexities of work and child-rearing, same-sex couples creating nurturing homes, cohabiting friends sharing parental responsibilities—and digital platforms can connect family members across the virtual expanse.

Yet despite this transformation, the essence of family endures. Family remains the pillar upon which we forge our identities, values, and connections, and it is an ever-evolving testament to the enduring power of love in all its forms. Family in all versions also remains the essential setting in which young children learn and thrive.

Evidence suggests that beyond the immediate family, the extended family contributes to the educational success of children.[1] Extended family—grandparents, aunts, uncles, cousins—all influence educational outcomes. Two effects in particular have been identified by researcher Mads Jæger, a sociologist at the University of Copenhagen. One is called the compensation mechanism, whereby resources in the extended family network are generally mobilized in times of need, which in turn promotes children's educational success. The second is the family quality mechanism, which describes how a family's interactions shape a child's overall development and understanding of the world.

Let's be clear: extended family structure is an ancient concept. We all know the African adage "It takes a village to raise a child."

In Latino and Filipino communities, the compadrazgo system places a significant emphasis on relationships between parents and chosen godparents, the "compadres," who are responsible both to their children/godchildren and to each other. Godparents become integral members of the family, providing support, advice, and assistance akin to that of blood relatives. This creates a supportive network that not only enriches the child's upbringing but also reinforces communal ties, often bridging socioeconomic gaps and fostering unity within the community. It's common in many cultures to refer to a godparent or a parent's close friend as "aunt" or "uncle" to signify their closeness to the family, despite the lack of a blood relationship. In a traditional Japanese family structure, known as *ie*, which prevailed from the late 1500s to the 1900s, family ties were defined less by blood relationships and more by who resided in the household and contributed to the family's work. Adults could be adopted into the family and could even assume the role of the household head if they served the household's social and economic needs better than blood relatives.

Many cultures are built around clan and lineage. In Scotland, clans are large kinship groups with a shared surname and a common ancestor. Being part of a clan like the MacLeods or the MacDonalds comes with a sense of belonging to a large extended family with its own history and heritage. In China, sharing a family name such as Chen or Lee (or Hau, my husband's family name) can imply belonging to a lineage or clan that may have its own history, ancestors, and sometimes even family temples or cemeteries. Membership in a Native American tribe or nation, like the Cherokee or Navajo, often implies a complex network of kinship that extends beyond immediate family to include the larger community as relations.

Today we are seeing emerging signs of a revival of this ancient concept, a resurgence of extended family ties that have been adapted, modified, and enhanced to foster relationships in our modern societies. This in turn could benefit our little learners.

From Biological to Chosen Bonds

The threads of family are no longer woven solely by the hands of biology. The concept of "chosen family," where the bonds of affection, solidarity, and mutual support transcend the traditional ties of bloodline, has emerged as a profound cultural shift. In 1975, sociobiologist Edward

(E. O.) Wilson introduced the term "alloparenting" to define the act of individuals other than the mother and father taking care of a young off-spring. People now forge familial bonds based on shared values, mutual care, and psychological affinity, crafting networks of support that rival the traditional family in emotional depth and stability. This cultural reframing has allowed for a more inclusive understanding of what it means to belong to a family, acknowledging the deep connections formed through friendship, shared experiences, and collective living.

Take Ashley Simpo, a Brooklyn-based writer who in 2018, at thirty-three years old, found herself divorced with a child. As she wrote in the *Huffington Post*, Ashley and her five-year-old son found themselves in need of a new place to live.[2] But because she was a single earner, options in New York were limited. Through a conversation with her best friend, Tia, who had also recently divorced and was struggling to afford her apartment as a single parent of two, a potential solution emerged. Why not share a living space? They made the choice to temporarily cohabitate, splitting expenses evenly and providing mutual support through the various challenges that arise in parenting and in daily life. They collaborated on meal preparation, assisted with homework, and raised their children together. In essence, they coparented, sans any romantic involvement. This meant not only a lighter financial burden for each family, but also a larger and stronger network of relationships and loving care. The arrangement lasted only a few years, but it established stability at a critical juncture and paved the way for long-term friendships and extended family support for all of them.

CoAbode is a platform where single mothers can locate other single moms to share housing and child-rearing as a way to defray costs, reduce isolation, and build connections and support for children to thrive. Danielle in Washington, DC, shares her experience:

> I was stressed. I was moving to a new town that I was ecstatic over, but everyone kept asking if I knew how expensive it was to live near Washington, DC. I really didn't. And then I read

about CoAbode in *USA Today*. I stayed up half the night during my first web visit reading people's profiles and imagining the possibilities. But even in all my hoping and dreaming, I never thought things would be *this* good.

I met my roommate at a CoAbode support group planned for people in our area. We all became friends first (we both have 5-year-old boys), which helped, and after a while began discussing what sharing a house would be like. We took the time to iron out a lot of details before we agreed to do it; how we'd handle different situations, what was important to us, what we valued, and what we hoped to get out of the experience. After we felt sure that we could mesh our lives under one roof, I was pretty certain that at the very least, this was going to be a "good arrangement." But I never dreamed it would be this amazing. Simpler. Better. Happier. Easier. Cheaper. Most importantly, our boys are having the time of their lives. No more boring weekends watching mom clean the house. No more watching lots of videos or entertaining themselves while she does laundry, pays bills, cooks, etc. Now, when we clean the house, there are two of us sharing the load—taking half the time and getting more done—and meanwhile the boys are peeing their pants laughing together! It's not been without its transitions, but it's gone amazingly well. And for me, having someone else to talk to, bounce ideas off of, learn from and share with is incredible. Not to mention that I now can have a bit of a social life, go see a movie, shop at night, go get a coffee . . . things I didn't do while living alone. And having a built-in baby-sitter that I care about and trust, and whom my son loves, is priceless. My roommate has even started to take classes at night, too, something she wasn't able to do while living alone![3]

Rachel Hope, author of *Family by Choice: Platonic Partnered Parenting*, advocates for a parenting approach where coparents reside separately yet in close quarters, such as in different homes on the same property.[4] She practiced this method herself while raising her first child.

Legal and societal recognition of same-sex marriages and parenting rights has been a watershed in redefining family structure. LGBTQ+ families have illuminated the richness that diversity brings to family life, challenging preconceived notions and showcasing the universality of love and parenting. These families, often built on the courageous pursuit of authenticity, have broadened the narrative of family life to include a spectrum of experiences and configurations, enhancing the social fabric with their unique stories and challenges. According to a survey carried out by Family Equality, 77 percent of LGBTQ+ millennials are either contemplating parenthood or are already parents.[5] Simply put, queer parents will likely continue becoming more prevalent.

Divorce rates have halved over the past two decades.[6] And when divorce does happen, an increasing number of parents are choosing shared custody arrangements. Moreover, many states are enacting laws that make shared custody the default.[7] Shared parenting is linked with favorable outcomes for children, including better relationships with each parent, and better performance in school.[8]

Platonic parenting—an arrangement in which individuals, whether LGBTQ+ or newer friends or long-term friends, choose to raise a child together, without a romantic relationship—is on the rise. Popular culture gets it: a new sitcom called *Platonic* debuted in 2023. The movement is still small, more signal than clear trend, but it is estimated that more than two hundred thousand people are registered on sites such as PollenTree and Modamily, which connect people who are interested in starting a family.[9] Charles Bourne, a forty-three-year-old nurse in Philadelphia, created a profile on Modamily in 2014, according to the BBC.[10] He had been contemplating becoming a parent and initially explored adoption, but the concept of platonic parenting was deeply appealing to him. He ultimately connected with Nisha Nayak, a forty-year-old psychologist, and together they pursued their shared dream of parenthood. In November 2015, Nisha underwent in vitro fertilization and gave birth to fraternal twins, making Charles and Nisha proud coparents of Ella and Vaughn, now seven years old.

The reasons for pursuing platonic parenting can vary, driven by the desire to form nontraditional family structures or by the need for support and shared responsibilities in child-rearing. The trend does have its critics. Some argue that the logistical challenges of children commuting between different homes can be stressful, although parents like Charles and Nisha work through these issues with the help of a family therapist. Critics also express concerns about children missing out on witnessing romantic love between their parents. However, proponents argue that children can still experience such love through their parents' romantic partners or by observing other couples. In any case, online communities for prospective platonic parents have grown significantly over the past decade. Legal recognition of these relationships is evolving. In the UK, rulings have recognized platonic parents living in separate homes as legal parents. Three-parent families are also emerging. Three-parent adoption is legal in California, Maine, Washington State, Rhode Island, and Vermont.

"In the same way that in the last 50 or 70 years we have decoupled sex and reproduction, I think we are in the process of decoupling love and relationships from parenting," says clinical social worker and family therapist Arlene Istar Lev.[11] The line between family and community is blurring for a substantial cross section of the American population. And children can flourish in a variety of family types and living arrangements.

This view is, of course, controversial. Some think that families headed by two married parents are key for children to thrive. In 1994, sociologists Sara McLanahan and Gary Sandefur analyzed data from four national surveys to assess the well-being of children raised in different family structures, including those with both biological parents, single parents, and stepparents. They concluded that children who don't live with both biological parents had approximately double the risk of experiencing poverty, facing behavioral and psychological issues, and failing to complete high school.[12] Their study makes several critical points: more adults around young children is generally better, and marriage can be a conduit to stable family formation and nurturing relationships for children. However, we also need to acknowledge that it is hard for researchers to distinguish the quality of the relationship from the commitment of marriage. For example, children raised in married households with high levels of conflict tend to have lower emotional well-being. In cases where parents have a tumultuous relationship, children often fare better if the parents choose to divorce.

As interest in different forms of families continues to grow, language and even the physical architecture of homes and neighborhoods may need to evolve to better accommodate the new family structures, emphasizing the need for spaces where families can collectively raise children and relationships are prioritized.

Collective Living Spaces

The US Census Bureau does not track cohousing, but parenting groups and housing specialists point to a surge in collective living. The *New York Times* documents the resurgence of "intentional communities," where people come together with the express purpose of living what they believe are more ethical, secure, and connected lives than those generally offered in mainstream society.[13] The Foundation for Intentional Community, a hub for resources for collective living spaces, estimates that there are more than thirty-five hundred in the US alone.[14]

In the 1960s, collective living was seen as a new model of liberation. More recently, cohousing has reemerged in response to tight housing markets. Some websites were established initially to target single professionals (like Coliving.com and Common.com) or retirees (like 55places.com and TheSeniorList.com). But the trend has now expanded to families, and communities have sprouted up that offer separate living spaces, shared play spaces, childcare services, community events, and family activities. Behind this movement are many young parents who are rethinking what constitutes a thriving family and understand the need to build relational networks around young children.

Although precise statistics are hard to obtain, collective housing seems to be expanding around the world. Collective housing, which was started in Denmark thirty years ago, features private homes with shared common space. At FrogSong, an intentional community of thirty households located an hour north of San Francisco, California, the members maintain private lives, but they share twelve to sixteen meals per month in a common house, which also provides laundry facilities, meeting spaces, a cozy sitting room for small-group socializing, and a kids' playroom. Children play together in a nurturing environment and benefit from an extended network of adult relationships. Parents often babysit or watch each other's youngsters. People living in FrogSong have chosen a "high-quality life with friends over an extravagant life with strangers." A study conducted by the Cohousing Research Network in 2011 found that 96 percent of people interviewed who lived in cohousing reported an improved quality of life.[15] Good research on the effects of cohousing on children's learning doesn't yet exist, but we have a decent proxy: affordable housing is linked with stronger child enrichment and cognitive development.[16]

In a similar vein, in downtown Madrid, Spain, parents residing in the Entrepatios ("between patios") cooperative housing development have established an on-site school.[17] Entrepatios hosts seventeen families and twenty-three children. Utilizing organized childcare rotations and a shared Google calendar, working parents are able to maintain their focus on their daytime jobs while their children participate in activities like yoga classes, sleigh rides, and performances in the communal playroom. According to a resident, "We take turns. . . . On Fridays, there's cinema. One family takes six children, so the rest of the parents have that evening for themselves. . . . On Mondays many of the children have a shared English class. Other evenings, a family might arrange an impromptu games night and send a message to the rest of the residents via Telegram."

Trends like cohousing and cohabitation, queer families, platonic parenting, and alloparenting are still rare. The cultural reframing of family to include these various forms also demands a reevaluation of societal support systems. It calls for policies and services that cater to the unique needs of nontraditional family structures, such as housing designed for multigenerational living and educational systems that recognize diversity in what constitutes a family.

We are just beginning. But new perspectives on what constitutes a family reflect a broader evolution in understanding and acceptance. They celebrate the myriad ways in which humans seek connection, support, and love. The traditional nuclear family may no longer be the sole blueprint for family life; instead, we are witnessing the rise of a more inclusive, flexible, and resilient concept of family—one characterized not just by its structure, but by the quality of the relationships and strength of the bonds among its members.

Sage and Seedling: Elders in Multigenerational Families

A majority of babies born today are expected to live past one hundred.[18] The global population is undoubtably aging. While the overall population is expected to reach a plateau at approximately ten billion past 2050, the number of older people is set to increase sharply. The number of people aged 60 and over has already reached one billion and is expected to double by 2050.[19] According to Guinness World Records, the most generations alive in a single family has reached seven—featuring a 109-year-old great-great-great-grandparent![20]

The aging population is spurring opportunities for multigenerational living by necessitating shared living spaces where families can pool resources and provide mutual support across different life stages. This model harkens back to more traditional societal structures while adapting to the contemporary needs of family members throughout the lifespan. The role of elders in these households is being reexamined; their wisdom, their experience, and sometimes their economic support are fundamental to the well-being of the family unit. Elders serve as culture bearers and caretakers, often bridging gaps in childcare and imparting values and knowledge that might otherwise be lost in a nuclear family model.

The intergenerational home also addresses practical concerns of the modern age, such as the high cost of living and caregiving for the youngest and the elders. It offers a solution to the isolation often felt by seniors, while providing younger members with a broader sense of identity and belonging. The benefits of such living arrangements are profound: they foster learning and empathy across ages, provide a sense of continuity and heritage, and contribute to the emotional and financial stability of the family. To cite one example, Latinx children living with grandparents at home are more likely to exhibit prosocial behaviors, such as sharing, comforting, helping, and cooperating, strong predictors of future learning and well-being.[21]

The construction industry, taking notice, is planning for bigger families. In-law units and architectural designs for multiple families living together are surging in popularity. Toll Brothers, one of the largest homebuilders in the US, advertises the "five benefits of living in a multi-generational home" on its website. Another homebuilder, Lennar, offers "Next Gen Homes," where separate living quarters are integrated within a single-family home, creating a space that honors both togetherness and independence. "Granny pods" provide high-tech, comfortable living spaces for elderly relatives that can be built or placed on the property of younger relatives, allowing family members to be near one another while also giving each generation its needed privacy. The number of multigenerational homes is at an all-time high in the US.[22]

But intergenerational living is not always easy, and not always a choice. It can be fraught with challenges due to differences in lifestyle and privacy needs, the care demands of the elderly, financial pressures, and the stress of caregiving. Additionally, conflicting values and busy schedules can strain family dynamics and household harmony. More than two-thirds of adults living in multigenerational households say it is stressful some, most, or all of the time. My friend Rashika Lee is a thirty-five-year-old grandma living in Grand Rapids, Michigan. She had her first child at seventeen, and her son had three children before he turned eighteen. She is raising one of her three granddaughters with help from her partner. She works for a health care provider, assisting patients to understand billing and insurance. Her son, who is pursuing his high school diploma, is unable to fully provide for his children. Her living situation is not one she had expected, and she has a lot of mouths to feed on her salary. Financial strain piles on top of emotional strain and worries about the future for her son and her grandchildren. These concerns highlight the need for support systems and resources for grandparents who find themselves in similar circumstances, including financial assistance, health care, legal advice, and emotional support. Rashika dreams of opening a group home for teen mothers one day.

Supporting Families to Support Children

An expanded understanding of what family means. The evolution of multigenerational and kinship-based extended families. Platonic parenting. Communal living spaces. Support networks. These are all hopeful examples of people figuring out new ways to support and nurture young children's development, despite the obstacles each presents. How can we as a society support the people and families who are pioneering these trends? How can we build on their innovations and encourage the evolution of resilient family networks that privilege emotional bonds and relational intelligence? I offer here a vision for collective action with four distinct aims: empowering, deepening, connecting, and centering.

Empowering

As we discovered in Chapter 4, our squeezed parents need support. In a 2023 report, the product of a year's effort involving experts from a wide political range, the Convergence Collaborative on Supports for Working Families identified consensus on key strategies to aid families.[23] You read that right: they achieved *consensus*, a major accomplishment in our highly polarized times! They found that families flourish when essential needs are met; when relational and community connectedness occur; when they are resilient in the face of challenges through access to a wide network of supports; and when they have actual choices when it comes to living their lives and caring for children. The report identifies three key actions:

1. Support parents with new children via paid leave.
2. Provide cash supports for families that need it the most.
3. Ensure more high-quality relational early care and education options for children.

I will add two more that I think are just as essential:
4. Deliver parent-friendly education pathways for parents who want or need to go back to school.
5. Design family support networks for the future.

Let's explore each in greater detail.

Support parents with new children via paid leave. Overwhelming evidence points to the profound benefits that accrue to both children and parents from spending time together during the initial weeks and months after birth. We have already belabored this point, which is at the core of relational intelligence, but here's one more piece of evidence: an analysis of forty years of survey data across two generations found that children whose parents benefited from paid leave achieved higher education levels and earned higher wages than those whose parents were not covered by such policies.[24] Intergenerational socioeconomic mobility was boosted, particularly for children of less educated mothers, who attained higher levels of education when their parents were covered by protected leave. Paid leave policies encouraged parents to invest more time and resources in their children's upbringing, potentially leading to these improved outcomes.

These findings are part of a broader body of research indicating that parental leave enables vital parent-child bonding time, reduces family stress, and contributes positively to a child's cognitive and language skills. The World Health Organization recommends fourteen to eighteen weeks of maternity leave to support breastfeeding and infant health. The US is an outlier among developed nations when it comes to maternity leave. Federal law mandates job protections for up to twelve weeks, but leave is *unpaid* and excludes many lower-income workers. Only eleven states have state-level paid family leave programs.[25] In addition to the benefits of paid leave for mothers, increasing evidence also shows the benefits of paid leave for fathers. A study of parental leave for fathers in Norway showed increases in test scores for children at high school graduation.[26]

Provide cash supports for families that need it the most. Support for our squeezed parents should extend to financial aid for lower-income families, especially in the first year of a baby's life. The Baby's First Year research, led by Kimberly Noble, a neuroscientist and pediatrician at Columbia University, examined the brain activity of one thousand babies born in low-income families in New Orleans, New York City, Omaha, and Minneapolis/St. Paul. Participating families were randomized to receive either a cash gift of $333 per month or a more modest gift card. The study concludes, "After one year of monthly cash support, infants in low-income families were more likely to show brain activity patterns that have been associated with the development of thinking and learning."[27] Similarly, Andrew Barr, an economics professor at Texas A&M University, analyzed four decades of federal tax information and educational data at the state level and discovered that low-income families who benefited from tax credits in the first year of their newborns' lives, rather than at a later time, experienced a lasting increase in family income. Children benefited even more. Those whose families obtained child-related tax credits earlier exhibited better performance in reading and math, along with reduced suspension rates, higher rates of graduation, and even increased incomes in adulthood.[28]

Ensure more high-quality relational early care and education options for children. Parents should have access to a wide variety of quality, affordable early care options, based on preferences and needs. One excellent example, found in Chile, is Chile Crece Contigo (Chile Grows with You). This initiative, which has been active nationwide since 2007, has reached 80 percent of the most economically disadvantaged mothers prior to childbirth and extends support until the child turns four (or in some cases nine).[29] The program provides tailored services ranging from home visits to medical screenings for genetic conditions, and even offers cash incentives for participation.

In St. Paul, Minnesota, a pilot program for early childhood education—the Minnesota Early Learning Scholarships (MELS) program—was launched in the mid-2000s under the leadership of economist Art Rolnick, former senior director of research at the Federal Reserve Bank of Minneapolis. Twenty years later, fifteen thousand low-income families annually receive support in the form of a mentor, prenatal nursing visits, and scholarships for a high-quality early childhood program chosen by the parents. Targeting the most at-risk children and empowering parental choice proved essential in delivering a significant return on investment (estimated at 18 percent). The MELS approach utilizes market forces to drive the availability of quality programs and is easily scalable.[30] Early childhood programs are currently being expanded in Minnesota.

A more complicated and cautionary example comes from Colombia, where in 2011, the government initiated the De Cero a Siempre (From Zero to Forever) program. It transitioned children from smaller, home-based, community childcare to larger centers that doubled the cost per child. This change to a less personal environment with fewer teachers per child negatively impacted the children's language and motor skills development.[31] Conversely, a more cost-effective program that involves home visits for younger children demonstrated superior outcomes.[32]

In the US, Tennessee's voluntary pre-K program yielded dismal results, due to low funding, poor quality, and an absence of support during the children's transition to elementary schools.[33] Teachers lacked access to training and supports, and spent more time than desired on academics and lecture-style instruction that was not developmentally appropriate for young children.

The quality of a child's early care environment has lifetime and intergenerational ramifications. Yet around the world, high-quality childcare is expensive, remaining out of reach for many families without government support.[34] In the US, childcare already accounts for nearly 30 percent of the median family income, and only 10 percent of existing early care and education offerings are considered high quality, a deeply sobering statistic.[35] Families need to have choices in securing loving networks around their young children. High-quality childcare should be one of those choices, and not the only one. We can take inspiration from Norway and Finland, which stand out both for providing high-quality childcare options and for offering substantial support to stay-at-home parents. This includes monthly home-care allowances amounting to several hundred dollars for parents with children under the age of three, caregiver credits that contribute to retirement pensions, and affordable services like flexible community childcare centers that allow parents to leave their children for a few hours during the day. In the US, a model like TrainingGrounds' We Play centers, in New Orleans—which welcome families for free, drop-in, play-based classes—merits being expanded or replicated.

Most importantly, childcare must evolve to adapt to the needs of today's modern families, offering flexible, high-quality options that cater to diverse family structures and working arrangements, and leveraging technology tools to connect families to quality care and education. Imagine childcare centers integrated with smart technologies for relational learning experiences, supported by policies akin to those in forward-thinking nations, emphasizing work-life harmony and the well-being of every family member. New innovation is making this possible. For example, the childcare-management software company Brightwheel already equips childcare providers with tools to reduce workload and is starting to provide families with access to curricula tied to an observational assessment app and communication tools. Through a partnership with the International Rescue Committee, Sesame Workshop designed an eleven-week intervention using WhatsApp for Syrian refugee parents in Lebanon, which yielded learning outcomes for little learners that were similar to those afforded by a year-long, in-person preschool program.[36] US-based Promise Venture Studio and South Africa's Innovation Edge support numerous comparable initiatives, ranging from gamified assessment tools to app-based curricula and a virtual reality game that demonstrates effective teaching practices. Successful programs like Early Head Start that serve pregnant women, infants, and young toddlers need to expand to serve the one-half of children from low-income homes that are not "ready to succeed in schools."[37]

Public-private partnerships are an important vehicle for change. Chile's Crece Contigo program showcases what a successful blend of public (federal and municipal) resources and private-sector childcare and neonatal health actors can accomplish. There are many places where private ventures can expand rapidly with minimal government support. In Kenya, both Kidogo and Tiny Totos train "mama-preneurs" to operate profitable childcare centers that provide both nutritious meals and suitable curricula. South Africa's SmartStart offers early learning programs to kids who otherwise would lack access by helping unemployed individuals establish franchises, equipping them with research-based care techniques, and ensuring quality standards. Their goal is to serve one million children by 2030. In the US, organizations like Wonderschool, All Our Kin, and Early Learning Ventures support care providers in launching and operating small childcare businesses out of their homes. Winnie helps families find quality care, while Upwards (formerly WeeCare), Bright Horizons, TOOTRiS, and Vivvi support families primarily through employers.

Deliver parent-friendly education pathways for parents who want or need to go back to school. Millions of parents aspire to better the life outcomes for themselves and for their children. In the US, four million parents are enrolled in two-year and four-year college institutions, and many more in other career-oriented technical-education programs.[38] These students are exceptionally motivated to succeed, and they academically outperform students who do not have families. But they face many barriers in going back to school and staying enrolled. Parent-friendly educational opportunities require a two-generation focus, supporting both parent and child and fostering their relationship. They need to take into account the fact that parents are squeezed for both money and time, and to promote, not hinder, parent-child interactions.

The story of Brittany Block is an example of what people who are given such opportunities can achieve. Block moved to Minnesota for a promotion and discovered she was pregnant. She juggled work and a tumultuous relationship, eventually going on furlough when her son, Grayson, was eighteen months old. After learning that her partner was unfaithful, she found herself jobless and without a home. Seeking help, she discovered the Jeremiah Program, which supports low-income single mothers aiming for career advancement through education. Despite Brittany's initial skepticism, a friend vouched for the program, so she joined. She and her son moved into the program's St. Paul campus rent-free, enabling her to pursue a bachelor's degree in two years. Grayson received childcare on-site at a high-quality Head Start center. Today, Block runs her own hairstyling business, illustrating the profound impact that well-designed support systems like the Jeremiah Program can have on a family's economic security, and setting an example for Grayson.

Ariel Ventura-Lazo, a father of two, is a first-generation American and the first of his family to graduate from college. Ventura-Lazo participated in the Generation Hope program, which offers services to students who are parenting, including tuition assistance, academic advising, childcare, peer mentoring, and parental counseling. Similar to the Jeremiah Program, Generation Hope employs what it calls a "two-generation model," supporting the students themselves while also providing services for their young kids. Jeremiah and Generation Hope are expanding. Organizations like Ascend at the Aspen Institute and the Institute for Women's Policy Research are promoting quality models and advocating for two-generation resources. But the demand is vast. College experiences were not designed for families and relational learning. Partnerships between Head Start programs and community colleges could be an avenue for enhancing both adult education and quality early childhood education through collaborative training programs, shared resources, and innovative educational strategies, ultimately benefiting children, families, and educators alike.[39] Some large employers are helping their employees with education expenses. Walmart offers 100 percent reimbursement for college tuition and books to its 1.5 million associates through Live Better U. In 2021, the corporation committed to investing $1 billion in career-driven training and development, and reported that more than fifty thousand associates had participated in the program since its launch in 2018.[40]

Design family support networks for the future. The social support network needs to be reimagined, utilizing digital communities and smart urban planning to foster real-world connections and provide seamless, integrated support services. Successful initiatives like the Nurse-Family Partnership's home-visiting program and its goal-setting app, Goal Mama, provide a model for how to leverage technology to enhance human connections and ensure that families have access to a supportive community. In the United Kingdom, Family Hubs offer a single place where families can find programs for children, young people, and parents, such as baby groups and parenting classes, well-being supports, and access to financial advice. In the US, there are three thousand Family Resource Centers, yet they do not receive dedicated federal funding.[41] Mirroring the UK's approach, family hubs in each community could integrate early childhood and parental resources from both the public and private sectors. New digital communities are also connecting families in innovative ways. Take, for example, the concept of time banking, in which the currency is time, not money.[42] In Rhode Island, for instance, the Parent Support Network helps parents of children with bipolar disorder, schizophrenia, or autism by using time banking to create an extended family. Parents earn time credits by providing childcare, coaching, transportation, or personal support to each other. Children earn credits through mutual support groups. These credits can be used for outings sponsored by the network. This system has helped prevent the institutionalization of children and has saved the state government millions of dollars in support services.

Deepening

In an age of screens, junk tech, and overscheduling, the project of deepening emotional bonds so that young children can thrive begins with adults who are more mentally and emotionally present. How might we make that happen? Well, by building on initiatives like the Basics Learning Networks, the Incredible Years, and Kaleidoscope Play and Learn.

A February 2011 profile of Ronald Franklin Ferguson in the *New York Times* reported, "There is no one in America who knows more about the [education achievement] gap than Ronald Ferguson."[43] Ron has been teaching at the Harvard Graduate School of Education and the Kennedy School of Government since 1983. In 1986, he ran his first educational study, and by the late 1990s, his work exclusively focused on the achievement gap. In 2005, he founded the Achievement Gap Initiative (AGI) at Harvard. Guess what? After twenty-five years spent researching the achievement gap, about a decade ago he chose to focus on the early years, and specifically on families who are raising young children. Essentially, he says, "the difference in life experiences begins at home." Seeking a way to contribute to the movement to support early learning and brain development, AGI convened a national conference and science advisory committee to formulate five tenets of caregiving practice, now called the Basics Principles, around which to mobilize a movement. The aim is "sociological saturation, meaning to infuse multiple settings in communities with information, social rein-forcements, and regular reminders regarding the benefits of using The Basics principles routinely in early childhood parenting/caregiving."[44] Those principles are: maximize love, manage stress; count, group, and compare; talk, sing, and point; explore through movement and play; and read and discuss stories. The idea took off, and the Basics Learning Network (BLN) was born. Today, there are BLN coalitions in cities, towns, and counties across the US, Brazil, and Australia; they actively engage their communities, participating in research and regularly con-vening to learn, innovate, and share best practices.

Other programs work with parents to enhance parenting skills and confidence, and to encourage parental engagement and self-care. The Incredible Years program teaches small groups of parents how to develop positive interactions with their kids. The classes start with a focus on improving parent-child relationships and positive attach-ment before moving on to consistent routines, rules, and setting lim-its. Finally, it covers strategies for dealing with issues such as ignoring, redirection, logical and natural consequences, time to calm down, and problem-solving. When we fly on a commercial airline, the cabin crew tells us that if the oxygen masks drop, we need to secure our own mask before helping children. This is good parenting advice in general. Kids undoubtedly have numerous needs and wants that require attention. However, for parents to effectively care for their children, they must also prioritize their own well-being. This ensures they have the energy necessary to provide the best care. Certain organizations promote self-care and leverage the power of parents supporting other parents. PEPS offers programs that support parents, connect families, and build community in the Puget region. Friends of Children with Spe-cial Needs and TACA (the Autism Community in Action) prioritize self-care for parents of children with special needs.[45]

Another inspiring program that focuses on deepening bonds between parent and child is Kaleidoscope Play and Learn (KPL), which facilitates play groups for young children, their caregivers, and their parents. By setting aside technology, families can focus on each other, participating in games, crafts, and outdoor adventures that strengthen ties and promote healthy child development. These activities emphasize the value of direct, undistracted interaction, highlighting the deep emotional security that caregivers who are fully present can provide to children. Eighty-nine percent of caregivers reported feeling more supported in their community after they began participating in KPL. A caregiver shares, "Before I found out about this program, I felt isolated and the kids in my care did not have opportunities to socialize, especially with a diverse group of people. Now we are part of a loving and diverse community!"[46]

Connecting

The future of families, in all their various configurations, hinges on the ability of family members to connect with each other and with their communities. It's clear that technology will play a pivotal role in strengthening familial and communal ties.

For parents from Gen Y and Gen Z, the intersection of identity and digital presence is becoming more pronounced. With over half of Gen Z claiming to have friends they know exclusively online, the influence of technology on parenting, relationships, and even the way people meet is undeniable. A study by Stanford sociologist Michael Rosenfeld highlights this shift, noting that online platforms have become the most popular way for heterosexual couples in the US to meet, surpassing traditional methods around 2013.[47]

Families, too, can leverage relationally focused platforms, like Peanut, a Tinder-like app that allows mothers to swipe and connect with other moms for parenting support, and Guardians Collective, which creates communities of parents to share experiences and advice, guided by an experienced early childhood educator. These platforms not only reduce feelings of isolation but also empower parents to form meaningful connections, thereby enhancing kinship and support networks.

Family storytelling also serves as a tool for connecting. Tools like StoryCorps and Amoofy, which capture and preserve personal narratives, can be adapted for family use. By recording and sharing stories across generations, children can develop a sense of their heritage and learn valuable lessons through the lived experiences of their relatives.

The burgeoning field of genealogy, facilitated by services like 23andMe, can help build a family tree history and connect distant relatives across continents. At the same time, however, discovering unexpected familial relationships or ethnicity can have significant emotional impacts, and it can be disappointing or life-altering to learn that DNA relatives don't share our values.

The future holds the promise of even more integrated digital systems, possibly leveraging advancements in holographic technologies, social robots, AI avatars, or other yet-to-be-invented mediums that could further enhance a sense of interconnectedness. In essence, technology-enhanced kinship isn't just about bridging distances; it's about enriching relationships and facilitating shared experiences that are dynamic and inclusive.

Centering

What happens to connections for millions of children affected by incarceration, homelessness, or foster care? Developing nurturing child-caregiver relationships is even more crucial in these circumstances. These bonds can enhance children's chances for a successful future. Some programs focus on centering family relationships during these life events.

At Bedford Hills Correctional Facility, the largest women's prison in New York State, Lindsay Landon shares a precious moment with her son Gabriel while reading to him during a video interview for NBC News.[48] Bedford Hills' nursery program, a rarity in the US, supports such vital bonds. The prison has a nursery section where every mother shares a cell with her baby for the first year. Commonly, babies are separated from their incarcerated moms after forty-eight to seventy-two hours and sent to a family member or foster care. Previously a struggling dairy farmer, Lindsay's financial desperation led her to drug trafficking, resulting in her arrest and incarceration while pregnant. The nursery program allowed her to have daily contact with her son, aiding his development and their relationship. The rise in the number of incarcerated mothers, which has surged by 700 percent since 1980, affects millions of innocent children. More than ten million live with a parent who has experienced criminal supervision at some point in the child's life.[49] Ten percent of incarcerated people are women, and 58 percent of all women in prison are mothers. Programs like the one at Bedford Hills show promise. A five-year study revealed that infants nurtured in prison nurseries develop secure attachments similar to those of children reared in traditional family settings.[50] Additionally, research at Bedford Hills showed that the recidivism rate for women who participated in the nursery program was half that of the general female released population.[51]

Homeless families often face so many challenges that early education may not be an immediate priority. For Ruth and her daughter Ava, who were living out of a car, preschool programs offer stability and educational foundations. However, awareness of available services is often lacking. When asked if she had told the staff at her daughter's preschool about their living situation, Ruth looked puzzled and responded, "No, why would I do that? They would think I am a bad mom!"[52] In San Francisco, Compass Family Services bridges this awareness gap, aiding hundreds of families, like Ruth and Ava, to access subsidized childcare, contributing to family housing stability. In Hawai'i, Ka Pa'alana ("a light for the future") goes one step further, providing the only preschool for homeless families in the US. At the core of Ka Pa'alana is the idea of teaching children and parents together. Four days a week, parents engage with their child for the first two hours of school, then participate in various adult education and life skills programs while their children receive an intensive, developmentally appropriate education from preschool teachers and assistants for another two hours.

This unique and highly accredited preschool has positively impacted thousands, illustrating the transformative power of combining early education with parental support.

For foster children in Easthampton, Massachusetts, the Treehouse Foundation has pioneered a new approach to community living by bridging the gap between two often overlooked populations: foster children and the elderly.[53] Established by Judy Cockerton, Treehouse is an intergenerational living space that provides a supportive network for foster families while also offering seniors a renewed sense of purpose. "Everybody coming out of their house has an opportunity to connect with somebody else," Cockerton notes. "So neighbors are always connecting. The affordable, vibrant community is designed to help foster children grow up in a nurturing environment, surrounded by people of all ages who care about them." Elders are titled "honorary grandparents." One says, "I never expected to be needed, valued, loved and supported so beautifully when I reached my 80's. Treehouse has changed my life. Every older American should have the opportunity to live in a Treehouse community." Sarah, who had been through twenty-five different foster homes, found a haven in Treehouse. It was there that she finally encountered the stable, loving relationships she needed to catalyze her learning and growth.[54] Ninety-five percent of children and youth at Treehouse will graduate from high school, compared with the national average for foster youth of 58 percent, and 100 percent of those who graduate high school will attend college or vocational training, compared with the national average of less than 10 percent for youths in foster care. Treehouse is expanding its replicable and scalable model into new communities. It is a beautiful example of the impact of loving relationships on child learning.

The programs at Bedford Hills, Compass Family Services, Ka Paʻalana, and Treehouse Foundation are small today, serving only a few thousand children and families. There is so much room to grow and create new relational possibilities for young children without a traditional home.

It is possible to create a future for our families that is characterized by interconnectedness and resilience, one in which diverse and inter-generational families can offer supportive, nurturing, and stable environments for the holistic development of children. In this future, relationships are the bedrock upon which young lives are built, guiding them through a world where the value of kinship is as enduring as it is profound. As family structures evolve in response to societal changes, it's increasingly apparent that the development of young children benefits from a broad relational network that extends beyond traditional family boundaries to include friends and ample play.

CHAPTER 10

Friends: Play Is Learning

Play matters because people matter. It reminds us of our inter-dependence and gives us a chance to really see other people. And in turn, to be really and truly seen.
— JILL VIALET, *THE POWER OF PLAY*, TEDMED, 2014

People tend to forget that play is serious.
— DAVID HOCKNEY, *THAT'S THE WAY I SEE IT*, 1993

Stuart Brown has been studying human play for over fifty years. His interest in the subject began with a horrific event: a tragic mass shooting at the University of Texas in 1966. Brown, at the time a young assistant professor of psychiatry at UT, joined the Tower Commission, named for the tower of the university's main building, from which Charles Whitman shot and killed fifteen people and injured thirty-one others. The commission was charged with delving into and deciphering the circumstances surrounding what was, at that point, the deadliest mass murder in the history of the United States. What drove Whitman, a twenty-five-year-old married student with no prior criminal record, and who was otherwise charming and smart, to perpetrate this heinous act?

Over a period of four months, the multidisciplinary commission thoroughly investigated every aspect of Whitman's life. As they pieced together his history, numerous potential influences on his violent behavior were considered. During these deliberations, the renowned child psychiatrist and commission member Robert Stubblefield repeatedly emphasized the significance of play, lamenting, "If only he had played." In the end, the commission reached a unanimous consensus that the root cause of Whitman's rampage was the chronic suppression of free and social play by his abusive, authoritarian father. (Whitman also had a brain tumor pressing on his amygdala. Although the original commission discounted the importance of the tumor, in the nearly sixty years since then, during which time the understanding of brain physiology has advanced greatly, experts in neurology have granted it much more importance as a potential additional root cause.)

Brown secured a research grant to further explore the meaning of play. He conducted interviews with male prison inmates convicted of homicide and compared their backgrounds to those of a control group without such criminal records. Concurrently, as part of his academic responsibilities, he compiled life histories of individuals convicted of felony driving offenses who had subsequently died in car accidents. His research uncovered a striking similarity between the inmates and the drivers: both groups played less as young children than their counterparts in their respective control groups. This finding highlighted a notable deficiency in play experiences among individuals with a propensity for high-risk or violent behaviors. Brown observed, "None of the murderers I studied participated in what could be considered normal rough-and-tumble play. And rough-and-tumble play and the ability to deal with hostility and still get along with your friends is a fundamental part of both animal and human experience."[1]

This work on social play parallels research on the linkage between attachment and prosocial behaviors. As this book has shown repeatedly, how a child is treated in early childhood greatly influences their ability to regulate emotions and cognitive abilities. Starving a child of social play is another way of depriving them of nurturing relationships and healthy brain development. Of course, not all young children who experience significant deficits in social playtime will become mass murderers, but most will face difficulties in forming relationships with others and in their learning journeys.

When other species of mammals are denied the opportunity for rough-and-tumble play, they struggle to differentiate between allies and rivals, exhibit heightened responses to stress, and have brains that are not only smaller but less complex in their neural connections.[2] In fact, play is deeply ingrained in the survival centers of the brain. Play is so essential and innate that when the cortex is removed from small mammals, they continue to engage in play as actively as those with an intact cortex.[3] However, as these animals age, those without a cortex fail to develop social skills and are unable to mate—unable to love, may I add. When faced with danger from a larger animal, both groups will hide, but those without a cortex remain in hiding long after the threat has vanished, often starving to death while avoiding a predator that has already left. The human brain shares similarities with the brains of these small mammals, with play originating from the same survival regions.[4] Play helps form the neural connections in our cortex, which are crucial for emotional stability and learning. Young children who experience severe play deprivation often have difficulties forming relationships and learning from their experiences.[5] Conversely, play drives social behaviors. A 1997 study conducted by the HighScope Educational Research Foundation in Ypsilanti, Michigan, found that children from underserved backgrounds who attended play-based preschools were better socially adjusted later in life compared with those who went to more structured, instruction-focused preschools. By age twenty-three, over a third of the individuals who had attended instruction-oriented preschools had been arrested for a felony, whereas fewer than 10 percent of those who had attended play-oriented preschools faced similar challenges. Additionally, as adults, fewer than 7 percent of those who attended play-based preschools had been suspended from work, compared to over 25 percent of those from instruction-based preschools.[6]

Play holds an irreplaceable role in the development of young minds and bodies and, for our youngest children, in developing friendships. The United Nations lists play as one of the basic rights of every child—it is that critical. Play is the cornerstone upon which children build their cognitive, physical, emotional, and social foundations. "Nearly all developmental psychologists, neuroscientists and education experts recommend play for kids 0–7 as the best way to nurture kids' development and ready them for success later in life," reports *Scientific American.*[7]

For a long time, education has focused on time spent in direct instruction and homework as the main driver of success. Friendships and social play have been implicitly considered a distraction, even impediments to academic performance in some cases. Children's free-play time has meaningfully shrunk, dropping by a quarter between 1981 and 1997.[8] Recess and play periods have been cut, limiting the time our little ones spend during the school day focused purely on developing friendships. Yet we know that friendships drive engagement in schools and higher grades.[9]

Education specialist John Hattie undertook the largest-ever synthesis of research into the factors that drive education outcomes. In a 2021 investigation of twenty-one hundred meta-analyses totaling more than one hundred thousand studies in education, Hattie showed that play with friends has a large positive effect on learning.[10] Having a best friend around can lessen negative emotions, reduce levels of stress hormones, and increase feelings of self-worth.[11] Supportive conversations with friends in the aftermath of stressful events can help bring stress hormone levels back to normal more quickly. The protective effect of friendship can help children cope with social and academic setbacks by fostering resilience rather than feelings of personal inadequacy.[12] Studies on adolescents have shown that working in pairs can lead to more exploratory learning, quicker learning, and better task performance than working alone.[13] The more a student perceives their study partner as a friend, the more they learn. Having a friend nearby can boost a child's willingness to try new things and tackle challenging intellectual tasks, while being alone might lead to less engagement.

The opposite is also true. Hattie's meta-analysis revealed that children who experience bullying or rejection show lower school performance and attendance. In fact, slipping grades is one of the first signs that a child is being bullied. Data for young children are admittedly scarce. However, one study on children's exposure to violence indicated that 20 percent of two- to five-year-olds had experienced physical bullying, and 15 percent had encountered verbal teasing.[14]

Psychologist Roy Baumeister has delved into the intricacies of social pain, exploring how our emotional responses to rejection and exclusion are intertwined with our need for social belonging. His work illuminates the profound impact that social pain can have on our psychological well-being, suggesting that the distress we feel from social disconnection is as impactful as physical pain. Baumeister's research has implications in education, revealing that students' experiences of social rejection or exclusion can significantly impact their intelligent thoughts and lower self-regulation.[15] The distress associated with social pain can diminish concentration, disrupt learning processes, and thus lower overall academic performance.

Over the years, evidence of the importance of social play has only grown stronger. Researchers have conclusively shown that play—and especially social play—has a profound and beneficial impact on brain development. In fact, the extent of a child's playtime significantly influences their learning abilities. Accumulating evidence has increasingly led scientists to advocate for more play opportunities, and to urge both parents and educators to embrace this approach.

Game On: Play Changes the Brain

In 1964, Marion Diamond and her team at the University of California, Berkeley, published a groundbreaking study on brain development in rats that marked a pivotal moment in our understanding of neurology and revolutionized perspectives on early childhood education and parenting.[16] Their seminal experiment compared two sets of rats raised from birth to adulthood under vastly different conditions. Members of one group lived in small, desolate, and isolated environments, while the others resided in stimulating, communal settings that contained lots of objects conducive to play. Upon examining the rats' brains, the researchers found that the rats that experienced "impoverished" conditions had noticeably smaller and thinner cerebral cortexes than their counterparts raised in "enriching" environments.

Diamond's initial experiment was conducted over eighty days. A colleague challenged the results, arguing that in light of brain plasticity, the rats were too young to conclusively demonstrate that environmental conditions would affect brain development long-term. Diamond conducted a follow-up experiment, allowing the rats to age. Some of them were exposed to an additional element in their enriched environments: daily physical contact with humans. She discovered that stroking the rats against her lab coat extended their lifespans. The rats that were petted also showed signs of improved brain development, evidenced by notably thicker cerebral cortices.[17] Nurturing and love boost learning and longevity.

Subsequent studies have repeatedly reinforced these findings. Rats that engage in social play—that is, those living in stimulating conditions—not only have larger brains but also demonstrate greater intelligence. They learn cause-and-effect relationships more quickly and navigate mazes with greater speed and efficiency.[18]

Social play is a common behavior across many species. A variety of animals, including cats, dogs, bears, tigers, and even certain birds, actively engage in playful interactions. Magpies exhibit playful behavior similar to that of puppies, engaging in mock fights and tussling.

Animals that exhibit higher levels of youthful playfulness tend to have increased longevity. Furthermore, there is a correlation between a species' brain size and the extent of playfulness in its members' younger years. Chimpanzees, dogs, cows, rats, and some birds even display behavior similar to human laughter during play. Rats "laugh" when they are tickled or when they play.[19]

Historically, scientists speculated that such playful wrestling in young animals served as practice for hunting, but more recent research challenges this view. Adult cats can efficiently hunt and capture prey, like mice, without having engaged in play during their kittenhood. Why, then, do animals engage in social play? The late researcher Jaak Panksepp of Washington State University, who coined the term "affective neuroscience," said in a 2014 interview with NPR, "The function of play is to build prosocial brains, social brains that know how to interact with others in positive ways."[20] This perspective emphasizes the role of play not only in preparing for predatory behaviors but in fostering positive social interactions, building social competence, making friends, and ultimately learning.

Research on rats suggests that play activates the whole neocortex. The next question, then, is: How much social play is necessary to trigger this effect? Surprisingly, it doesn't take much. Panksepp observed that out of the twelve hundred genes he analyzed in the rat brain, about one-third showed significant change after just thirty minutes of play every day.[21]

Given that this research has predominantly been conducted on rats and other animals, it doesn't directly confirm the hypothesis that play has the same effect on human brains. But there's substantial reason to believe that it does. Different species exhibit a remarkable similarity in what "play" means and how it is conducted.

"Play is not frivolous: It enhances brain structure and function and promotes executive function (i.e., the process of learning, rather than the content), which allow us to pursue goals and ignore distractions," states an American Academy of Pediatrics report.[22] "When play and safe, stable, nurturing relationships are missing in a child's life, toxic stress can disrupt the development of executive function and the learning of prosocial behavior; in the presence of childhood adversity, play becomes even more important."

The Play's the Thing

The science of play is now a vibrant field that reveals a simple truth: play is not just an activity; it's a crucial part of how children learn, grow, and interact with the world. Social play thus has a critical role to play within the educational sphere. Play offers a natural and safe way for children to engage with peers from diverse backgrounds and rejoice by celebrating and achieving shared goals. It's beneficial for young children to interact with those who differ from them.

Research has consistently demonstrated that social play facilitates children's adaptation to school environments and bolsters their readiness to learn, their positive behavior during learning activities, and their problem-solving abilities. Play fosters cognitive growth and drives higher IQ and even greater earnings in adulthood. Play builds imagination and skills for the future.[23] It delivers social, emotional, and behavioral benefits, and it improves literacy and math. You are reading right: guided play can be a better way for kids to learn math than traditional teaching methods, at least until they're eight years old.[24] Play *is* learning.[25]

Cognitively, play is a child's laboratory. It's where they test hypotheses, solve problems, and build neural pathways. When toddlers stack blocks, they're not just creating a tower; they're learning about gravity, balance, and geometry. As children engage in pretend play, they develop language skills and executive function. They practice self-regulation as they follow the rules of their imagined scenarios and switch roles, fostering cognitive flexibility. This kind of imaginative play is linked to the development of narrative skills and abstract thinking, laying the groundwork for literacy and numeracy. Karyn Purvis, the late director of the TCU Institute of Child Development, estimated, "It takes four hundred repetitions of an act or a learning skill [performed] four hundred times to get one new synapse, or twelve repetitions with joy and laughter and you get a synapse because there's a release of a chemical, dopamine."[26]

Socially, play is the universal language of childhood. It's through play that children learn to negotiate, cooperate, and navigate social hierarchies. Social play requires children to interpret verbal and nonverbal cues, a fundamental aspect of social intelligence. They learn to manage emotions and impulses, to take turns, to empathize, and to understand the perspectives of others. These are the building blocks of relationships and community. In essence, play is the training ground for the social roles we will assume in later life.

Emotionally, play is a safe haven where children can express feelings and manage stress. It provides a natural outlet for emotions, allowing children to work through anxiety, frustration, and fear in a context where they have control. Emotional resilience is bolstered through the trials and triumphs of play scenarios. For children who have experienced trauma or who struggle with emotional regulation, play can be a powerful therapeutic tool, helping them to communicate their experiences and feelings in a nonthreatening way.

In more concrete terms, play can also have a significant impact on academic achievement. Increased playtime can lead to immediate improvements in children's grades. One study found a strong correlation between a child's social skills in third grade and their academic achievement in eighth grade.[27] Another study from Penn State University even showed that prosocial behavior in kindergarten is one of the greatest predictors of long-term success in adulthood. Kindergarten teachers assessed seven hundred children eight times, using a five-point scale to rate their performance on social tasks such as helpfulness and sharing materials. The researchers conducted follow-up assessments when the participants reached their twenties. Children who had displayed positive prosocial behaviors like sharing and problem-solving in kindergarten were more likely to have achieved higher levels of education and secure employment and to have fewer records of criminal activity in their twenties.[28] These results can likely be attributed to the fact that play enhances the development of the prefrontal cortex, the brain region associated with planning, problem-solving, and emotion regulation—all crucial for successful social interaction and learning, or what I call relational intelligence.

More Play, Please

"When did play become a dirty word?" asks Kathy Hirsh-Pasek, a professor of psychology at Temple University and senior fellow at the Brookings Institution. "We need a new mindset that builds on what we know about how children learn."[29] As this chapter makes clear, play isn't just fun—it's the key to unlocking young minds. We need a societal shift in how we think about play. We need more play-based curricula, more green time relative to screen time. We need to introduce play across all the environments young children inhabit. A number of inspiring global initiatives can illuminate our path.

For Families: A Prescription for Play

As families face increasing academic demands and schools prioritize test prep, it's ever more important to define *why* play is so valuable to learning and to child development. Pediatric research has transformed these insights into actionable advice for parents and caregivers. The American Academy of Pediatrics now recommends that doctors write "prescriptions for play" at every well-child visit in the first two years of life.[30] This advice is not just metaphorical; it's a clinical push to ensure that play is recognized as a vital sign of health, as crucial as any vaccine or vitamin. The prescription for play underscores the importance of unstructured, unplugged, and creative play—not as a luxury or an add-on, but as a fundamental part of a child's daily routine. In a world where structured activities and screen time often dominate, ensuring that children have ample opportunity for free play is a public health issue.

We also need to support families and caregivers in learning *how* to play with children. In 1994, Johann Olav Koss, a champion speed skater from Norway, embarked on a missionary trip to Eritrea, where he witnessed the indomitable spirit of play in a land recovering from the ravages of prolonged conflict. Surrounded by the remnants of war tanks, children competed in a makeshift soccer game using a ball fashioned from a tattered shirt. Their undaunted joy amidst desolation stirred something deep within Koss, prompting him to establish the nonprofit Right to Play.[31] Two decades later, the organization has touched the lives of millions of youngsters across fifteen nations in Africa, Asia, the Middle East, and Canada. It offers play-based learning programs and builds the capacity of local schools. Its impact is wide-ranging. In Pakistan, children taught by Right to Play–trained teachers scored 10 percent higher on standardized tests than children without trained teachers. Peer violence, a challenge faced by as many as 94 percent of boys in some Pakistani schools, was reduced by 25 percent in schools with Right to Play programs.

In rural Ghana and Uganda, there are virtually no childcare or early childhood centers. This is not for a lack of children. The average number of children per mother exceeds five. Yet these youngsters often have few opportunities to learn, and their families lack knowledge about early education. The nonprofit organization Lively Minds seeks to change these realities by unlocking the enormous potential of marginalized, rural parents through play.[32] Parents are trained to run free educational classes called Play Schemes for all the preschoolers in their community. Each Play Scheme generally welcomes two hundred children and families every week. It features various stations where kids can play in a child-led and participatory manner. Teaching, conducted in groups of six children, is discovery-based. The kids rotate through activity stations equipped with cardboard puzzles, dominoes, sorting games, and wooden blocks. Mothers are also trained to make their own games. Given the fun they are having, the children do not even realize they are learning: the organization ran a rigorous evaluation and estimated the education gains for children participating in the Play Schemes to be the equivalent of an extra year of school! Lively Minds is also seeing meaningful impact in helping mothers spend more time on developmentally appropriate activities with their children and improving their teaching style. Lively Minds is partnering with governments to continue to scale the program, which now reaches over two hundred thousand little ones and ninety thousand parents in rural communities.

Back here in the US, I saw the benefits of outdoor social play and "co-play" firsthand when I served on the board of Tinkergarten.[33] American sociologist Mildred Parten's theory of social play suggests that children evolve through six stages of play, starting with unoccupied play in infancy, where they explore their environment, and evolving to solitary play with toys as toddlers, then to observing others' play, engaging in parallel play near peers, participating in associative play with separate objectives, and finally cooperative play or co-play, where they work together toward a common purpose. Tinkergarten provides outdoor, experiential learning sessions for children aged eighteen months to eight years, with an accompanying adult. Children and adults engage in a learning journey together, in the ultimate classroom—nature. Tinkergarten embraces the idea that by encouraging independent discovery, embracing risks, and being unafraid to get a little dirty, children can accomplish amazing things—a philosophy I wholeheartedly endorse. Sessions, conducted in local green spaces, follow a flexible structure that includes an introductory circle, a main activity, a concluding circle, and a shared snack time. Activities range from making a "nature curtain," when little ones can turn a small corner of the outdoors into a fort, a fairy house, or even a doorway into another magical world, to building sun catchers, which always dazzle and delight, especially when kids have made them with their own hands. The activities promote unstructured exploration and play, encouraging children to use their imagination and problem-solving skills. Although an adult plans and oversees the activity, and other adults accompany the children as they play, it is the children's interests that significantly shape the experience. Tinkergarten claims that 85 percent of kids improve their ability to focus attention, 90 percent of kids play independently often and for longer, and 93 percent of parents and caregivers feel better prepared to engage their child in playful learning. Not bad. Tinkergarten, now part of Highlights for Children, is currently on pause as they explore future directions for the program.

For Schools: More No-Cost Miracles

The educational landscape must evolve to acknowledge that play is an essential part of learning, and that academic learning, in a school setting, involves social and emotional skills best developed through social play. Kevin Stinehart, an elementary teacher in South Carolina, shared this student story in *eSchool News*:

> A few years ago I had a student who walked around with a chip on his shoulder. He never smiled, never laughed, and always seemed angry. He was cruel to other kids, had frequent behavior issues in class, and in the course of one week had three principal office referrals from three different teachers for his extreme behaviors. Other kids would label him a bully, but where they saw a bully, we as teachers saw a hurting and lonely child in need of friends. He was the kind of student who was always disciplined by losing recess time, so I eventually added it up and realized he was getting only about 30 minutes of playtime in an entire week on average.
>
> Realizing his lack of play and knowing play's immense benefits, I arranged a conference with his parent and asked if I could have him join my Play Club—a one-hour afterschool club dedicated to unstructured free play. His parent agreed to let him join, and before I knew it, his first day at Play Club had

arrived. I was a little nervous that his behavior issues would continue, and he would wreak havoc on my other Play Club students, but I knew play could help him, so I was committed to the process. For the first half hour of Play Club he just walked around by himself. Eventually a student kicked a ball to him and he kicked it back. After a few more kicks, he eventually started running around and playing with the other kids. By the end of that first day of Play Club he was smiling, laughing, and playing in a healthy way—and with other kids! It was shocking to see the transformation in him after just one hour of complete unstructured free play. The teacher supervising Play Club with me had tears in her eyes at the dramatic change she was witnessing. . . .

Free play not only helps the student who is bullying, but it helps those on the receiving end of the behavior. Students who participate in large amounts of unstructured free play are far better at coping with other students who are aggressive, hurtful, and irritating. As children encounter more and more real-life experiences with other children, they learn how to handle others in profound ways as their interpersonal skills are acquired and sharpened.[34]

Stinehart noted other benefits: Behavior issues decreased and academic outcomes improved. Participating students did better on reading and math tests. "We didn't start Play Club to raise test scores," he wrote. "All of that was just icing on the cake."

In other schools, play is integrated into the curriculum. Welcome to teacher Mary Martinez's elementary school class in Florida, where the performance of the Miami Dolphins is employed to teach students math. Martinez has become a social media sensation after getting the attention of several well-known football players and fans. The class tracks various stats, including the team's wins and losses, and key players' total and average receiving yards. "They love it," Martinez said on ESPN *SportsCenter*'s

"Feel Good Friday," during an interview on how she incorporates sports into her teaching.[35] "We're excited to come to school on Mondays now. There's no 'Sunday Scaries' when on Monday morning, you get to talk Miami Dolphins football." Martinez has provided an incentive to get all students invested in the endeavor. If the Dolphins win, the class wins, and the kids are awarded ten extra minutes of recess. "Not all are Dolphins fans," she concedes. "They are eight. They are recess fans."

"Make it fun, and children will learn more" is the premise of Tools of the Mind, an early childhood curriculum and professional development program anchored in the theory of social learning. Tools classrooms prioritize play, dramatization, and interaction among peers. At McGlone Academy, one of the Denver schools that implements the curriculum, preschoolers engage in role-playing activities like bartering. Children create "play plans" by drawing pictures of the activity centers they want to visit and writing descriptions of their planned activities using a scaffolded writing approach. After completing their plans, little learners engage in small-group activities, like planning a party in the kitchen, working on cars in the garage, or building a road in the block area. Later they engage in free play. This unique play-based curriculum is favored by educators and parents, who appreciate seeing their children learn through play that's structured yet imaginative. Moreover, the program supports the development of self-regulation, aiding children in overcoming distractions and frustrations, which is crucial for both immediate classroom harmony and long-term academic and personal success.

Direct teaching methods may have their place, such as in phonics, but integrating play-based learning is crucial. Some states, including New Hampshire, have mandated a play-based curriculum in kindergarten since 2018, emphasizing activities that promote movement, creativity, exploration, and social skills. New Hampshire even compiled a guide, "What Is Play-Based Learning in Kindergarten?"[36] Oklahoma and Connecticut have also adopted measures to encourage play-based learning practices. The state of Washington became the first state to license outdoor, nature-based childcare, after a successful pilot across five sites that launched in 2017 and a meaningful increase in parent demand. Outside the United States, Rwanda's educational reform initiative stands out for having incorporated play-based learning into its revised curriculum at all school levels.[37]

The Play and Learning Gap

Play is not equitably distributed. As crucial as play is to childhood learning and development, there is disparity in how much playtime children get, based on their socioeconomic situation. The Real Play Coalition, a nonprofit initiative that includes UNICEF, National Geographic, Arup, IKEA, and LEGO Foundation, uncovered significant differences in playtime based on gender and socioeconomic status among children in seventy countries. It aims to narrow the play gap for one hundred million kids by 2030. Young children from underprivileged environments have a 20 percent lower chance of playing with blocks and an 11 percent reduced likelihood of singing songs with their parents compared with their more affluent peers. Children hailing from families with higher socioeconomic status have a 10 percent greater probability of participating in play.[38]

KABOOM! is a national nonprofit organization focused on ensuring that all kids get the balanced and active play they need to thrive. It has been instrumental in highlighting and addressing the play gap across the United States. KABOOM! has found that play inequity is a significant issue, particularly in underserved communities. In majority-Black and -brown neighborhoods, parks are on average half the size and five times more crowded than those that serve a majority-white population.[39] This means that millions of kids are missing out on the childhood they deserve, one filled with play. The organization has identified "play deserts," where there is a lack of accessible, safe places for children to play. These areas disproportionately affect

Black, Indigenous, and other communities of color, exacerbating social and health disparities.

Play holds transformative potential. Some research posits it as a means to bridge educational disparities among children ages three to six. A review of twenty-six studies across eighteen nations discovered that in underresourced areas from Rwanda to Ethiopia, there were notably higher improvements in literacy, motor skills, and social-emotional growth among children who attended childcare centers that incorporated a blend of direct instruction with both free and structured play, compared with centers that exclusively focused on academic instruction.[40]

More Green Time, Less Screen Time

The rise of outdoor preschools in the US, whose numbers grew from 250 in 2017 to more than 800 in 2022, marks a notable shift in early childhood education.[41] These schools, often referred to as "forest kindergartens" or "nature preschools," forgo traditional indoor classrooms for the boundless learning opportunities provided by the great outdoors. Rooted in the philosophy that nature itself is the best learning environment in which children can explore, develop critical thinking skills, and cultivate creativity, they encourage play, discovery, and hands-on experiences. This educational trend, a nod to the pioneering vision of Friedrich Froebel's "children's garden," is shaping a generation of learners who are environmentally conscious and well-rounded in their physical, emotional, and social development, combatting what some experts have called "nature deficit disorder."[42]

Outside of school, other organizations are promoting outdoor play. Outdoor Afro was started by social entrepreneur Rue Mapp in Oakland in 2009 to encourage outdoor play for Black children and adults alike. One of their programs, Making Waves, ensures that every child and caregiver in Outdoor Afro's sphere of influence learns to swim and enjoys water. Sixty-five percent of Black American children do not know how to swim.[43]

Play and Learn Everywhere

"Play and learn everywhere" is a burgeoning movement advocating for the integration of play and learning into all environments where children spend time. KABOOM!'s "Play Everywhere" playbook outlines design principles and provides grants to turn concept into reality. It encourages people to think about spaces that could become *play*ces—a laundromat, sidewalk, bus stop, airport. Any unexciting situation can turn into a stimulating, creative outlet for play, socialization, and learning.

The Supermarket Speak project has mounted signs in grocery stores prompting caregivers to engage in conversation with their children as they shop. Three supermarkets situated in low- and middle-income neighborhoods across Philadelphia and Delaware have participated. The project's website reports that "parent-child talk" increased by 33 percent when the signs were up.[44]

Look around. On your street, in your local park, in your community, where might you create a *play*ce to play?

CHAPTER 11

Schools: Relational Hubs

It is the supreme art of the teacher to awaken joy in creative expression and knowledge.

—ALBERT EINSTEIN, 1931

When teachers teach with love, combining care, commitment, knowledge, responsibility, respect, and trust, we are often able to enter the classroom and go straight to the heart of the matter, which is knowing what to do on any given day to create the best climate for learning.

—BELL HOOKS, *TEACHING COMMUNITY*, 2004

Only by abolishing the situations of oppression is it possible to restore the love which that situation made impossible. If I do not love the world—if I do not love life—if I do not love—I cannot enter into dialogue.

—PAOLO FREIRE, *PEDAGOGY OF THE OPPRESSED*, 1968

O ur educational system was historically predicated on information scarcity; our schools were conceived at a time when teachers and textbooks were the primary sources of knowledge. These circumstances fostered the belief that education should be conducted in a controlled environment, largely closed to families and the broader community. Teaching was constructed as a unidirectional transfer of knowledge. Current educational practices still often reflect this: a 2021 study revealed that teachers account for 89 percent of the talking time in classrooms.[1] Whereas a teacher asks 120–160 questions per class, students ask on average 11 questions per class (of which 9 are procedural, such as "Can I go to the bathroom?" or "Can you say that again?").[2] Students speak for just twenty-seven seconds per hour of instruction time.[3] Students in historically marginalized communities, such as English learners, students with disabilities, and students from low-income backgrounds, get even fewer opportunities to speak.[4]

Meanwhile, the rate at which human knowledge is doubling is a subject of debate. But it's frequently stated that until the early twentieth century, human knowledge doubled approximately every century. By the end of World War II, knowledge was estimated to double every twenty-five years. Now, with the existence of the internet and other advancements such as AI technology, experts suggest that the doubling of knowledge occurs at an even faster rate. These advancements have also made *more* information widely available. McKinsey estimates that global data doubles every three years; according to some, it could be doubling every twelve hours.[5] The overwhelming amount of available information alters not only teaching methods but also the content that needs to be taught and learned. We can't possibly learn all there is to know. So we need to learn how to navigate the abundance; how to sort the data; how to figure out what we need to know and what is peripheral; how to determine what information is trustworthy and what isn't. Learning goes beyond merely transferring knowledge; it also involves nurturing a child's ability to discern meaning from an overabundance of data, as well as fostering their imagination and responsible creativity based on that data. What we need to know depends on context, and contexts can be socially driven. The necessary skills and competencies of today and of the future can no longer be taught through unidirectional knowledge transfer.

In today's world, where information abounds and knowledge development has accelerated, schools need to adapt. Forward-thinking educators are adopting new teaching methods informed by advances in the science of learning and relationships and by an understanding of brain development. The mom of a young son recently asked me why her son needed to go to school if he is teaching himself more using digital resources. The answer is that in the long run, social connections are fundamental to the learning process, and schools play a major role as relational hubs. Effective instruction is now seen to depend on the establishment of nurturing relationships between a caring, knowledgeable teacher and a child who is both emotionally secure and motivated to learn. Equally important is that the child be supported beyond the classroom by a broader network of relationships, not just with teachers but also with family members, peers, and the larger community. They all play a pivotal role in the child's learning journey.

In East Palo Alto, California, the Primary School is piloting a new model of education that brings together all the adults in a child's life—parents, educators, medical providers, and mental health providers—to help ensure that children learn and thrive starting from a very early age. It is reimagining schools as *relational hubs*.

Drawing on her experience as both pediatrician and educator, Priscilla Chan, spouse of Meta cofounder and CEO Mark Zuckerberg, recognized the prevailing limitations in providing the necessary support for children's health and educational success. In 2016, she joined forces with the late Meredith Liu, an innovator in K–12 education and an advocate for children and families, to work on improving integration between health and educational systems. Their extensive dialogues with educators, health care workers, social workers, and other professionals highlighted the common barriers to children's classroom success: health issues and trauma, and the inability to address them within existing systems. These conversations led them to found the Primary School, which currently serves over four hundred children ages one through twelve, with more than 80 percent of families considered low-income.

At the Primary School, educators strive to foster a sense of community and to make the school environment feel like a second home for the children. They adopt a distinctive two-generation strategy aimed at nurturing bonds by supporting both the child and the adults in the child's life. One of the school's tenets states, "We believe when a parent is well, a child can thrive."

The school assigns a dedicated parent-wellness coach to each family. Parent-wellness coaches, sourced from the community, meet parents in both individual sessions and group sessions called parents' circles. A session might delve into the benefits of establishing routines for children; another might address the importance of adults getting sufficient sleep. Valentina Helo-Villegas, a licensed therapist who works as director of the program, explains, "Parents are usually seen as adults in the service of children, but we forget to acknowledge that they are also individuals with their own hopes and dreams." She adds that, when she worked as a therapist, she "was often charged to fix the child, and I was working in wraparound services serving children with very, very high needs. It was very clear that the funding of the system was paying attention to the child and forgetting the adults and systems around the child." The Primary School operates under what she calls "a better working hypothesis": the well-being of the adult who is caring for that child is of central importance. Guadalupe Virruela, a parent of a young child at the Primary School, shares in her native Spanish that the school "has given me time and space to know myself, which personally did not occur to me before. I wouldn't give myself time and explore my potential and serve as a role model for my child."[6]

In addition to parents' circles, a children's circle convenes three times a year for each student. During the meeting, the family, teacher, parent-wellness coach, and, if appropriate, medical staff assess the child's academic progress, health, and social-emotional development—or, in the language of the school, their soul.

Helo-Villegas is hopeful about the early results of this program, especially in terms of its effect on family relationships. "We're seeing that our families are . . . learning to recognize a lot better and address the impact and toxic stress in their families and in their communities. The most important thing for me is that they're building effective networks of support well beyond the small things that we're doing at the Primary School."

Imagine a future where schools evolve from being settings for information transmission into vibrant relational hubs at the heart of each community—like the Primary School. In this vision, teachers are regarded not just as academic content providers but as relational brain builders, crucial for nurturing both the educational and cultural fabric of society. And other adults—pediatricians, counselors, family members—participate in the project of unlocking a child's full potential.

Sadly, this is not what most of our children experience today. Many families lack access to early care and education, let alone *quality* early care and education. The United States and many other countries have struggled to support families. The result is a suboptimal patchwork of solutions for our youngest learners, a fragmented nonsystem of preschools, childcare centers, family childcare, faith-based early education, kin care, nannies, babysitters, neighbors, and friends that is challenging for most families to navigate.

In the US, there were three critical moments in our long-standing failure to adopt a universal system of care and education for our little learners. One was right after World War II. During the war, the US had established federally funded childcare centers under the Lanham Act.[7] Every family, irrespective of their financial status and race, had access to childcare up to six days a week, including summer breaks and holidays—albeit in racially segregated programs. Parents would pay only about nine or ten dollars a day in today's currency. By the end of the war, six hundred thousand children were estimated to have received some care from the Lanham Act programs. Beyond its affordability, the care provided was high quality, with numerous centers maintaining favorable child-to-teacher ratios, offering nutritious meals and snacks, and engaging children in artistic and educational enrichment programs. The program had a lasting impact on the future success of children: higher school graduation rates, higher college completion rates, and a boost in employment rates.[8] However, postwar, priorities shifted in the absence of a broad public consensus on the importance of early childhood education and the role of mothers in society.

The second missed opportunity was in the early 1970s. Head Start, the federal preschool program for children from low-income backgrounds, was authorized as a pilot in 1965 and expanded nationally shortly thereafter. On the back of the success of Head Start, a landmark piece of legislation called the Comprehensive Child Development Act emerged to create a universal early care and education system. It passed in both the House and the Senate. Under the system proposed by the bill, the most economically disadvantaged Americans would be exempt from paying for childcare, while those in the middle and higher income brackets would face fees adjusted based on their earnings. But despite having initially campaigned on childcare as part of his legislative agenda, President Richard Nixon vetoed the bill in light of concerns over government intrusion into family life, the potential economic impact of the program, and ideological opposition to expanding the federal government's role in childcare.

The third critical moment of failure to establish a national childcare system occurred in 2022. A proposal responding to disruptions in the childcare services essential to many working families during the COVID pandemic was dropped from the Biden Administration's Build Back Better legislation due to concerns related to costs and inflation, and a lack of bipartisan support.

Despite those three policy failures to create a coherent system, there has been significant success in what may be a surprising setting: the US military. The Department of Defense offers the best childcare system in the nation for its military personnel. More than 95 percent of childcare centers on US military bases meet the high standards of quality for curriculum, teaching, and community relations established by the National Association for the Education of Young Children. The education-focused Hechinger Report describes the child development center at the Meridian Naval Air Station in Mississippi this way: "Each classroom has its own playground and each has an area where children can play house, with a mini stove and sink. The rooms are full of books, blocks, puppets, dolls and other toys and staffed by at least two teachers at all times."[9]

In the wake of the pandemic, as families continue to struggle to find affordable quality childcare, we are also experiencing a meaningful decline in school enrollment. This is especially true for our youngest children, a population in which a rise in chronic absenteeism is widely documented. Concerns over COVID-19 have played a significant role, influencing some parents to delay their children's entry into early care and education. Some parents worry that their child is not ready for the structure and expectations of formal settings. Others don't see value in rigid educational programs, which fail to fit their schedules the way online programs did. Parents are choosing forms of childcare that better fit their lifestyle, including homeschooling, driven by reasons ranging from dissatisfaction with the traditional educational system to a desire for more involvement in their child's learning—especially families with neurodiverse or Black children. An increasing number of parents are choosing homeschooling for nonreligious reasons, reflecting a significant shift in the motivations behind the movement. One survey highlighted that only 1 percent of new homeschooling parents cited religious beliefs as their top reason for homeschooling, down from 14 percent of those who were homeschooling prior to the pandemic.[10]

These trends underscore the importance of understanding and addressing the diverse needs and concerns of families in redesigning early childhood education that fits the future.

In an ideal future, the heart of learning would involve nurturing relationships, joyful play, and the foundational principle of love. Every child would be welcomed into an environment rich with opportunities for connection, where educators act as guides fostering warm, supportive relationships with and among children. Play would be recognized as the natural language of children and the main avenue for learning, creativity, problem-solving, and collaboration. The aspirational goal would be to create a learning environment where every child feels valued and connected, ready to step into a world where relational intelligence and digital intelligence go hand in hand. To accomplish this goal, we need to build on three foundational pillars:

1. relational schools that connect families, children, and peers;
2. relational teachers who inspire a love of learning through meaningful, nurturing connections; and
3. relational pedagogy that embraces love as a new form of literacy.

Relational Schools That Connect Families, Children, and Peers

In South Africa, DataDrive is running an experiment called the Early Learning Positive Deviance Initiative to determine why some younger children from lower socioeconomic backgrounds outperform their peers. What they've found so far is that the key is for schools to be relational. Focused engagement in early education, dedicated pedagogy, fostering relationships, community integration, effective leadership, and active family involvement are key to impactful care and learning.[11]

Early education environments are much more than mere caretaking facilities; they embody a comprehensive strategy for fostering the growth of young minds. This approach weaves together play and the development of skills with the active involvement of families and the broader community, thereby nurturing a child's learning journey holistically. In the K–12 years, such places are often called community schools. Community schools are public schools that provide services and supports that fit the needs of the neighborhood they're in; they're created and run by the people who know our children best. In Kentucky, the Berea Pre-K Pirates program exemplifies a statewide initiative embracing the community school approach, specifically targeting early childhood education. This program focuses on offering early intervention and educational services to three- and four-year-old children with diagnosed disabilities who come from households with incomes not exceeding 160 percent of the federal poverty threshold. Families can read on Berea's website about what the school teaches: "Preschool often looks like play, but their play is their work." "We do finger paint and explore messy activities."[12] The school emphasizes socialization through small and larger groups, as well as lots of outdoor time. They even have a "dinosaur lady," a guidance counselor who uses dinosaur puppets to teach a variety of social skills and safety skills. Through trusting relationships and well-coordinated supports, Berea ensures that learners and families receive the health, social service, and learning opportunities they need to be successful.

Relational schools connect with families in many other innovative ways. Briya Public Charter School in Washington, DC, offers language and GED classes for parents in the same location and at the same time as early childhood education for little ones. Briya is colocated with a family clinic, a gift of convenience for families. Other schools leverage text-messaging platforms to connect to families, or technology tools, like Along or Sown to Grow, that aim to foster better connection between teachers and learners.[13] Teachers can use Along to send research-backed reflection questions to students, who can respond via text, audio, or video. Some schools in Connecticut offer home visit programs, yielding positive attendance results.[14] A study at Head Start centers in New York City conducted by Harvard sociologist Mario

Small found that mothers with children enrolled at a center had larger social networks, which led to less hardship and better well-being. A low-cost experiment, consisting of grouping kids by neighborhood and promoting parent connections, improved attendance by 5–7 percent and doubled parental support networks.[15]

Home-based childcare caters to the unique local needs of families. Wonderschool was founded by Chris Bennett, who was inspired by the impact of family childcare on his own educational path. Raised in part at Yoli's home-based childcare, located around the corner from his house in Miami, Bennett was the first in his family to go to college. Wonderschool provides a technology platform for families to find childcare and for childcare providers to collect tuition, track expenses, and access training, licensing, and peer-support systems to turn their homes into childcare settings. It empowers educators to start their own businesses, promoting accessible, culturally resonant childcare, and it partners with state agencies to enhance the availability of quality care. Home-based care offers the benefits of a nurturing environment, adaptable schedules, and a sense of community, reinforcing children's holistic growth and offering a viable, relational alternative for early education.

Relational schools also connect with grandparents. Tūtū and Me is a traveling preschool in Hawai'i that offers education and support to *keiki* (children) and their families, particularly the *tūtū* (a Hawaiian term of endearment for grandparents), in underserved communities. This part-time program, active two mornings weekly, involves families in learning, celebrates Hawaiian culture, and helps with caregiving challenges. It delivers a flexible, culturally relevant curriculum focused on cognitive, social, and language development. Mobile teams of early childhood professionals travel to designated locations, setting up an engaging educational environment that is dismantled at the end of each session, ready to be transported to the next location. The curriculum is thoughtfully designed around thematic learning that honors and incorporates Hawaiian cultural values, ensuring that it aligns with the keiki's heritage and the community's diverse needs. By third grade, 86 percent of the children who attend Tūtū and Me are proficient in reading, compared with a statewide average of 65 percent.[16]

Many schools leverage peer learning, long known for beneficial outcomes.[17] At Bing Nursery School, an early childhood research center at Stanford University, mixed-age classrooms are a tradition.[18] Mixed-age interaction leads to higher-quality play, improved social skills, and greater academic growth.[19]

These different models of connected learning are not just educational interventions. By promoting a philosophy of learning as a shared journey and integrating learning with other important aspects of the human experience, these schools become the lifeblood of their communities. They demonstrate that when education is crafted with the whole family in mind, when it's embedded within the community's fabric, it does more than educate; it also empowers, uplifts, and unites.

Relational Teachers Who Inspire a Love of Learning Through Meaningful, Nurturing Connections

If you had to choose between a relational teacher, a high-quality curriculum, or a small classroom to drive academic performance, which would you pick? Well, the quality of interactions between teachers and children is a better enabler of academic success than the content of what is taught, the way it is taught, or even the number of children in the classroom.[20] Results from the large longitudinal Finnish First Steps study indicate that warm, secure relationships with educators meaningfully increase children's reading, writing, and math skills.[21] We also know that when teacher-learner relationships are positive, teachers are more likely to use complex and high-impact instructional practices, driving better academic outcomes.[22]

What is a relational teacher, you may ask? Aren't all teachers relational? A relational teacher is one who prioritizes and actively cultivates positive, supportive relationships with and among their students. This approach to teaching emphasizes the importance of understanding and responding to students' individual needs, backgrounds, and experiences to create an inclusive, respectful, and engaging learning environment. Building trust, fostering a sense of belonging, facilitating peer connections, and promoting learner and family engagement are key.

Let's be clear: the thousands of teachers I've met all aspire to be relational. When asked what motivates educators to teach in the field of early childhood learning, the common response is "working with kids and their families." As one early childhood teacher put it, "The kids. That's my number one motivator. They are whimsical and beautiful and lovely and smart and everything wonderful and amazing."[23] This is why people enter the teaching profession, and why they stay. But institutional constraints get in the way, including class size, time limitations, compensation, inadequate training, and/or ineffective administrative support.[24]

Of course, there are many notable successes. Every night before bedtime, toddler Nevaeh tells her mother, "I want to go to Ms. Kelly's house!"[25] She is not talking about a neighbor or family friend, but about her beloved teacher. Shortly after her first birthday, Nevaeh attended Debra Kelly's home-based childcare through the All Our Kin Early Head Start program in New Haven, Connecticut. There, Nevaeh thrives, listening to stories, playing with her friends, and dancing to her favorite songs. Nevaeh's mother, who often lingers after drop-off, says, "It's not just daycare; it's an educational environment." Of Ms. Kelly, she says, "It's like she's kin. Like All Our Kin, she's like kin to me. If you work together, it will create a good outcome for the child." Ms. Kelly echoes this sentiment: "The care, the love, and the expertise [family childcare educators] put into the work they do for young children, especially infants and toddlers—it's more than just caring for the children; we care for the parents and families also." All Our Kin supports Ms. Kelly with personalized coaching to refine her teaching approach, with group classes on diverse topics from entrepreneurship to gardening for children, and with assistance in obtaining her teaching license. As with Wonderschool, "We're right in the same neighborhoods as the families we service, and so we have a perspective on where they're coming from and what their needs are and what they experience on a daily basis." Ms. Kelly's relational approach creates a nurturing learning space and strong community ties, embodying the essence of relational brain building by fostering children's and families' development and connectivity.

The relational approach to brain building also extends to discipline and classroom management. In fostering cognitive and social growth, educators are shifting from punitive discipline to restorative practices that promote empathy and understanding. These methods, which include discussing consequences and actively involving children in resolution processes, support the development of strong social-emotional skills and a cohesive classroom community. A punitive approach to a little one drawing on the wall might involve scolding the child and imposing a time-out, thus focusing on punishment for the action. A restorative practice would involve discussing with the child why drawing on the wall is inappropriate, exploring the consequences of their actions, and involving them in the cleanup process. This approach aims to teach responsibility and the impact of actions, fostering understanding and empathy rather than just obedience. Studies show that such approaches, which emphasize explanation over punishment, significantly boost long-lasting positive social behaviors among young learners.[26]

Relational teachers reach children and families, like Nevaeh and her mom, to ensure that education is woven into the very fabric of family life, expanding a child's sense of home and the family's sense of connectedness to a larger community.

A Relational Pedagogy That Embraces Love as a New Form of Literacy

As this book has repeatedly shown, love—defined here as a series of micromoments that arise during positive, resonant interactions when two or more individuals share a moment of emotional attunement—is at the root of relationships for young children, driving relational intelligence. Thus, the primacy of relationships and love should be at the core of our educational systems and central to our mission as educators. Love is a driving force that fosters connection, attachment, understanding, learning, and growth. When educators approach teaching with a focus on love, they create a fertile environment for holistic development, one where little learners are valued, understood, and more deeply engaged. This theory advocates for a compassionate pedagogy that doesn't just emphasize academic success but cultivates relationships, emotional intelligence, and resilience, essential qualities for thriving in all areas of life.

This theory is not new. Paulo Freire's educational philosophy presents love not merely as an emotion but as a transformative force in learning. In his seminal 1968 work, *Pedagogy of the Oppressed*, he posits that love is a foundational element for humanization and liberation. His approach to teaching is one in which love transcends the personal and becomes a vehicle for engaging with the world, particularly in the context of addressing and overcoming oppression. Love, in this sense, is an act of resistance against the dehumanization that accompanies oppression. It becomes the thread that connects learners to life, to the world, and to each other, making meaningful dialogue and transformation possible.

Zaretta Hammond's work on culturally responsive teaching outlines a pedagogy grounded in love and brain science.[27] She details six "brain rules":

1. The brain's drive for social safety and connection
2. The role of positive relationships in calming the brain's threat response
3. The influence of culture on information processing
4. The centrality of attention in learning
5. The need to integrate new knowledge with what is already known

6. The brain's growth through challenges that promote complex thinking

Hammond's approach, which resonates with Freire's vision, nurtures an education that balances cognitive growth with relational and emotional connection, embraces a holistic view of human experience, and enriches students' minds and hearts.

Relational pedagogy is "an educational approach that places a strong emphasis on building positive and meaningful relationships between educators and students," as defined by Catherine Bovill at the University of Edinburgh.[28] It views learning not merely as the transfer of knowledge but as a social process in which the connections and interactions within the classroom are as important as the content being taught. Teachers are facilitators who nurture a classroom environment of trust and collaborative engagement. It emphasizes the importance of understanding each learner's context. Techniques like co-designed learning and teaching, open discussions, group projects, and individualized feedback exemplify the approach. It is often associated with improved learner engagement, better academic outcomes, and the development of critical life skills such as communication, collaboration, and problem-solving.

Finland exemplifies the incorporation of relational pedagogy within its national education system. They even have a term for it: pedagogical love. The concept was introduced in the nineteenth century by Uno Cygnaeus, often considered the father of the Finnish public school system, who advocated that a good teacher should "blaze with the spirit of sacred love."

Outside the school system, one of my favorite examples of relational pedagogy is the Suzuki method, which has influenced millions of children globally through music. Shinichi Suzuki's approach is based on a belief in every child's potential and emphasizes children's natural learning processes, which are akin to language acquisition. Kids are taught to play an instrument starting at an early age in a supportive learning environment that also emphasizes parental involvement. The method also focuses on positive reinforcement, building self-esteem, developing a caring relationship between teacher and student, and group lessons for collective learning and motivation. Although the Suzuki method is specifically music oriented, its foundational principles echo the broader ideals of developing character and fostering a love for lifelong learning.

Relational pedagogy is not without its controversies. The idea of co-designing lessons with a child rather than knowing what is needed challenges the traditional view of education as a process of knowledge transfer. And the idea of underpinning that collaboration with love and care further provokes those who hold a conventional view of education. Relational approaches to learning are not easy, especially for children and families who have not experienced trust with schools or institutions before. But that's why we must welcome the integration of love and relational practices in education. It's essential to challenge traditional frameworks and support every student, particularly those who might feel marginalized or distrustful of educational systems.

Incorporating love as a new literacy within our schools bridges the gap between the empirical science of relationships and the practice of teaching, fostering an education system that values heart-centered engagement. The literacy of love transcends mere sentimentality; it is an evidence-based strategy that reinforces the neural pathways conducive to learning and well-being. Embedding this literacy into our educational ethos invites a profound rethinking of success, one in which academic accomplishments are celebrated alongside the development of compassionate, socially conscious citizens. As such, love becomes not just an ideal, but a practical, guiding principle that shapes the educational journey into one of holistic growth and interconnectedness.

Other countries have started to include the teaching of love and relationships in their curricula. Denmark's education system includes *Klassens Tid*, an hour of class time each week dedicated to discussing emotional well-being and interpersonal dynamics, which can involve relationship building.[29]

In Canada (and beyond), Roots of Empathy is an innovative classroom program designed to foster empathy and build stronger, more caring relationships among students. A baby and its parent are invited into the classroom at intervals throughout the year, allowing the children to observe the baby's development. Children are guided to understand and label emotions, and are encouraged to reflect on their own feelings and those of their peers. This direct engagement lays a foundation for more respectful and compassionate relationships.

In New Zealand, the Te Whāriki is the national curriculum for early childhood education.[30] The name translates into "the woven mat," a symbol of the diverse yet interconnected nature of learning and development. New Zealand's early learning standards are among the highest in the world, and almost all children participate. The curriculum is underpinned by four principles: empowerment for the children to learn and grow; holistic development; family and community; and responsive and reciprocal relationships with people, places, and things.

Relationally focused learning should be a core tenet of pedagogy and curriculum. It is the path to a better future for our children, the next generations, and our society as a whole. This is not just a pipe dream. Innovative funders are recognizing the need for love as a new literacy. Laura Arnold, Priscilla Chan, MacKenzie Scott, Connie Ballmer, Jackie Bezos, Susie Buffett, Melinda French Gates, Lisa Mennet, Pam Omidyar, Signe Ostby, Laura Overdeck, and Liz Simons, to name a few, are pushing the boundaries of philanthropy and investing to transform the face of early childhood education and care. They are all remarkable leaders. Most are signatories to the Giving Pledge, a commitment to give away a majority of their wealth during their lifetime. They are also all women. They are all mothers and grandmothers. And this is likely not a coincidence.

Edtech funders—like Amy Klement, Vinice Davis, and Enyi Okebugwu at Imaginable Futures; Jennifer Carolan, Shauntel Garvey, and

Wayee Chu at Reach Capital; Deborah Quazzo and Michael Moe at GSV Ventures; Andre Bennin, Ebony Brown, Monique Malcom-Hay, Matt Greenfield, and Rick Segal at Rethink Education; and Jenny Abramson and Heidi Patel at Rethink Impact—are supporting innovative models for the early years. Foundations like Bainum Foundation, Burke Foundation, Einhorn Collaborative, Omidyar Network, Packard Foundation, and Pritzker Children's Initiative are dedicating large initiatives to "elevate the power of human connection," "build cultures of belonging," "build strong partnerships for community and care in the first 1,000 days," and "prioritize the importance of children having a healthy start and promoting resilience and vibrant communities where children and families thrive," respectively. They all understand the outsized impact that investments in relationally focused care and education in early childhood can have on children, families, communities, and societies.

Let's turn to one more influential philanthropist, Harry Rosen, who single-handedly funded the community transformation of Tangelo Park.

CHAPTER 12

Communities: Thriving Together

Now, more than ever, the illusions of division threaten our very existence. We all know the truth: more connects us than separates us. But in times of crisis the wise build bridges, while the foolish build barriers. We must find a way to look after one another, as if we were one single tribe.
                                    —KING T'CHALLA, *BLACK PANTHER*, 2018

Love should be at the heart of our community efforts, inspiring us to come together to fight systemic oppression and inequality.
                                    —BELL HOOKS, *ALL ABOUT LOVE*, 1999

Let your teacher be love itself.
                                    —RUMI, THIRTEENTH CENTURY

When we think about relationships, we often focus on the beautiful dance between two partners: child-parent, child-child, child-teacher. Yet it's clear that these connections are part of a larger web of human interaction, existing in communities that either facilitate or hinder the interactions. Now imagine communities that are relationship-centered, care-full, and learning-focused, where social connectedness and intergenerational solidarity support our future generations of little learners. Where mothers and fathers, grand-adults and tūtūs, educators and coaches, health professionals and civil servants, young and old friends share time and energy as a form of mutual aid to develop young children's minds, talents, and creativity.

This can happen. The transformation of Tangelo Park, to name one example, is nothing short of a miracle.

Tangelo Park is a neighborhood in Orange County, Florida, just outside Orlando, where Walt Disney World Resort and other amusement parks are located. The community was built in the 1950s where orange groves once flourished, to house workers at the former Martin Marietta headquarters (now Lockheed Martin). Its name derives from the citrus fruit that is a cross between a tangerine and a pomelo.

In the early 1990s, Tangelo Park was going through challenging times, earning a reputation as the neighborhood with the highest crime rate in central Florida. Its population, 90 percent of which was composed of African American and African Caribbean residents, was struggling with patterns too familiar in low-income communities: drugs, violence, incarceration, an exodus of young talent, low high school graduation rates. Nearly half of Tangelo Park's students were dropping out of their designated school, Dr. Phillips High School, located in a nearby majority-white suburb.[1]

The community tried to organize around these challenges. As resident Sam Butler recounted in an interview with researcher Elaine Weiss, "We were a community of people who had been places, did things—served in the military, worked for corporations like Lockheed Martin—and knew something about what we would like for our community. We had a nucleus of people who were not willing to accept the crime, the drugs, the 'mischief' that some other neighborhoods sort of laid down for. We wanted a better place for our children, a safer environment to raise our children. About ten men got together and said, 'Hey, we can do something about this.'"[2]

Meanwhile, Harry Rosen, an immigrant born poor in the Lower East Side of Manhattan, had built substantial wealth in the hotel industry and was aspiring to give back. He was familiar with the troubled community of Tangelo Park. At the time, Tangelo Park "was just in very, very bad shape, crime was an epidemic," Rosen said.[3] The community advised him that focusing on children, especially young children, was crucial to making a real difference. Rosen decided to support Tangelo Park by funding three parallel interventions: free high-quality childcare for anyone, family engagement programs, and "full-ride" (fully paid) postsecondary education for anyone graduating from high school.

Rosen's investment fueled a transformation. Now, less than twenty years later, the community boasts high school graduation rates close to 100 percent, meaningfully higher college graduation rates, low crime, and a tripling of housing value. Most residents stay in Tangelo Park to build on the progress, while spreading the hope and the love to other communities. Rosen recounts a conversation from a few years back with Jerry Demings, sheriff of Orange County at the time and now the mayor of Tangelo Park, who highlighted the program's positive outcomes. "He said, 'Let me tell you something: We now consider Tangelo Park to be a quiet oasis.'"

Tangelo Park resident Jamez Morris remembers what things were like when she was growing up and her community seemed to lack prospects for the future: "Living in this neighborhood, you don't see too many success stories walking down the street. . . . Don't nobody really believe in us! That was our mindset back in the day: Don't nobody care about us!" Despite the challenges, Morris's mother did her best to support her and her four sisters. "My biggest fear was where am I going to end up after high school." Morris seized the opportunity provided by the Rosen-funded scholarship, earning her bachelor's degree in psychology with a minor in criminal justice from Florida A&M University. Now she is pursuing her master's degree to fulfill her goal of becoming a school counselor, aiming to inspire children to realize their own potential, just as the Tangelo Park program did for her. "This scholarship was not just money to get into school," she says. "It was my foundation."

The initiative's emphasis on early childhood education has been particularly impactful. By ensuring that children have access to a high-quality preschool, the program lays a solid foundation for academic achievement and development. Tangelo Park's 2-3-4-Year-Old Program is myopically focused on quality, with a low ratio of caregiver to child (one to six) and the highest state certification required for all caregivers. Caregivers are supervised by a specialist certified in early childhood, who visits each home-based center four times per week to support their curriculum and program. The 2-3-4-Year-Old Program is tailored to foster the development, social skills, and emotional competencies of children, providing care from 7:30 a.m. to 5:00 p.m., Monday through Friday, for fifty weeks each year. Rosen furnishes each childcare center with computers and printers. Websites like Starfall offer interactive games that teach children about shapes, colors, numbers, and letters, simultaneously introducing them to technology. Additionally, a nurse is available to assist care providers, working in partnership with parents and families to support the children's development, education, and psychological well-being across both home and childcare settings.

In addition to the core offerings of the 2-3-4-Year-Old Program, parents are encouraged to participate in parenting education sessions; those with two-year-old children must attend at least two such classes annually. Assessments are conducted three times a year for children nearing kindergarten age, or those about to start in Tangelo Park's pre-K program, to evaluate a variety of academic abilities. The evaluations are utilized by the program coordinator to guide parents in supporting their child's educational readiness. The coordinator then maintains ongoing communication with pre-K and kindergarten educators to bridge any readiness gaps, ensure a seamless transition into formal schooling, and monitor the children's academic advancements.

The success of Tangelo Park was not solely due to Rosen's generosity. It was a product of deep community involvement. The initiative was designed with input from those it aimed to help, leading to programs that were tailored to their specific needs. This collaborative approach fostered a sense of ownership among the residents, and the positive outcomes were a testament to the power of partnership between philanthropy and community.

The program's longevity has also been essential to its success. Rosen's commitment went beyond short-term intervention. It spanned years, allowing for sustained growth and giving residents the confidence that their educational and social support structures would remain in place so they could plan for the future. Tangelo Park's success story demonstrates that strategic, sustained investment in education starting in the early years, combined with an inclusive, community-driven approach and attention to wider social needs and relationships, can lead to substantial and enduring positive change.

Rosen reflects on the broader significance of the efforts: "The word is hope. There is so little hope in so many underserved communities now . . . and hope is what it's all about."

Tangelo Park highlights three main drivers of change in building relational communities that emphasize learning for little ones: places, people, and programs.

Places

Our young children need to be nurtured in modern relational villages like Tangelo Park, where education, care, and human connections are a celebrated part of the everyday landscape. In the ideal village, early care settings and schools would transcend their traditional roles and become vibrant centers of community life where learning intertwines with day-to-day activities, and where programming bridges ages and cultures, knitting a rich and mutually supportive social fabric. Safe, nurturing play areas within a web of walkable, educational landscapes form the heartbeat of neighborhoods designed for families to flourish. Green spaces, accessible family services, and inclusive educational structures create a fertile environment for dynamic engagement by diverse community members. You may think this is all theoretical. But the community and financial investment that transformed Tangelo Park is also fueling transformation in other places.

Designing Modern Relational Villages

Take the city of Curitiba, Brazil, which has been called the "most innovative city in the world," the "green capital," and the "greenest city on earth."[4] Curitiba also boasts the highest literacy rate and ranks number one in education among Brazilian state capitals.

In 1971, Curitiba's green spaces were limited to just one park in downtown, the Passeio Público. Now the city boasts over fifty square meters of green space per person, a stark contrast to the mere two square meters per person available in the city of Buenos Aires or even the twenty square meters per person available in Paris or New York City. Curitiba has become a testing ground for innovative urban planning under the leadership of Jaime Lerner, a three-time mayor and two-time governor who trained as an architect and urban planner.

Transportation was a catalyst for Curitiba's transformation. When the need for a transit system arose, the city innovatively opted for an "above-ground subway," where passengers board elongated express cars at tube-like stations. Despite a high number of cars in the city, 85 percent of commuters choose this efficient mass transit, significantly lowering fuel consumption compared with the national average. Curitiba has built parks instead of canals to reduce flooding, and has used parks to make the city more livable, while pedestrianizing the downtown area. The city's "garbage that is not garbage" initiative has propelled it to become a global leader in recycling, with over 70 percent of its waste being repurposed. This impressive figure dwarfs the 25 percent recycling mandate of Los Angeles and the national average in the United States. According to the city's estimates, their paper-recycling efforts alone save approximately twelve hundred trees daily.[5]

Beyond transportation and recycling, what I find the most intriguing about Curitiba's innovative urban design is its educational system. In the 1990s the city introduced the Faróis de Saber, or Lighthouses of Learning, in each neighborhood. These colorful buildings, inspired by the great lighthouse in Alexandria, Egypt—one of the ancient world's seven wonders—contain libraries and reading rooms, providing free access to internet and a safe space for learners. Each library is named after an illustrious Brazilian novelist or poet and is crowned by a rooster weathervane, a symbol of awakening and a sharp mind. About the libraries, the current mayor states, "This is very important in a country where the schools have no books . . . and where people for 500 years have been forbidden to think."[6] Moreover, the centers have become community beacons, reducing crime rates and costing just a fraction of what is typically spent on road infrastructure. "It's cheaper to build libraries than prisons," the mayor, an engineer, points out.

In addition to Lighthouses of Learning, the city has invested in maker spaces, called mini-fab labs—learning environments adjacent to schools that teach kids how to be creative and agile. The innovation does not stop here: young children's educational materials teach numbers through examples from the local biodiverse ecosystems, and students can pay for textbooks and school supplies with recyclable trash, creating a cycle of environmental consciousness. Curitiba also houses the Free University for the Environment, which disseminates environmental knowledge to all strata of society.

All these elements collectively contribute to a learning-friendly city where educational opportunities are embedded within the community infrastructure, fostering a holistic growth environment for its young citizens.

In another part of the planet, Abu Dhabi is on a mission to become the world's most family-friendly city—a noble goal! The city has undertaken comprehensive initiatives across education, health care, public spaces, and safety to improve the quality of life for families. This includes investing in world-class educational institutions and medical facilities, developing safe and accessible parks and recreational areas, providing affordable housing, and ensuring the city's safety and security through advanced measures. The Abu Dhabi Early Childhood Authority, established to develop a comprehensive framework for youngsters' development, aims to ensure that all children in Abu Dhabi have access to high-quality early learning programs, health services, and family support from birth to eight years old. One of the programs, We Grow with You, provides parents and caregivers the tools and knowledge to support their young children's achievement of developmental milestones. Other programs are innovating to provide high-quality early childhood education. Abu Dhabi is also committed to inclusivity, offering support for families with special needs and policies that promote work-life balance. Environmental sustainability plays a key role, with efforts to preserve natural habitats and promote green urban spaces, showcasing Abu Dhabi's holistic approach to fostering a supportive, safe, and enriching environment for all families.

Elsewhere in the Middle East, NEOM is a futuristic city in Saudi Arabia, being built from the ground up to become a "new land of the future, where the greatest minds and best talents are empowered to embody pioneering ideas and exceed boundaries in a world inspired by imagination."[7] It will span thirty-four square kilometers and host nine million people by 2045. Loads of money is being invested behind this project. When I say loads, I mean it: we are speaking about $500 billion! (For context, that's more than Austria's 2021 GDP.) NEOM is intended to embody the values of care, curiosity, diversity, passion, and respect—and to be a catalyst for change. While some of the initial construction is focused on luxury tourism, there is a vision to build a family-friendly city with no cars and no emissions, and easy access to facilities. The NEOM Education, Research, and Innovation Sector plans to develop a fully integrated education ecosystem to promote life-long learning, starting in early childhood.

Near San Francisco, plans are forming for another new city, California Forever, intended to house fifty thousand residents by the late 2030s in a walkable middle-class community. The concept of walkability is a positive in fostering community and human connections, although disappointingly not much has been disclosed about the city's plans for childcare and education.

Time will tell if the plans for NEOM or California Forever fully materialize. But meanwhile, I am inspired by these innovative urban projects and the opportunity they afford to prioritize family, care, play, and learning while focusing on sustainability.

Playful Learning Landscapes

Another way to redesign urban (or village) infrastructure to support communitywide connection can be found in initiatives like Playful Learning Landscapes and Play Everywhere (described in Chapter 10) that integrate playful learning opportunities into public spaces. The idea is to transform everyday places into interactive and engaging environments that encourage children and families to play and learn together. The various environments are designed based on the principles of cognitive and developmental science to promote language development, numeracy, spatial reasoning, and social skills. Cityscape Playgrounds turn imaginative role-play into lessons on social roles. Interactive Sidewalks blend hopscotch with math puzzles, weaving numeracy into every step. Storybook Paths invite families to follow tales through parks, fostering a love of reading amidst nature's backdrop. Musical Playgrounds encourage people to co-create rhythms as they explore sound. Nature Exploration Areas prompt scientific curiosity through hands-on interaction with the natural world. Bus Stop

Puzzles turn waiting times into brain-teasing games, enriching mundane moments.

One of my favorites is Math Trails, which challenge young minds with environmental shapes and numbers, turning parks into giant classrooms. If you are ever in the Boston, Massachusetts, area, check out the Bob Moses MathTrail, a one-mile path running through several parks in the Port neighborhood of Cambridge. It features activities and games to teach mathematical concepts interactively. You can even download an app and explore activities using augmented reality. The trail was designed by MathTalk—an organization that creates opportunities for young children and their families, particularly those in economically distressed communities, to discover and enjoy math everywhere—under the umbrella of a citywide partnership called Math Matters for Equity.

Why is it one of my favorites? Let's admit that math makes most of us a little uncomfortable. Nine in ten adult Americans indicate that they experience some level of math anxiety.[8] Yet our daily lives are shaped by math. "Every time you're cooking, you're doing math," says Omo Moses, the founder and CEO of MathTalk.[9] For young children, who absorb their emotional and physical surroundings, math anxiety among the adults in their lives can seep into their own learning, especially in their crucial early years, and have lifelong ripple effects. Starting young children off on the right foot with math has been shown to be a better predictor of success than early reading, but American children regularly underperform on math assessments compared with children in other countries.[10]

Early math learning that is facilitated through adult and parent guidance can become more engaging and effective with the use of technology.[11] Moses was inspired by his father, Bob Moses, who was a civil rights leader, a MacArthur "Genius" Fellow, and the founder of the Algebra Project, a math literacy nonprofit for children of color. Omo joined his father at the Algebra Project when he graduated from college. The elder Moses saw math literacy as the key to economic mobility among people of color, especially as technology-based jobs began out-numbering traditional industrial jobs. "People clearly understand that education is a kind of vehicle for upward mobility," Omo says. "Within that, math has become much more important for people to be able to have that same type of upward mobility." Yet research shows that math education is less accessible to Black and Latinx students, and the way it is taught may even favor white students.[12] While working with his father at the Algebra Project, Omo learned a lot about what barriers keep students from embracing math. The way most of us learn math is through memorization, but to Omo, math is a language, a way to explore ideas and discover new things. "I know how strange it can sound to say that math literacy—and algebra in particular—is the key to the future of disenfranchised communities, but that's what I think and believe with all of my heart." He adds, "As you learn and see math around you, and you're able to interact and engage with it, a world opens up."[13]

Generations United Metropolis

Imagine a city that embraces the concept of intergenerational living, where people aren't self-segregated by age, and friendships blossom between old and young. Or visit Singapore.

Singapore's approach to being an intergenerational city includes the development of housing policies that encourage multigenerational living, such as the Multi-Generation Priority Scheme, which facilitates younger and older generations of the same family living in close proximity. The city also has facilities and spaces that promote inter-generational interaction, like community centers and parks that host activities catering to all ages. For example, Kampung Admiralty is Singapore's first integrated public housing development specifically designed to foster intergenerational interaction and support among residents of all ages. Opened in 2017, this innovative project combines housing for the elderly with childcare and community facilities in a single complex. Kampung Admiralty features studio apartments for seniors, a medical center, childcare and eldercare centers, and collective spaces that encourage social interaction among residents. The design includes shared community gardens and open spaces where residents can participate in activities together, from gardening to exercise classes, creating natural opportunities for intergenerational bonding. The government also supports initiatives that involve seniors in volunteer roles that leverage their skills and experience, thereby fostering a sense of purpose and contribution. Other programs aim to keep older adults engaged and integrated in the broader community by promoting life-long learning and active aging.

In the United States, the Intergenerational Learning Center at Providence Mount St. Vincent, in Seattle, Washington, is an innovative childcare program located within a nursing home, allowing children and seniors to interact regularly through structured activities such as reading, art, and music. These interactions benefit both the children and the seniors, promoting learning and understanding across generations, improving the mood and well-being of the elderly residents, and providing children with unique learning experiences.

Similarly, St. Ann Center for Intergenerational Care in Milwaukee, Wisconsin, supports a holistic model of care that recognizes the benefits of connecting different generations. It provides day services for individuals of all ages, including childcare, adult day care, and specialized care for those with disabilities. The center is designed to foster intergenerational relationships, with programs that encourage interaction between seniors and children, such as shared meals, educational activities, and entertainment.

The Village to Village Network, a movement that began in Boston in 2002 and has spread to more than three hundred locations across the US, exemplifies a community-led approach that supports aging in place, enabling seniors to maintain their independence while still benefiting from the security and companionship provided by a network of local families. Through shared resources, intergenerational wisdom, and a commitment to mutual support, these living arrangements are redefining residential life, showcasing the full potential of family structures to adapt and flourish in today's diverse population.

These examples reflect a growing recognition of the value of intergenerational programs and living arrangements for building stronger communities and addressing social isolation among the elderly, while also providing educational and developmental benefits for younger generations. Despite the clear benefits, there are operational challenges to scaling up such initiatives. Funding constraints, regulatory hurdles, and public awareness are some of the barriers that must be overcome. Nevertheless, the existing models provide a blueprint for success, demonstrating that with community support and innovative utilization of resources, intergenerational programs can thrive.

Pioneering communities rooted in and revivified by learning, sustainability, and mutual support are not only possible; they're already blossoming. In these visionary places, structured to cultivate human connections, peers and mentors become the living heart of the community, guiding, inspiring, and enriching the lives of little learners.

People

As we saw in Tangelo Park, people in the community play an instrumental role in designing and activating solutions for young children to thrive. The establishment of support networks and mentoring opportunities plays a crucial role in nurturing children's potential, offering them the wisdom and encouragement of compassionate adults during critical periods of growth. Two particular initiatives are especially inspiring. The first involves creating support groups that begin at a child's birth, providing a strong foundation of collective support from the very start. The second is the development of large-scale programs to equip children with dedicated mentors who can guide and inspire them throughout their formative years. These programs fill a vital need, ensuring that every child can benefit from meaningful relationships.

Moais at Birth

The secret to immortality might be closer than we think. Okay, maybe not immortality, but certainly a long, happy, and healthy life. In the village of Ogimi, located in the rural northern part of Okinawa Island, Japan, a stone marker contains a few carved sentences. In rough translation, they read, "At 80, you are merely a youth. At 90, if your ancestors invite you into heaven, ask them to wait until you are 100—then, you might consider it."[14]

This is not false advertising. Okinawa is home to more centenarians—people older than one hundred—per capita than just about any place on earth. It has nearly twice the concentration of centenarians as the whole of Japan does, and, remarkably, four times the concentration as the US.[15] The proportion of centenarians is so high that "you can't walk down the street without running into one," reports Brad Willcox, a geriatric expert who has studied longevity in Okinawa.[16]

Longevity expert Dan Buettner has studied the secrets behind these exceptionally long, happy lives.[17] Among them are *moais*, small groups whose members have made a commitment to each other for life. Moais were originally conceived as an alternative to a public tax system to finance village projects, and as a quasi-banking system through which villagers could support each other during hardship. Traditionally, moais were formed in early childhood in groups of about five. As extended families, moais met regularly for work, play, and to pool financial resources.

Today, the idea has expanded to become more like a social support network, a cultural tradition to provide companionship. More than half of Okinawans participate in a moai, and many are in more than one. Some moais have been in existence for over ninety years. The moai tradition helps to create lifelong community and trusted networks. Klazuko Manna is one of the Okinawan women featured in Buettner's book, *Blue Zones*. At 77 years old, she was the youngest of her moai, of which the aggregate age was 450 years. She stresses that a moai isn't just about chatter or gossip—it is about a deep level of support and respect for each other. "Each member knows that her friends count on her as much as she counts on her friends. If you get sick or a spouse dies or if you run out of money, we know someone will step in and help. It's much easier to go through life knowing there is a safety net."

Could moais be replicated elsewhere? In the US, several models have been developed based on a similar concept of providing a support group at birth. The nonprofit organization Centering Healthcare offers group classes for expectant and new parents at pediatricians' offices; they are fully reimbursed by Medicaid and private insurers. When I visited Clínica Alta Vista, a health clinic for young adults in Oakland, California, I met the Xena group, which included six mothers and their five-month-old babies. They had joined a nurse practitioner and a health specialist for a two-hour well-baby visit coordinated by Centering Healthcare. They exchanged stories about their life events over the preceding few weeks, then played games along the lines of Two Truths and a Lie, and Memory. These versions had been designed to playfully inform the moms about which solid and liquid foods were appropriate for five-month-olds. The session ended with a three-minute mindfulness breathing exercise. Research on the programs has shown that parents who attend the sessions are less isolated, and also more informed, confident, and empowered to make healthier choices for themselves, their babies, and their families.[18] If they were extended over time, the group classes could lead to moai-type structures of support among parents and little ones as they grow up together.

The nonprofit UpTogether offers financial support to individuals and families using unrestricted cash donations. It connects families in small groups with the aim of helping them achieve their goals. The results of combining cash with relationships and a support network are impressive. The Gonzalez family—Flor, her husband, and their four children—were able to invest in Flor's childcare business, increase their financial resilience, and in turn provide critical support for neighborhood children to grow into healthy, productive adults. Although they do not start at birth, these support groups are reminiscent of moais.

Mentoring at Scale

In addition to peer groups, evidence strongly suggests that mentorship can have a transformative impact on young children. Young individuals with mentors, whether through formal arrangements or informal connections, are more likely to achieve academic success, engage in extracurricular activities, assume leadership roles, and set ambitious personal goals.

Among the leading mentorship efforts worldwide is Big Brothers Big Sisters, whose proven approach of matching adult volunteers with children has enhanced the lives of countless young individuals. Notable improvements among participants include academic achievements, enhanced self-esteem, and expanded social interactions, illustrating the profound influence mentorship can have.[19] These benefits start kicking in after a minimum mentoring period of approximately nine months. Yes, establishing trusted relationships takes time.

A local example of this philosophy in action is the Everyone Mentors LA initiative of the Los Angeles Unified School District. This program envisions public education as a collective asset and responsibility, and aims to aid students facing academic challenges through mentorship. The district calls upon the community to contribute to the educational journey of more than twenty-seven thousand students, emphasizing that such involvement benefits not only individuals but also the broader society. Also in Los Angeles, the Generation Xchange (GenX) program is making strides by pairing seniors with elementary school students to boost academics. Celeste Madal, a six-year-old learner, reports, "I feel like somebody is counting on me, and somebody knows that I can do it. It is good because you have somebody when you need help." Linda Ricks, a retired office manager and longtime community volunteer, says, "GenX is an excellent program. It's a win-win: the school wins because it gets more adults in the schools that can support teachers' efforts, the children win because they get more caring adults in the classroom and more personal attention, and the volunteers win because they get to help in their local community and improve their health in the process."[20] This strategy of marrying the wisdom of seniors with the vibrancy of youth is showing remarkable outcomes: improved behavior and attendance for the students, and enhanced health and well-being for the seniors, exemplified by weight loss and increased stamina.[21] Similarly, in AARP's Experience Corps, volunteers over age fifty mentor children and support their education, fostering intergenerational connections, community involvement, and relational skills.[22]

While I applaud these initiatives, they generally start for children age five and older, thereby missing the sensitive window of the early years. The potential to expand such initiatives into early care and education settings is vast. A "Caring Corps" that would enroll grand-adults in early childhood education would present a transformative opportunity to shape the social and cognitive landscapes of young minds.[23] The concept, initially promoted by Marc Freedman, founder and co-CEO of CoGenerate who also started Experience Corps, and Carol Larson, senior research scholar at the Stanford Center on Longevity, could attract elders to help young children read, learn, and develop, and could expand to engage millions more elder/child pairs. People in the second half of life are a natural "army" to assist in educating little ones. Research shows that elders have attributes that make them perfectly suited for this task: more patience, greater emotional regulation, persistence, and often time.[24] The question is how many seniors will want or be able to afford to devote themselves to such a project. To rally a vast network of elders in support of early childhood development, the Caring Corps could harness a blend of government, philanthropic, and corporate funds. That way, seniors could take on either remunerated or volunteer roles, from assisting in educational settings to mentoring in literacy to supervising play areas. Furthermore, the corps could synchronize local initiatives to cultivate a collective sense of identity, purpose, and solidarity.

Programs: Community-Led Innovation Meets Connection

After places and people come programs. To foster the well-being and growth of young children, community-led programs serve as critical initiatives leveraging grassroots ingenuity and a network of support to ensure that our children don't just grow, but thrive. I will highlight two promising examples.

Taylor Toynes was working at the Dallas County district attorney's office in 2013 when he uncovered a dire statistic. In the area designated by zip code 75216, where he'd grown up, also known as the "super-block" of Dallas's Oak Cliff neighborhood, there were 681 former prison inmates and only 2 college-ready high school graduates. Toynes decided to be part of the solution. His goal, which would later become the mission statement for his nonprofit organization, For Oak Cliff, is "to liberate Oak Cliff from systemic oppression through a culture of education, while increasing social mobility and social capital."[25]

Before founding the nonprofit, Toynes left the district attorney's office and began teaching at South Oak Cliff's Bushman Elementary through Teach for America. He saw that a majority of his students did not have school supplies, an issue that he realized stemmed from the community's extreme poverty. In the summer of 2015, Toynes rallied students, local residents, and organizations to launch the first Back to School Festival, aimed at providing Oak Cliff students with backpacks filled with essential supplies and with information about resources and service providers that could help kids have a successful academic year. This event has seen significant growth in the years since, aiding more than four thousand students and parents each summer.

The festival quickly became a yearly highlight and led to the creation of For Oak Cliff, but it now represents only a small part of the impactful work being done in the 75216 superblock. In 2016, For Oak Cliff leased an office space in the Black-owned Glendale Shopping Center to offer invaluable two-generation education programs. For Oak Cliff finds it more effective to create radical change by engaging everyone in the home, both students and guardians. For example, they offer early childhood programming for "budding students" ages zero to three, after-school programs and tutoring for kids ages six through twelve, and GED classes for parents and other adults.

Taking a major leap forward, For Oak Cliff recently acquired a twenty-thousand-square-foot facility on ten acres of land, the site of the former Moorland YMCA. Now called the For Oak Cliff Community Campus, it is dedicated to enhancing the organization's mission-driven programs, which include summer sports camps, "yoga in the hood" classes, bimonthly farmers' markets, and community mixers for the "OGs."[26] It boasts a food pantry, a community garden, and a movie theater. Outside the building are walking trails, a sand volleyball court, a fruit orchard, and flexible field and event space. "I'm excited to bring so much love," Toynes shares. "I'm excited to bring people together." The results in Oak Cliff are growing by the day, with nearly fifty adults having completed a GED and seven thousand little learners growing up with quality early childhood education.

Harlem Children's Zone (HCZ), in New York City, founded by Geoffrey Canada, has long been an example of cradle-to-career community change, including its Baby College program. When fourteen-year-old Kiara Molina stood at the White House podium to introduce President Barack Obama in 2014, she had no doubt where she was headed after high school. "I used to want to be a veterinarian. But now I'm thinking, maybe I'll be a lawyer, because I love *Law and Order*," she said at the event celebrating the president's Promise Zones initiative. "But either way, I am going to college."[27] Though her remark got a laugh from the president, she wasn't joking about her plans. She has since graduated from the Newhouse School of Public Communications at Syracuse University.

Kiara is proof of the amazing potential of young people and a shining example of the HCZ model. She started her HCZ journey in the Harlem Gems pre-K program, then enrolled in the Promise Academy charter school, and later became a participant in the Center for Higher Education and Career Support. From babyhood to adulthood, HCZ does whatever it takes to help scholars like Kiara thrive. Now Kiara hopes to give back to the next generation of scholars so that they can achieve the same success. "Seeing the impact HCZ has had on me is motivation to help out other kids who look like me get to the places I've been," she says.

HCZ is an example of a Promise Neighborhoods program, funded by the US Department of Education, which strives to turn neighborhoods of concentrated poverty into neighborhoods of opportunity. They work to improve kids' lives throughout their young lifespan. The effectiveness of Promise Neighborhoods can be challenging to evaluate. As with any large-scale social initiative, outcomes can vary based on execution and local context. Success depends on a variety of factors, including the quality and fidelity of implementation, community engagement, funding stability, and the breadth of services provided. However, initial research and reports from various Promise Neighborhoods have shown positive results in some areas, such as increased kindergarten readiness, greater high school graduation rates, and improved family and community support for children's education.[28] Although Promise Neighborhoods face challenges and require substantial investment and time to realize their objectives, the overall consensus is that they have the potential to make significant impacts on the communities they serve.

As this book demonstrates, love is the most potent force in a child's education. Love inspires, motivates, and heals. When a community is built on a foundation of love, the learning that occurs within it is imbued with compassion, empathy, and a sense of belonging. The ultimate goal is to create places, empower people, and support programs where love and learning are so intertwined that one cannot exist without the other, where every child knows they are valued, and where education is not just about the mind, but also about the heart.

CONCLUSION

A Call for System Change

In the summer of 2015, my team at Omidyar Network built a system map of the US educational system. A system map is a visual depiction of relationships and interactions between stakeholders within a given system; its purpose is to provide a simplified conceptual understanding of a larger, complex structure. The large-formatted visual we created, which was covered in Post-it notes, bubbles, and arrows, laid out a child's learning journey from cradle to career. Our goal was to illustrate the key forces and factors that drive learning and allow kids to thrive in life. The pictorial representation and accompanying narrative captured the collective intelligence of hundreds of diverse stakeholders who had collaborated with us in the mapping process. These contributors included learners, educators, caregivers, school administrators, parents, grandparents, policymakers, researchers, community-based organizations, funders, edupreneurs, and other system leaders.

The visual sequences sought to tell a story of why inequities in the US educational system have persisted, and most importantly to identify leverage points where change can happen. The map highlighted many systems within one system. It also revealed that the US educational system generally works as it was intended to—that is, it works well for certain children and not for many others. This is in sharp contrast to the belief that education is a meritocracy and a path to opportunity. A child's education outcomes primarily depend on their starting points: their family, community, socioeconomic status, race, and ethnicity, and to some extent their gender. Overall, the US education system yields little social mobility, and less than most peer nations. A mere 16 percent of learners from families in the lowest income quartile will graduate from college.[1] It's better to be born rich than smart to succeed in America: a low-performing kindergartner from a higher income family has a greater chance of completing college than a math genius born into a low-income family.[2]

Pam and Pierre Omidyar became extraordinarily wealthy after their company, eBay, went public in 1998. Forbes ranked Pierre Omidyar as the twenty-fourth-richest person in the world in 2021, with an estimated net worth greater than $20 billion. At the time of eBay's initial public offering, Pam and Pierre were in their early thirties. They made a thoughtful decision about what to do with their wealth: give it away. They reckoned that since their affluence had been generated by eBay, a marketplace that had helped connect sellers and buyers, their wealth should be redistributed for the good of others.

Since then, they have both exhibited a rare combination of humility and determination in devoting their net worth to the betterment of humanity. After testing different modalities of philanthropic giving, in 2004 they founded Omidyar Network, a pioneering organization in impact investing and venture philanthropy. I worked at this remarkable organization for nearly ten years, funding both for-profit companies and nonprofit organizations to create opportunity for individuals around the world to improve their own lives. I established and led Omidyar's work in the field of US education (renamed Imaginable Futures in 2020). Pam and Pierre also signed the Giving Pledge, a commitment for billionaires to give away at least 50 percent of their wealth during their lifetime. As of 2022, they had spent billions of dollars funding philanthropic projects. More importantly, a 2018 analysis showed that their philanthropic efforts had reached over one billion lives globally.[3]

The question that Pierre and Pam Omidyar had framed for me was straightforward: Should Omidyar Network invest in US education, and if so, where? It was a simple question with no simple answer. After all, there is no easy solution to any complex social issue, and certainly not to learning and education. For reference, our government (state, local, and federal combined) spends over a trillion dollars every year in education, so any amount of philanthropy fares modestly in comparison—even $20 billion! Moreover, while many philanthropic efforts have been targeted at education, it is not always clear how much difference they have made. Some critics go so far as to say that philanthropy interferes with a public education system that should be governed by the people and for the people.

In analyzing the system map, clear areas emerged where philanthropic funding could be additive, if not catalytic. Two opportunities in particular jumped off the page: early childhood development and relationships.

Recognizing the greatest leverage point in the system map was an aha moment, to use a highly technical system-thinking term. Right at its center, the map showed two deeply interwoven circles—the child and the primary caregiver. The map guided us toward acknowledging a profound and well-studied truth: the criticality of intergenerational relationships in child development and learning, and how they affect generational cycles of poverty. I will admit that as I stared at the map, I almost ignored that connection. I was myopically focused on an individual child's trajectory rather than the context in which the child learns and the web of relationships—including families, communities, and governments at all levels—that foster the child's learning. As it turns out, our educational system and society at large very often overlook that linkage too.

As I hope this book has made clear, relationships have long been the greatest catalyst of learning and thriving. Countless scientists have highlighted the importance of relationships in child development, whether they frame it in terms of bonding, attachment, attunement, "two-gen," "three-gen," "four-gen" strategies, or even love. Yet relationships are also the most undervalued and neglected component of education. In effect, we take relationships for granted, as opposed to intentionally prioritizing them. We do not teach children, parents, or educators about relationships. The word "love" is taboo in most educational settings. We do not track or measure the relationships that impact young children. Our education and health systems are not built around relationships. In essence, relationships—especially early ones—are the best scientifically proven secret for how children learn and thrive, and the most underutilized.

To act on the two key revelations of the system map, I invested in dozens of organizations and projects. My team and I at Omidyar Network and Imaginable Futures built a portfolio of nearly fifty innovative education organizations shaping the future of learning. In my role as a philanthropic and for-profit funder and investor, I seeded many promising ideas and helped them grow into proven solutions that have improved millions of lives and influenced the field of early care and education. I also had the opportunity to advise hundreds of inspiring nonprofit and for-profit edupreneurs, educators, parents, policymakers, advocates, and researchers. One of my greatest joys is seeing the transformational impact of early learning and early relationships on children, educators, and families. I visited early learning and family programs in forty-two states (if you are wondering, I am still working on North and South Dakota, Alaska, Wyoming, Mississippi, Arkansas, Missouri, and Iowa). I even toured early learning settings in Brazil, China, Denmark, France, India, Kenya, Morocco, Qatar, and South Africa. I also witnessed joy, resilience, hope, and courage from children, families, educators, and communities everywhere.

At the onset of the global pandemic, I realized that my work as a philanthropist and impact investor was not enough to address this silent crisis of relational deprivation in the foundational early years of life. So I decided to leave the Omidyar Group and work on this book, hoping to find answers along the way. I found instead many more questions.

I realized that it was not enough to address this major silent crisis: a neglect of human capital that starts in the foundational early years of life. We need a radical societal shift toward focusing on the early years in such a way that elevates and prioritizes relationships and relational intelligence. And as an optimist, I believe we can innovate with a renewed energy and hope, especially in embracing an increasingly diverse population and empowering families and communities.

When I started this journey, I aspired to touch hearts and minds and to inspire new ideas and collaborative solutions in early childhood education. I now realize that the process of listening to families, educators, child advocates, and children themselves fundamentally changed my own heart and mind. It strengthened my belief in the need to focus on early relationships. It also made me realize the complexity of such a vision.

More than ever, I appreciate that building a brighter future for our little learners, and ultimately for our society, requires a profound change in mindset on how we value childhood, and how we support families and early educators. None of us can address this systemic crisis alone. But together there is hope for better relationship-centered solutions that enable every child to learn and thrive.

We cannot simply say "provide children with better relationships" without addressing the systemic issues at the root of relational deprivation. By highlighting promising solutions, my hope is to spark more innovations to drive system change that prioritizes relationships during the prenatal period, the early years, and throughout childhood. In writing about the many relational innovations underway globally, I came to see that we stand on the brink of reimagining kinship for our future generations as evolving family dynamics, new science and technology, and growing intergenerational unity enhance the exchange of wisdom, resources, and values, reinforcing bonds and mutual understanding between the ages.

The love of learning and the need to love and be loved are not just parallel lines in the human narrative. They are, in fact, interlaced strands that form the very fabric of our growth and development. To thrive in a world that is in constant flux, a love of learning guides us through uncharted territories, igniting our curiosity and fueling our journey toward innovation. And this flame of learning is kindled and sustained by the loving and nurturing relationships we receive from those around us. It is by being loved that we find the gift of connection, the capacity to engage, the courage to question, the strength to persevere, and the freedom to imagine.

In a world that yearns for renewal, may we all be learners, may we all love and be loved, and may we all discover the power that lies in the union of both.

This is merely the opening salvo. Let's craft a bright future of learning for our next generation, a bright relational future for all, together.

ACKNOWLEDGMENTS

This book is a testament to the power of relationships and the profound impact they have on our lives. It is with deep gratitude and appreciation that I acknowledge the many individuals and communities who have supported and inspired this work. It takes a village to raise a child. It also takes a village to deliver a book. Here is to my incredible "book village."

To my family, whose unwavering love and encouragement have been my bedrock, thank you for nurturing my curiosity and passion for learning. Your belief in me is the driving force behind this journey. To Peter, the love of my life, your constant support and love have been my greatest source of strength. Your critical role in reviewing countless versions of the manuscript, offering insightful feedback and unwavering encouragement, has been indispensable in shaping this book. To my daughter Olivia, a talented writer and designer in her own right, thank you for reviewing countless early versions and for building the website that brings this vision to the world. And to Sophia, watching you grow up to be the beautiful, smart, and articulate young woman you are today is the inspiration that fuels my passion and commitment to this work.

To my parents and in-laws, your love and wisdom have shaped who I am today. Your support has been invaluable throughout this journey.

Thank you, Papa, for translating to Mom every word of this book into French.

Coming from a lineage of educators, I am deeply honored to carry forward this tradition. A special note of gratitude to my mom and to my sister Florence, a veteran early childhood teacher, who have each received the Palmes Académiques, the highest distinction in education in France, for their work in education. Your remarkable achievements and dedication to the field are a source of immense pride and inspiration. Your contributions to education have profoundly impacted countless lives, and your legacy will continue to inspire future generations. In loving memory of my grandparents, who were dedicated teachers and whose legacy lives on through this work. Their passion as educators and commitment to nurturing young minds have deeply influenced me and inspired this book. Thank you to my brother Antoine, whose sense of humor always keeps me going with optimism and a smile.

To my book's "board of directors," Carol Carter, Betsy Corcoran, Steven Dow, Luis Duarte, Ellen Galinsky, Derrick Johnson, Martha Kanter, Amy Klement, Anne Mosle, Michel Levine, Joan Lombardi, Linda Roberts, and Marjorie Sims, thank you for your unwavering support and guidance. Your strategic insights and steadfast commitment have been crucial in shaping the direction of this book and ensuring its success.

To my early readers, Kate Jerome, Victoria Dimitrakopoulos, and Jenn Clark, who catalyzed new ideas, your feedback and reflections were instrumental in refining the concepts and arguments presented in this book. Your enthusiasm and supportive critical perspectives have made this work richer and more impactful.

To my twenty-year-old and still-going book club, to my colleagues at Stanford University, and to my friends and partners in the education field, whose insights and wisdom have enriched this book, thank you for your invaluable contributions. Your dedication to the field of education and your commitment to nurturing the potential within every child have been a constant source of inspiration.

Acknowledgments

To my publishers at PublicAffairs/Hachette Book Group, Clive Priddle and Lara Heimert, who believed in this vision from the start and offered unwavering support throughout the process, thank you for helping bring this book to life. To the PublicAffairs/Hachette Book Group team, including Anupama Roy-Chaudhury, Shena Redmond, Brieana Garcia, Jenny Lee, Liz Wetzel, and Kelley Blewster, thank you for supporting me. To my agent extraordinaire, Jill Marsal at Marsal Lyon Literary Agency, who shaped every step of this project. To my editor, Lisa Kauffman, for partnering on every detail and helping bring this vision to life. Your expertise and dedication have been invaluable.

To Amy Klement, Ashley Beckner, Vinice Davis, Luis Duarte, Enyi Okebugwu, and the team at Imaginable Futures, and to Pam and Pierre Omidyar, who generously sponsored me to start this project and guided me throughout, your belief in my vision and your support were pivotal in bringing this book to life. Thank you for your trust and encouragement.

To the edupreneurs, advocates, and innovators who are tirelessly working to transform education, your pioneering spirit and dedication are a source of great inspiration. Your efforts are paving the way for a future where learning is more inclusive, innovative, and impactful.

To the educators, parents, grandparents, and caregivers, who tirelessly devote themselves to the growth and development of young minds, this book is for you. Your work is a labor of love, and it is through your hands that the seeds of future generations are sown. Thank you for your relentless dedication and for believing in the transformative power of relationships.

To the children, whose boundless curiosity and joy remind us of the wonder and potential of the early years, thank you for being the heart of this work. You inspire me to imagine a future where learning is a joyous and relational journey, and where every child is given the opportunity to thrive.

Finally, to all the readers, thank you for embarking on this journey with me. It is my hope that this book inspires you to imagine, innovate, and prioritize love and relationships in your own lives and work. Together we can unlock the potential that lies within each of us and create a future where learning is truly transformative. Together, this is just the beginning.

With heartfelt gratitude and boundless inspiration,
Isabelle C. Hau

RESOURCES

Here is a list of organizations referred to in the book.

23andme www.23andme.com/
55places www55places.com/
Abu Dhabi Early Childhood Authority https://eca.gov.ae/
Algebra Project https://algebra.org/wp/
All Our Kin https://allourkin.org/
Along www.along.org/
Amoofy www.amoofy.com/
Basics Boston https://thebasicsboston.org/our-story/
Bedtime Math https://bedtimemath.org/
Berea Pre-K Pirates www.berea.kyschools.us/schools-1/preschool
Big Brother, Big Sister www.bbbs.org/
Bing Nursery School https://bingschool.stanford.edu/
Bright Horizons www.brighthorizons.com/
Brightwheel https://mybrightwheel.com/
Briya Public Charter School https://briya.org/
California Forever https://eastsolanoplan.com/
Caribu https://caribu.com/
Centering Healthcare Institute https://centeringhealthcare.org/
Character.ai https://character.ai/
Chile Crece Contigo www.crececontigo.gob.cl
CK-12 Foundation's Flexi www.ck12.org/flexi/subjects/
Climate of Healthy Interactions for Learning & Development (CHILD) https://
    socialemotionalchild.org/
CoAbode www.coabode.org/
Cohousing Research Network www.cohousingresearchnetwork.org
Coliving.org www.coliving.org
Common www.common.com/

Compass Family Services www.compass-sf.org/

DataDrive2030 https://datadrive2030.co.za/about/

De Cero a Siempre https://deceroasiempreterritorial.icbf.gov.co/

Early Learning Ventures www.earlylearningventures.org/

Early Relational Heath Screen (ERHS) www.allianceaimh.org/early-relational-health-screen

Early Start Denver Model (ESDM) www.esdm.co/

Eldera.ai www.eldera.ai/

Ello www.ello.com/

Everyone Mentors LA Initiative www.lausd.org/everyonementors

Experience Corps www.aarp.org/experience-corps/our-impact/

Family Hubs Network https://familyhubsnetwork.com/

The Fatherhood Project https://thefatherhoodproject.org/

For Oak Cliff www.foroakcliff.org/

Friends of Children with Special Needs https://fcsn1996.org/

FrogSong www.cotaticohousing.org/

Generation Hope www.generationhope.org/

Generation Xchange (GenX) www.uclahealth.org/departments/medicine/geriatrics/research
/generation-xchange-genx

Goal Mama (app information) https://hopelab.org/case-study/goal-mama/

Google Glass or Autism Glass Project https://autismglass.stanford.edu/

Google ReadAlong https://readalong.google.com/

Guardians Collective www.aboutgc.com/

Harlem Children's Zone https://hcz.org/

High 5s Project www.mdrc.org/work/projects/high-5s-project

The Incredible Years www.incredibleyears.com/

Innovation Edge https://innovationedge.org.za/

The Intergenerational Learning Center www.providence.org/locations/wa/mount-st-vincent
/facility-profile/intergenerational-learning-center

Jeremiah Program https://jeremiahprogram.org/

KABOOM! https://kaboom.org/

Kaleidoscope Play & Learn www.brightspark.org/kaleidoscope-play-and-learn/

Kampung Admiralty www.archdaily.com/904646/kampung-admiralty-woha

Ka Paʻalana https://pidf.org/kapaalana/

Khan Academy Khanmigo www.khanmigo.ai/

Khan Academy Kids https://learn.khanacademy.org/khan-academy-kids/

Kidogo www.kidogo.co/

LENA www.lena.org/

Lennar www.lennar.com/

LitLab www.litlab.ai/

Live Better U https://corporate.walmart.com/about/working-at-walmart/live-better-u

Lively Minds www.livelyminds.org/

Lourie Center www.louriecenter.org/LC/

MathTalk www.math-talk.com

Math Trail www.cambridgema.gov/STEAM/MathTrail

Resources

Microsoft ReadingCoach https://coach.microsoft.com/

Minnesota Early Learning Scholarships https://education.mn.gov/MDE/dse/early/elprog
/sch/

Minnie https://robotics.wisc.edu/robots/minnie/

Modfamily https://modfamily.com/

Moxie https://moxierobot.com/

National Family Support Network www.nationalfamilysupportnetwork.org/family
-support-programs

NAO Robot www.aldebaran.com/en/nao

NEOM www.neom.com/en-us/about

Nurse Family Partnership www.nursefamilypartnership.org/

Outdoor Afro https://outdoorafro.org/

Paradot.ai www.paradot.ai/

Parent Support Network of Rhode Island https://psnri.org/

Peanut www.peanut-app.io/

PEPS www.peps.org/

Play Everywhere https://kaboom.org/grants/play-everywhere-design-challenge

Playful Learning Landscapes https://playfullearninglandscapes.com/

Playful Learning Landscapes Supermarket Speak https://playfullearninglandscapes.com
/project/supermarket-speak/

The Primary School www.theprimaryschool.org/

Promise Venture Studio www.promisestudio.org/

Ready4K, a product of ParentPowered https://parentpowered.com/

Replika.ai https://replika.ai/

Right to Play https://righttoplayusa.org/en/impact/

Roots of Empathy https://us.rootsofempathy.org/

The Senior List www.theseniorlist.com

Sesame Workshop's Welcome Sesame Program (for refugees) https://sesameworkshop.org
/our-work/impact-areas/support-for-families-affected-by-crisis/

SmartStart https://smartstart.org.za/

Soul Machines www.soulmachines.com/

Sown to Grow www.sowntogrow.com/

St. Ann Center for Intergenerational Care https://stanncenter.org/

Story Corps https://storycorps.org/

Synapse School www.synapseschool.org/

TACA https://tacanow.org/family-resources/self-care-for-parents-ofchildren-with-autism/

Tangelo Park Program www.rosengivesback.com/providing-hope-through-education
/tangelo-park-program/

Tega Robot www.media.mit.edu/projects/tega-a-new-robot-platform-for-long-term
-interaction/overview/

ThinkEqual https://thinkequal.org/

TimeBanks.org https://timebanks.org/

Tinkergarten www2.tinkergarten.com/

Tiny Totos www.tinytotos.com/

Tobii Eye Tracking www.tobii.com/
Toll Brothers www.tollbrothers.com/
Tools of the Mind www.toolsofthemind.org/
TOOTRiS https://tootris.com/
TrainingGrounds WePlay www.mytraininggrounds.org/we-play
Treehouse Foundation www.treehousefoundation.net/
Tūtū and Me https://pidf.org/tutuandme/
UpTogether www.uptogether.org/
Upwards (formerly WeeCare) https://upwards.com/
Village to Village Network www.vtvnetwork.org/
Vivvi https://vivvi.com/
WeLive https://coliving.com/company/welive
Wildflower Montessori www.wildflowerschools.org/our-beliefs
Winnie https://winnie.com/
Wonderschool www.wonderschool.com/corp/

NOTES

Introduction. Planting the Seeds of Connection

1. Garner, A., and Yogman, M., "Preventing Childhood Toxic Stress: Partnering with Families and Communities to Promote Relational Health," *Pediatrics* 148, no. 2 (2021), https://doi.org/10.1542/peds.2021-052582.

2. Office of the Surgeon General, *Our Epidemic of Loneliness and Isolation: The US Surgeon General's Advisory on the Healing Effects of Social Connection and Community* (US Department of Health and Human Services, 2023), https://pubmed.ncbi.nlm.nih.gov/37792968/.

3. America's Promise Alliance, *Every Child, Every Promise: Turning Failure into Action* (2006), https://eric.ed.gov/?id=ED505358.

4. Margolius, M., Doyle Lynch, A., Hynes, M., Flanagan, S., and Pufall Jones, E., *What Drives Learning: Young People's Perspectives on the Importance of Relationships, Belonging, and Agency* (Center for Promise, 2020), https://files.eric.ed.gov/fulltext/ED617364.pdf.

5. Dumitriu, D., "Life-Long Negative Impacts of COVID-19 on Mother-Infant Outcomes," Early Childhood Funder Collaborative, March 18, 2021, www.youtube.com/watch?v=GVrXdC4FP1w.

6. "Time Spent in Leisure and Sports Activities, 2022," US Bureau of Labor Statistics, July 7, 2023, www.bls.gov/opub/ted/2023/time-spent-in-leisure-and-sports-activities-2022.htm; "American Time Use Survey—2012 Results," news release, US Bureau of Labor Statistics, June 20, 2013, www.bls.gov/news.release/archives/atus_06202013.pdf.

7. Press Association, "Children Spend Only Half as Much Time Playing Outside as Their Parents Did," *The Guardian*, July 27, 2016, www.theguardian.com/environment/2016/jul/27/children-spend-only-half-the-time-playing-outside-as-their-parents-did.

8. Twenge, J. M., Haidt, J., Blake, A. B., McAllister, C., Lemon, H., and Le Roy, A., "Worldwide Increases in Adolescent Loneliness," *Journal of Adolescence* 93 (2021): 257–269, https://doi.org/10.1016/j.adolescence.2021.06.006.

9. Goodwin Cartwright, B. M., Smits, P. D., Stewart, S., Rodriguez, P. J., Gratzl, S., Baker, C., and Stucky, N., "Time-Series Analysis of First-Time Pediatric Speech Delays from 2018 to 2022," *JAMA Pediatrics* 178, no. 2 (2024), https://doi.org/10.1001/jamapediatrics.2023.5226.

10. Gotlib, I. H., Miller, J. G., Borchers, L. R., Coury, S. M., Costello, L. A., Garcia, J. M., and Ho, T. C., "Effects of the COVID-19 Pandemic on Mental Health and Brain Maturation in Adolescents: Implications for Analyzing Longitudinal Data," *Biological Psychiatry Global Open Science* 3, no. 4 (2023): 912–918, advance online publication, https://doi.org/10.1016/j.bpsgos.2022.11.002.

11. Dworak, E. M., Revelle, W., and Condon, D. M., "Looking for Flynn Effects in a Recent Online U.S. Adult Sample: Examining Shifts Within the SAPA Project," *Intelligence* 98 (2023), article 101734, https://doi.org/10.1016/j.intell.2023.101734; Dutton, E., van der Linden, D., and Lynn, R., "The Negative Flynn Effect: A Systematic Literature Review," *Intelligence* 59 (2016): 163–169, https://doi.org/10.1016/j.intell.2016.10.002; Pietschnig, J., and Gittler, G., "A Reversal of the Flynn Effect for Spatial Perception in German-Speaking Countries: Evidence from a Cross-Temporal IRT-Based Meta-Analysis (1977–2014)," *Intelligence* 53 (2015): 145–153, https://doi.org/10.1016/j.intell.2015.10.004; Sundet, J. M., Barlaug, D. G., and Torjussen, T. M., "The End of the Flynn Effect? A Study of Secular Trends in Mean Intelligence Test Scores of Norwegian Conscripts During Half a Century," *Intelligence* 32, no. 4 (2004): 349–362, https://doi.org/10.1016/j.intell.2004.06.004; Bratsberg, B., and Rogeberg, O., "Flynn Effect and Its Reversal Are Both Environmentally Caused," *Proceedings of the National Academy of Sciences of the United States of America* 115, no. 26 (2018): 6674–6678, https://doi.org/10.1073/pnas.1718793115; Amundsen, B., "Our IQ Is Steadily Declining. Should You Be Worried?," *ScienceNorway.no,* April 4, 2023, www.sciencenorway.no/health-intelligence-iq/our-iq-is-steadily-declining/2180595.

12. Shen-Berro, J., "Student Behavior Remains Concerning Among COVID's Impact, Educators Say," Chalkbeat, March 7, 2023, www.chalkbeat.org/2023/3/7/23628032/student-behavior-covid-school-classroom-survey/.

13. Dumitru, O., "How Are Teachers Changing Their Students' Lives?," August 22, 2022, YouGov, https://today.yougov.com/society/articles/43501-how-teachers-changing-their-students-lives-poll.

14. van Dyck, L. I., and Morrow, E. M., "Genetic Control of Postnatal Human Brain Growth," *Current Opinion in Neurology* 30, no. 1 (2017): 114–124, https://doi.org/10.1097/WCO.0000000000000405.

15. Paschall, K., and Moore K. A., "National Outcome Measure of Healthy and Ready to Learn," Child Trends, November 7, 2018, https://cms.childtrends.org/project/national-outcome-measure-healthy-ready-to-learn.

16. UNICEF, "175 Million Children Are Not Enrolled in Pre-Primary Education" (press release), April 9, 2019, https://tinyurl.com/4azbhk65.

17. Hau, I. "Education Has Been Hammering the Wrong Nail. We Have to Focus on the Early Years," *EdSurge,* December 21, 2021, https://www.edsurge.com/news/2021-12-21-education-has-been-hammering-the-wrong-nail-we-have-to-focus-on-the-early-years; Reich, R., "Class 13: 'Reducing Inequities in Education,'" UC Berkeley, YouTube video, 2022, https://youtube/W9rtmYxwvD0.

18. Pritzker, J. B., Bradach, J. L., and Kaufman, K., *Achieving Kindergarten Readiness for All Our Children: A Funder's Guide to Early Childhood Development from Birth to Five* (Bridgespan Group and Pritzker Children's Initiative, 2015), www.bridgespan.org/getmedia/c7b49388-b3b3-4e31-999d-91f0749cf5e1/early-childhood-funder-guide-2015.pdf.

19. See Love Quotient website, accessed June 15, 2024, https://thelovequotient.org/.

Part I. The Early Childhood Relational Crisis

Chapter 1. The Predictive Value of Early Relationships

1. William T. Grant Foundation website, accessed June 17, 2024, https://wtgrantfoundation.org/about/history.

2. Harvard Study of Adult Development website, accessed June 17, 2024, www.adultdevelopmentstudy.org/.

3. Waldinger, R., "What Makes a Good Life? Lessons from the Longest Study on Happiness" (video), TEDxBeaconStreet, November 2015, www.ted.com/talks/robert_waldinger_what_makes_a_good_life_lessons_from_the_longest_study_on_happiness?language=en; Waldinger, R., and Schulz, M., *The Good Life: Lessons from the World's Longest Scientific Study of Happiness* (New York: Simon and Schuster, 2023).

4. Vaillant, G., "Happiness Is Love: Full Stop," Harvard Medical School and Brigham and Women's Hospital, 2013, www.duodecim.fi/xmedia/duo/pilli/duo99210x.pdf.

5. Werner, E. E., and Smith, R. S., "An Epidemiologic Perspective on Some Antecedents and Consequences of Childhood Mental Health Problems and Learning Disabilities: A Report from the Kauai Longitudinal Study," *Journal of the American Academy of Child Psychiatry* 18, no. 2 (1979): 292–306; Werner, E., "Resilience and Recovery: Findings from the Kauai Longitudinal Study," *Research, Policy, and Practice in Children's Mental Health* 19, no. 1 (2005): 11–14, www.pathwaysrtc.pdx.edu/pdf/fpS0504.pdf.

6. "Public Spending on Childcare and Early Education," OECD Family Database, February 2023, www.oecd.org/els/soc/PF3_1_Public_spending_on_childcare_and_early_education.pdf. OECD countries spent on average 0.8 percent of GDP on early childhood and care in 2019; the US spent 0.3 percent of GDP on early childhood and care in 2019. Lawrence, S., and Fine, M., *Trends in Education Philanthropy: Benchmarking 2018–19* (Grantmakers for Education, February 2019), https://files.eric.ed.gov/fulltext/ED595154.pdf. Funding for early learning is 4 percent of the share of grant dollars as part of 2018 funding for early learning/elementary/secondary education and postsecondary education (page 5).

7. LENA website, accessed June 17, 2024, www.lena.org.

8. Gilkerson, J., *Inside Early Talk* (LENA, 2020), https://3975639.fs1.hubspotusercontent-na1.net/hubfs/3975639/03.%20Backgrounders/Inside%20Early%20Talk_20210303.pdf.

9. Gilkerson, J., Richards, J. A., Warren, S. F., Oller, D. K., Russo, R., and Vohr, B., "Language Experience in the Second Year of Life and Language Outcomes in Late Childhood," *Pediatrics* 142, no. 4 (2018), https://doi.org/10.1542/peds.2017-4276.

10. Richards, J. A., Gilkerson, J., Xu, D., and Topping, K., "How Much Do Parents Think They Talk to Their Child?," *Journal of Early Intervention* 39, no. 3 (2017): 163–179, https://doi.org/10.1177/1053815117714567.

11. "National Parent Survey Overview and Key Insights," Zero to Three, June 6, 2016, www.zerotothree.org/resource/national-parent-survey-overview-and-key-insights/.

12. McLean, C., Austin, L. J. E., Whitebook, M., and Olson, K. L., *Early Childhood Workforce Index 2020* (Center for the Study of Child Care Employment, 2021), https://cscce.berkeley.edu/workforce-index-2020/report-pdf/.

13. Pfitzer, S., interview with Shonkoff, J., "Serve and Return: Supporting the Foundation," *The Brain Architects* podcast, 2019, https://developingchild.harvard.edu/resources/the-brain-architects-podcast-serve-and-return-supporting-the-foundation/.

14. "Family Engagement and School Readiness," Administration for Children and Families, 2018, https://eclkc.ohs.acf.hhs.gov/sites/default/files/pdf/rtp-school-readiness.pdf.

15. Sawhill, I. V., Winship, S., and Searle Grannis, K., *Pathways to the Middle Class: Balancing Personal and Public Responsibilities* (Center on Children and Families at the Brookings Institution, September 20, 2012), 8.

16. Children participating in high-quality early learning programs have higher graduation rates: "Lifelong Gains," First Five Years Fund, accessed June 17, 2024, www.ffyf.org/by-topic/lifelong-gains/; Gray-Lobe, G., Pathak, P. A., Walters, C. R., "The Long-Term Effects of Universal Preschool in Boston" (NBER Working Paper 28756, May 2021), www.nber.org/system/files/working_papers/w28756/w28756.pdf; Bailey, M., Sun S., Timpe, B. D., "Prep School for Poor Kids: The Long-Run Impacts of Head Start on Human Capital and Economic Self-Sufficiency," (NBER Working Paper 28268, December 2020), www.nber.org/system/files/working_papers/w28268/w28268.pdf.

Adults who had quality early childhood education are more likely to be employed full-time, own a home, and have a savings account: Campbell, F. A., Ramey, C. T., Pungello, E., Sparling, J., and Miller-Johnson, S., "Early Childhood Education: Young Adult Outcomes from the Abecedarian Project," *Applied Developmental Science* 6, no. 1 (2002), https://doi.org/10.1207/S1532480XADS0601_05.

Adults who participated in high-quality early education programs as children, like Head Start, saw long-term health benefits, including reduced rates of depression, alcohol and tobacco use, and cardiovascular disease: Hoagland, C., Fumia, D., and Reynolds, M., *Early Childhood Education for Low-Income Students: A Review of the Evidence and Benefit-Cost Analysis* (Washington State Institute for Public Policy, 2019), www.wsipp.wa.gov/ReportFile/1547/Wsipp_Early-Childhood-Education-for-Low-Income-Students-A-Review-of-the-Evidence-and-Benefit-Cost-Analysis_Full-Report.pdf.

Early social experiences can influence adult behavior in romantic relationships: Simpson, J. A., Collins, W. A., Tran, S., and Haydon, K. C., "Attachment and the Experience and Expression of Emotions in Romantic Relationships: A Developmental Perspective," *Journal of Personality and Social Psychology* 92, no. 2 (2007), https://doi.org/10.1037/0022-3514.92.2.355; Rauer, A. J., Pettit, G. S., Lansford, J. E., Bates, J. E., and Dodge, K. A., "Romantic Relationship Patterns in Young Adulthood and Their Developmental Antecedents," *Developmental Psychology* 49, no. 11 (2013), https://doi.org/10.1037/a0031845; Crouter, A. C., and Booth, A., *Romance and Sex in Adolescence and Emerging Adulthood: Risks and Opportunities* (London: Psychology Press, 2014).

17. Kuhl, P. K., "Brain Mechanisms in Early Language Acquisition," *Neuron* 67, no. 5 (2010), https://doi.org/10.1016/j.neuron.2010.08.038.

18. Kuhl, P. K., "The Linguistic Genius of Babies" (video), TEDxRainier, October 2010, www.ted.com/talks/patricia_kuhl_the_linguistic_genius_of_babies?language=en.

19. Kuhl, P. K., "Early Language Learning and Literacy: Neuroscience Implications for Education," *Mind, Brain and Education* 5, no. 3 (2011), https://doi.org/10.1111/j.1751-228X.2011.01121.x.

20. Kuhl, "Brain Mechanisms in Early Language Acquisition."

21. Kuhl, P. K., Tsao, F. M., and Liu, H. M., "Foreign-Language Experience in Infancy: Effects of Short-Term Exposure and Social Interaction on Phonetic Learning," *Proceedings of the National Academy of Sciences of the United States of America* 100, no. 15 (2003), https://doi.org/10.1073/pnas.1532872100.

22. Friederici, A. D., Friedrich, M., and Christophe, A., "Brain Responses in 4-Month-Old Infants Are Already Language Specific," *Current Biology* 17, no. 14 (2007), https://doi.org/10.1016/j.cub.2007.06.011.

23. Schaadt, G., Zsido, R. G., Villringer, A., Obrig, H., Männel, C., and Sacher, J., "Association of Postpartum Maternal Mood with Infant Speech Perception at 2 and 6.5 Months of Age," *JAMA Network Open* 5, no. 9 (2022), https://doi.org/10.1001/jamanetworkopen.2022.32672; Fernald, A., "Approval and Disapproval: Infant Responsiveness to Vocal Affect in Familiar and Unfamiliar Languages," *Child Development* 64, no. 3 (1993), https://doi.org/10.2307/1131209.

24. Izard, V., Sann, C., Spelke, E. S., and Streri, A., "Newborn Infants Perceive Abstract Numbers," *Proceedings of the National Academy of Sciences of the United States of America* 106, no. 25 (2009), https://doi.org/10.1073/pnas.0812142106; Beck, J., and Clarke, S., "Babies Are Born with an Innate Number Sense," *Scientific American*, March 1, 2021, www.scientificamerican.com/article/babies-are-born-with-an-innate-number-sense/.

25. Gilmore, C. K., McCarthy, S. E., and Spelke, E. S., "Symbolic Arithmetic Knowledge Without Instruction," *Nature* 447, no. 7144 (2007), https://doi.org/10.1038/nature05850.

26. Bedtime Math website, accessed June 17, 2024, https://bedtimemath.org/.

27. Berkowitz, T., Schaeffer, M. W., Maloney, E. A., Peterson, L., Gregor, C., Levine, S. C., and Beilock, S. L., "Math at Home Adds Up to Achievement in School," *Science* 350, no. 6257 (2015), https://doi.org/10.1126/science.aac7427; Schaeffer, M. W., Rozek, C. S., Berkowitz, T., Levine, S. C., and Beilock, S. L., "Disassociating the Relation Between Parents' Math Anxiety and Children's Math Achievement: Long-Term Effects of a Math App Intervention," *Journal of Experimental Psychology* 147, no. 12 (2018), https://doi.org/10.1037/xge0000490.

28. High 5s project website, accessed June 17, 2024, www.mdrc.org/work/projects/high-5s-project.

29. Mattera, S., Tepper Jacob, R., MacDowell, C., and Morris, P., "Long-Term Effects of Enhanced Early Childhood Math Instruction," MDRC, December 2021, www.mdrc.org/work/publications/long-term-effects-enhanced-early-childhood-math-instruction; Guest, G., "Math Games: High 5s Program Brings the 'Math Out of Play,'" *Michigan News*, April 11, 2022, https://news.umich.edu/math-games-high-5s-program-brings-the-math-out-of-play/.

30. Durand, V. N., Loe, I. M., Yeatman, J. D., and Feldman, H. M., "Effects of Early Language, Speech, and Cognition on Later Reading: A Mediation Analysis," *Frontiers in Psychology* 4, no. 586 (2013), https://doi.org/10.3389/fpsyg.2013.00586.

31. Lieberman, M. D., *Social: Why Our Brains Are Wired to Connect* (Oxford, UK: Oxford University Press, 2013).

32. "Child Abuse and Neglect Prevention," CDC, May 16, 2024, www.cdc.gov/child-abuse-neglect/about/index.html.

33. "Child Maltreatment," World Health Organization, September 19, 2022, www.who
.int/news-room/fact-sheets/detail/child-maltreatment.

34. "National Statistics on Child Abuse," National Children's Alliance, accessed August
6, 2024, www.nationalchildrensalliance.org/media-room/national-statistics-on-child-abuse.
National child abuse statistics are cited from US Administration for Children and Families,
Child Maltreatment 2022. These data, released annually, are the most current federal data available. The annual reports are available at www.acf.hhs.gov/cb/data-research/child-maltreatment.

35. Wang, L., Liang, W., Zhang, S., Jonsson, L., Li, M., Yu, C., Sun, Y., Ma, Q., Bai, Y.,
Abbey, C., and Luo, R., "Are Infant/Toddler Developmental Delays a Problem Across Rural
China?," *Journal of Comparative Economics* 47, no. 2 (2019): 458–469.

36. Graham, B., "Bob Graham on Uncovering the Plight of Romanian Orphans,
31 Years Ago," *Telegraph Magazine*, 2021, www.pressreader.com/uk/the-daily-telegraph
-telegraph-magazine/20210102/282437056736262.

37. Koch, C., "Does Brain Size Matter?," *Scientific American*, January 1, 2016, www
.scientificamerican.com/article/does-brain-size-matter1/.

38. Fox, N. A., Almas, A. N., Degnan, K. A., Nelson, C. A., and Zeanah, C. H., "The
Effects of Severe Psychosocial Deprivation and Foster Care Intervention on Cognitive Development at 8 Years of Age: Findings from the Bucharest Early Intervention Project," *Journal of Child Psychology and Psychiatry, and Allied Disciplines* 52, no. 9 (2011), https://doi
.org/10.1111/j.1469-7610.2010.02355.x.

39. Fay Greene, M., "30 Years Ago, Romania Deprived Thousands of Babies of Human
Contact. Here's What's Become of Them," *The Atlantic*, July/August 2020, www.theatlantic
.com/magazine/archive/2020/07/can-an-unloved-child-learn-to-love/612253/.

40. Davis, N., "Severe Childhood Deprivation Reduces Brain Size, Study Finds,"
The Guardian, January 6, 2020, www.theguardian.com/science/2020/jan/06/severe-childhood
-deprivation-reduces-brain-size-study-finds.

41. Bucharest Early Intervention Project website and list of publications, accessed June
17, 2024, www.bucharestearlyinterventionproject.org/publications.

42. Bakermans-Kranenburg, M. J., Steele, H., Zeanah, C. H., Muhamedrahimov, R. J.,
Vorria, P., Dobrova-Krol, N. A., Steele, M., van IJzendoorn, M. H., Juffer, F., and Gunnar,
M. R., "Attachment and Emotional Development in Institutional Care: Characteristics and
Catch-Up," *Monographs of the Society for Research in Child Development* 76, no. 4 (2011),
https://doi.org/10.1111/j.1540-5834.2011.00628.x.

43. Luby, J. L., Barch, D. M., Belden, A., Gaffrey, M. S., Tillman, R., Babb, C., Nishino,
T., Suzuki, H., and Botteron, K. N., "Maternal Support in Early Childhood Predicts Larger
Hippocampal Volumes at School Age," *Proceedings of the National Academy of Sciences of the
United States of America* 109, no. 8 (2012): 2854–2859; Luby, J. L., Belden, A. C., Harms,
M. P., Tillman, R., and Barch, D. M., "Preschool Is a Sensitive Period for the Influence of
Maternal Support on the Trajectory of Hippocampal Development," *Proceedings of the
National Academy of Sciences* 113 (2016): 5742–5747.

44. Luby et al., "Maternal Support in Early Childhood Predicts Larger Hippocampal
Volumes."

45. Luby et al., "Preschool Is a Sensitive Period."

46. "A Father's Impact on Child Development," All4Kids, May 12, 2023, www.all4kids .org/news/blog/a-fathers-impact-on-child-development/; Fatherhood Project website, accessed June 17, 2024, https://thefatherhoodproject.org/.

47. "The Importance of Grandparents in Development," Motherhood Center, April 28, 2023, www.motherhoodcenter.com/the-importance-of-grandparents-in-development/.

48. Brody, B., "Want to Live Longer? Play with Your Grandkids. It's Good for Them Too," *Washington Post*, August 6, 2023, www.washingtonpost.com/wellness/2023/08/06 /children-grandparents-play-health-benefits/; Di Gessa, G., Glaser, K., and Tinker, A., "The Impact of Caring for Grandchildren on the Health of Grandparents in Europe: A Lifecourse Approach," *Social Science and Medicine* 152 (2016), https://doi.org/10.1016 /j.socscimed.2016.01.041.

49. Ramenzoni, V. C., and Liszkowski, U., "The Social Reach: 8-Month-Olds Reach for Unobtainable Objects in the Presence of Another Person," *Psychological Science* 27, no. 9 (2016), https://doi.org/10.1177/0956797616659938; Chase, C. C., Chin, D. B., Oppezzo, M. A., and Schwartz, D., "Teachable Agents and the Protégé Effect: Increasing the Effort Towards Learning," *Journal of Science Education and Technology* 18 (2009), https://doi.org/10.1007 /s10956-009-9180-4.

50. Sell, M. A., Ray, G. E., and Lovelace, L., "Preschool Children's Comprehension of a 'Sesame Street' Video Tape: The Effects of Repeated Viewing and Previewing Instructions," *Educational Technology Research and Development* 43, no. 3 (1995), www.jstor.org/stable/30221007.

51. Lytle, S. R., Garcia-Sierra, A., and Kuhl, P. K., "Two Are Better than One: Infant Language Learning from Video Improves in the Presence of Peers," *Proceedings of the National Academy of Sciences of the United States of America* 115, no. 40 (2018), https://doi.org/10.1073 /pnas.1611621115.

52. Bryk, A. S., "Organizing Schools for Improvement," *Phi Delta Kappan* 91, no. 7 (2010), https://doi.org/10.1177/003172171009100705.

53. Yale School of Medicine, Child Study Center, Comer School Development Program, https://medicine.yale.edu/childstudy/services/community-and-schools-programs/comer/; Stannard, E., "Comer Began Movement to Educate Whole Child in 1968," *New Haven Register*, November 26, 2018, https://www.nhregister.com/news/article/Comer-began-movement-to -educate-whole-child-in-13421830.php.

54. Roy, J., Maynard, M., and Weiss, E., *The Hidden Costs of the Housing Crisis* (Partnership for America's Economic Success, 2008), www.pewtrusts.org/-/media/legacy/uploadedfiles /wwwpewtrustsorg/reports/partnership_for_americas_economic_success/paeshousingreportfinal1 pdf.pdf.

55. Hanford, E., "Early Lessons, The Perry Preschool Changed Their Lives," *American Public Media* (2018), https://americanradioworks.publicradio.org/features/preschool/teachers.html.

56. Dunn, E. C., Nishimi, K., Powers, A., and Bradley, B., "Is Developmental Timing of Trauma Exposure Associated with Depressive and Post-Traumatic Stress Disorder Symptoms in Adulthood?," *Journal of Psychiatric Research* 84 (2017), https://doi.org/10.1016/j .jpsychires.2016.09.004.

57. Osofsky, H. J., Osofsky, J. D., Kronenberg, M., Brennan, A., and Hansel, T. C., "Posttraumatic Stress Symptoms in Children After Hurricane Katrina: Predicting the Need

for Mental Health Services," *American Journal of Orthopsychiatry* 79, no. 2 (2009), https://doi.org/10.1037/a0016179.

58. Perry, B. D., and Winfrey, O., *What Happened to You? Conversations on Trauma, Resilience, and Healing* (New York: Flatiron Books, 2021); Hambrick, E. P., Brawner, T. W., and Perry, B. D., "Timing of Early-Life Stress and the Development of Brain-Related Capacities," *Frontiers in Behavioral Neuroscience* 13 (2019), https://doi.org/10.3389/fnbeh.2019.00183.

59. Heckman, J., Garcia, J. L., Bennhoff, F., and Duncan Ermini L., "The Dynastic Benefits of Early Childhood Education" (Working Paper No. 2021-SSRN 77, Becker Friedman Institute for Economics, June 30, 2021), http://dx.doi.org/10.2139/ssrn.3877620.

60. Other inspirations for Head Start include the Peabody Experimental School, later renamed the Susan Gray School in Tennessee, and a program in New Haven, Connecticut, led by Jennette Galambos Stone.

61. Dixon, M. R., Paliliunas, D., Barron, B. F., Schmick, A. M., and Stanley, C. R., "Randomized Controlled Trial Evaluation of ABA Content on IQ Gains in Children with Autism," *Journal of Behavioral Education* (2019), http://doi.org/10.1007/s10864-019-09344-7.

62. Park, A., "Top 10 Medical Breakthroughs," *Time*, December 4, 2012, https://healthland.time.com/2012/12/04/top-10-health-lists/slide/hope-for-reversing-autism/.

63. Dawson, G., Rogers, S., Munson, J., Smith, M., Winter, J., Greenson, J., Donaldson, A., and Varley, J., "Randomized, Controlled Trial of an Intervention for Toddlers with Autism: The Early Start Denver Model," *Pediatrics* 125, no. 1 (2010), https://doi.org/10.1542/peds.2009-0958.

64. Holt, L. E., *The Care and Feeding of Children: A Catechism for the Use of Mothers and Children's Nurses* (New York, 1907; Project Gutenberg, 2005), www.gutenberg.org/files/15484/15484-h/15484-h.htm.

65. Watson, J. B., *Psychological Care of Infant and Child* (New York: W. W. Norton, 1928).

66. Bowlby, J., "Forty-Four Juvenile Thieves: Their Characters and Home-Life," *International Journal of Psychoanalysis* 25 (1944), https://psycnet.apa.org/record/1945-00751-001.

67. Ainsworth, M., Boston, M., Bowlby, J., and Rosenbluth, D., "The Effects of Mother-Child Separation: A Follow-up Study," *British Journal of Medical Psychology* 29 (1956), https://doi.org/10.1111/j.2044-8341.1956.tb00915.x.

68. Harlow, H. F., "The Nature of Love," *American Psychologist* 13 (1958), https://doi.org/10.1037/h0047884; Harlow, H. F., "Early Social Deprivation and Later Behavior in the Monkey," *Unfinished Tasks in the Behavioral Sciences*, ed. A. Abrams, H. H. Gurner, and J. E. P. Toman (Philadelphia: Lippincott Williams and Wilkins, 1964), 154–173.

69. Bowlby, J., *Maternal Care and Mental Health* (World Health Organization Monograph, Serial No. 2, 1951), 13.

70. Ainsworth, M. D., and Bell, S. M., "Attachment, Exploration, and Separation: Illustrated by the Behavior of One-Year-Olds in a Strange Situation," *Child Development* 41, no. 1 (1970), https://doi.org/10.2307/1127388.

71. Main, M., and Solomon, J., "Procedures for Identifying Infants as Disorganized/Disoriented During the Ainsworth Strange Situation," in *Attachment in the Preschool Years*, ed. M. T. Greenberg, D. Cicchetti, and E. M. Cummings (Chicago: University of Chicago Press, 1990), 121–160.

72. Wang, R., "The Influence of Attachment Styles on Academic Performance," *Proceedings of the 2021 4th International Conference on Humanities Education and Social Sciences (ICHESS 2021)*, 2021, www.atlantis-press.com/proceedings/ichess-21/125966960.

73. Madigan, S., Prime, H., Graham, S. A., Rodrigues, M., Anderson, N., Khoury, J., and Jenkins, J. M., "Parenting Behavior and Child Language: A Meta-analysis," *Pediatrics* 144, no. 4 (2019), https://doi.org/10.1542/peds.2018-3556.

74. Pong, S. L., Johnston, J., and Chen, V., "Authoritarian Parenting and Asian Adolescent School Performance: Insights from the US and Taiwan," *International Journal of Behavioral Development* 34, no. 1 (2010), https://doi.org/10.1177/0165025409345073.

75. Gershoff, E. T., and Font, S. A., "Corporal Punishment in U.S. Public Schools: Prevalence, Disparities in Use, and Status in State and Federal Policy," *Social Policy Report* 30, no. 1 (2016), www.ncbi.nlm.nih.gov/pmc/articles/PMC5766273/; Falcone, M., Quintero, D., and Valant, J., "Ending Corporal Punishment of Preschool-Age Children," Brookings Institution, October 20, 2020, www.brookings.edu/articles/ending-corporal-punishment-of-preschool-age-children/.

Chapter 2. Shrinking Networks

Epigraph: Margaret Mead's book *Culture and Commitment* originated from the Man and Nature lectures, which she delivered at the American Museum of Natural History in March 1969 in conjunction with the museum's centennial celebration.

1. Gagnet, M., dir., *Hikikomori: The Locked Generation* (film), Java Films, 2021, https://vimeo.com/ondemand/hikikomorilockedgen.

2. Yeung, J., and Karasawa, M., "Japan Was Already Grappling with Isolation and Loneliness. The Pandemic Made It Worse," CNN, February 7, 2023, https://tinyurl.com/zp2um7dt.

3. Eun Gong, S., "Social Isolation Takes a Toll on a Rising Number of South Korea's Young Adults," NPR, February 11, 2024, www.npr.org/2024/02/11/1229437757/social-isolation-south-korea.

4. Krieg, A., and Dickie, J. R., "Attachment and Hikikomori: A Psychosocial Developmental Model," *International Journal of Social Psychiatry* 59, no. 1 (2013), https://doi.org/10.1177/0020764011423182; Malagón-Amor, Á., Martín-López, L. M., Córcoles, D., González, A., Bellsolà, M., Teo, A. R., Bulbena, A., Pérez, V., and Bergé, D., "Family Features of Social Withdrawal Syndrome (Hikikomori)," *Frontiers in Psychiatry* 11, no. 138 (2020), https://doi.org/10.3389/fpsyt.2020.00138.

5. Pozza, A., Coluccia, A., Kato, T., Gaetani, M., and Ferretti, F., "The 'Hikikomori' Syndrome: Worldwide Prevalence and Co-Occurring Major Psychiatric Disorders: A Systematic Review and Meta-Analysis Protocol," *BMJ Open* 9, no. 9 (2019), https://doi.org/10.1136/bmjopen-2018-025213.

6. The Google search was inspired by the following report: Baskin, C., Gentry, E., Gillan, G., Hamamoto, B., English-Lueck, J., Maher, T., Mason, V., Rodgers, N., and Vian, K., *Families in Flux: Imagining the Next Generation of the American Family* (Institute for the Future, August 2020), https://familystoryproject.org/wp-content/uploads/2020/08/Families-in-Flux-Report.pdf.

7. Parker, K., Menasce Horowitz, J., Livingston, G., Wang, W., Stepler, R., Patten, E., López, G., Deane, C., Suh, M., Keegan, M., and Kramer, M., "The American Family Today," Pew Research Center, December 15, 2015, www.pewresearch.org/social-trends/2015/12/17/1-the-american-family-today; Aragão, C., Parker, K., Greenwood, S., Baronavski, C., and Carlo Mandapat, J., "The Modern American Family: Key Trends in Marriage and Family Life," Pew Research Center, September 14, 2023, www.pewresearch.org/social-trends/2023/09/14/the-modern-american-family/.

8. MassMutual, *2018 State of the American Family Study: Insights from African American Families—Executive Summary* (2018), www.massmutual.com/global/media/shared/doc/MC1133AA_09248MR-FINAl.pdf.

9. Fry, R., "The Number of People in the Average U.S. Household Is Going Up for the First Time in Over 160 Years," Pew Research Center, October 1, 2019, www.pewresearch.org/short-reads/2019/10/01/the-number-of-people-in-the-average-u-s-household-is-going-up-for-the-first-time-in-over-160-years/.

10. Alburez-Gutierrez, D., Williams, I., and Caswell, H., "Projections of Human Kinship for All Countries," *Proceedings of the National Academy of Sciences of the United States of America* 120, no. 52 (2023), https://doi.org/10.1073/pnas.2315722120.

11. Lee, J., and Kim, C., "In South Korea, World's Lowest Fertility Rate Plunges Again in 2023," Reuters, February 28, 2024, www.reuters.com/world/asia-pacific/south-koreas-fertility-rate-dropped-fresh-record-low-2023-2024-02-28/.

12. Mackenzie, J., "Why South Korean Women Aren't Having Babies," BBC, February 27, 2024, www.bbc.com/news/world-asia-68402139.

13. Kazmin, A., "Italy's Births Drop to Historic Low," *Financial Times*, March 29, 2024, www.ft.com/content/ad9c108f-32a6-4cb1-8394-fbad78864f4c.

14. Roser, M., "50 Years Ago the Average Woman Had Five Children; Since Then the Number Has Halved," Our World in Data, September 3, 2019, https://ourworldindata.org/global-fertility-has-halved.

15. Baranowska-Rataj, A., Styrc, M., and Chihaya da Silva, G., "The Impact of Family Size on Educational Attainment in Cross Country Comparative Perspective" (Population Association of America, 2015), https://paa2015.populationassociation.org/papers/151825.

16. Maralani, V., "The Changing Relationship Between Family Size and Educational Attainment over the Course of Socioeconomic Development: Evidence from Indonesia," *Demography* 45 (2008): 693–717; Rhodes, K. W., Orme, J. G., Cox, M. E., and Buehler, C., "Foster Family Resources, Psychosocial Functioning, and Retention," *Social Work Research* 27, no. 3 (2003): 135–150.

17. Merry, J., Bobbitt-Zeher, D., and Downey, D., "Number of Siblings in Childhood, Social Outcomes in Adulthood," *Journal of Family Issues* 41, no. 2 (2020), https://doi.org/10.1177/0192513x19873356.

18. Downey, D. B., and Condron, D. J., "Playing Well with Others in Kindergarten: The Benefit of Siblings at Home," *Journal of Marriage and Family* 66, no. 2 (2004), https://doi.org/10.1111/j.1741-3737.2004.00024.x.

19. Kramer, S., "U.S. Has World's Highest Rate of Children Living in Single-Parent Households," Pew Research Center, December 12, 2019, https://tinyurl.com/4kfcvxu6.

20. Livingston, G., and Parker, K., "Living Arrangements and Father Involvement," Pew Research Center, June 15, 2011, https://tinyurl.com/5amc6bjm.

21. Link, E., Watson, T., and Kalkat, S., "More Kids Are Living with Their Grandparents. Can Safety Net Policy Keep Up?," Brookings Institution, December 20, 2023, www.brookings.edu/articles/more-kids-are-living-with-their-grandparents-can-safety-net-policy-keep-up/.

22. Fry, R., "The Number of People in the Average U.S. Household Is Going Up for the First Time in 160 Years," Pew Research Center, October 10, 2019, www.pewresearch.org/short-reads/2019/10/01/the-number-of-people-in-the-average-u-s-household-is-going-up-for-the-first-time-in-over-160-years/.

23. David, P., and Nelson-Kakulla, B., "Grandparents Embrace Changing Attitudes and Technology," AARP, April 2019, www.aarp.org/research/topics/life/info-2019/aarp-grandparenting-study.html.

24. Cohn, D., Menasce Horowitz, J., Minkin, R., Fry. R., and Hurst, K., "The Demographics of Multigenerational Homes," Pew Research Center, March 24, 2022, www.pewresearch.org/social-trends/2022/03/24/the-demographics-of-multigenerational-households/.

25. McPherson, M., Smith-Lovin, L., and Cook, J. M., "Birds of a Feather: Homophily in Social Networks," *Annual Review of Sociology* 27, no. 1 (2001), https://doi.org/10.1146/annurev.soc.27.1.415.

26. Chopik, W. J., "Associations Among Relational Values, Support, Health, and Well-Being Across the Adult Lifespan," *Personal Relationships* 24, no. 2 (2017), https://doi.org/10.1111/pere.12187.

27. Cox, D. A., "The State of American Friendship: Change, Challenges, and Loss," Survey Center on American Life, June 8, 2021, www.americansurveycenter.org/research/the-state-of-american-friendship-change-challenges-and-loss/.

28. Gilbert, E., "Americans More than Ever Have No Friends. Here Are 5 Steps to Make More Friends," Big Think, April 15, 2023, https://bigthink.com/neuropsych/americans-no-friends/.

29. Bhattacharya, K., Ghosh, A., Monsivais, D., Dunbar, R. I. M., and Kaski, K., "Sex Differences in Social Focus Across the Life Cycle in Humans," *Royal Society Open Science* 3, no. 4 (2016), https://doi.org/10.1098/rsos.160097.

30. Tomova, L., Tye, K., and Saxe, R., "The Neuroscience of Unmet Social Needs," *Social Neuroscience* 16, no. 3 (2021), https://doi.org/10.1080/17470919.2019.1694580.

31. Schnall, S., Harber, K. D., Stefanucci, J. K., and Proffitt, D. R., "Social Support and the Perception of Geographical Slant," *Journal of Experimental Social Psychology* 44, no. 5 (2008), https://doi.org/10.1016/j.jesp.2008.04.011.

32. Kovacs, B., Caplan, N., Grob, S., and King, M., "Social Networks and Loneliness During the COVID-19 Pandemic," *Socius* 7 (2021), https://journals.sagepub.com/doi/10.1177/2378023120985254.

33. Kannan, V. D., and Veazie, P. J., "US Trends in Social Isolation, Social Engagement, and Companionship—Nationally and by Age, Sex, Race/Ethnicity, Family Income, and Work Hours, 2003–2020," *SSM—Population Health* 21 (2022), https://doi.org/10.1016/j.ssmph.2022.101331; "American Time Use Survey—2022 Results," news release, US Bureau of Labor Statistics, June 2023, www.bls.gov/news.release/pdf/atus.pdf.

34. Jones, D. E., Greenberg, M., and Crowley, M., "Early Social-Emotional Functioning and Public Health: The Relationship Between Kindergarten Social Competence and Future Wellness," *American Journal of Public Health* 105, no. 11 (2015), https://doi.org/10.2105/AJPH.2015.302630.

35. Wentzel, K. R., Barry, C. M., and Caldwell, K. A., "Friendships in Middle School: Influences on Motivation and School Adjustment," *Journal of Educational Psychology* 96, no. 2 (2004), https://doi.org/10.1037/0022-0663.96.2.195.

36. Burdette, H. L., and Whitaker, R. C., "Resurrecting Free Play in Young Children: Looking Beyond Fitness and Fatness to Attention, Affiliation, and Affect," *Archives of Pediatric and Adolescent Medicine* 159, no. 1 (2005), https://doi.org/10.1001/archpedi.159.1.46.

37. Jarrett., O. S., "Recess in Elementary School: What Does the Research Say?," ERIC Digest ED466331, 2002, www.isbe.net/Documents_IIRTF/recess_elem_school.pdf.

38. Hüttenmoser, M., "Children and Their Living Surroundings: Empirical Investigations into the Significance of Living Surroundings for the Everyday Life and Development of Children," *Children's Environments* 12, no. 4 (1995), www.jstor.org/stable/41514991.

39. Bassok, D., Latham, S., and Rorem, A., "Is Kindergarten the New First Grade?," *AERA Open* 2, no. 1 (2016), https://doi.org/10.1177/2332858415616358.

40. Pressman, R. M., Sugarman, D. B., Nemon, M. L., Desjarlais, J., Owens, J. A., and Schettini-Evans, A., "Homework and Family Stress: With Consideration of Parents' Self-Confidence, Educational Level, and Cultural Background," *American Journal of Family Therapy* 43, no. 4 (2015), https://doi.org/10.1080/01926187.2015.1061407.

41. Livingston, G., "The Way U.S. Teens Spend Their Time Is Changing, but Differences Between Boys and Girls Persist," Pew Research Center, February 20, 2019, https://tinyurl.com/2rrhcmbk.

42. Wenyu, S., "Chinese Students Spend Almost 3 Hours on Homework Daily, 3 Times the World Average," *People's Daily Online*, December 21, 2017, http://en.people.cn/n3/2017/1221/c90000-9307187.html.

43. Chen, X., Ke, Z. L., Chen, Y., and Lin, X., "The Prevalence of Sleep Problems Among Children in Mainland China: A Meta-Analysis and Systemic-Analysis," *Sleep Medicine* 83 (2021), https://doi.org/10.1016/j.sleep.2021.04.014.

44. Zeng, C. Q., Zhou, L. H., Zhang, P., Wang, J., Ye, M. H., Yi, B. X., Xiong, X. W., and Liang, X. C., "The Epidemiology of Myopia in Primary School Students of Grade 1 to 3 in Hubei Province," *Zhonghua yan ke za zhi* [Chinese journal of ophthalmology] 54, no. 10 (2018), https://doi.org/10.3760/cma.j.issn.0412-4081.2018.10.007; "The Overall Myopia Rate of Chinese Children and Adolescents Is 52.7%," Ministry of Education of the People's Republic of China, October 27, 2021, www.moe.gov.cn/fbh/live/2021/53799/mtbd/202110/t20211027_575366.html.

45. Barker, J. E., Semenov, A. D., Michaelson, L., Provan, L. S., Snyder, H. R., and Munakata, Y., "Less-Structured Time in Children's Daily Lives Predicts Self-Directed Executive Functioning," *Frontiers in Psychology* 5 (2014), https://doi.org/10.3389/fpsyg.2014.00593.

46. De Visé, D., "Teens Are Spending Less Time than Ever with Friends," *The Hill*, June 7, 2023, https://thehill.com/blogs/blog-briefing-room/4037619-teens-are-spending-less-time-than-ever-with-friends/.

47. Resnick, B., "22 Percent of Millennials Say They Have 'No Friends.' Loneliness Can Be Helpful, Unless It Becomes Chronic," *Vox*, August 1, 2019, www.vox.com/science-and-health/2019/8/1/20750047/millennials-poll-loneliness.

48. Tate Sullivan, E., "16,000 Shuttered Childcare Programs Push the Sector Closer to Collapse," *EdSurge*, February 11, 2022, www.edsurge.com/news/2022-02-11-16-000-shuttered-child-care-programs-push-the-sector-closer-to-collapse.

49. Mader, J., "A Wave of Childcare Center Closure Is Coming as Funding Dries Up," *Hechinger Report*, August 24, 2023, https://hechingerreport.org/a-wave-of-child-care-center-closures-is-coming-as-funding-dries-up/.

50. Miranda, B., "Higher Child-to-Staff Ratios Threaten the Quality of Childcare," Child Trends, June 15, 2017, www.childtrends.org/blog/higher-child-staff-ratios-threaten-quality-child-care.

51. Bassok, D., Markowitz, A. J., Bellows, L., and Sadowski, K., "New Evidence on Teacher Turnover in Early Childhood," *Educational Evaluation and Policy Analysis* 43, no. 1 (2021), https://doi.org/10.3102/0162373720985340.

52. Pilarz, A. R., and Hill, H. D., "Unstable and Multiple Childcare Arrangements and Young Children's Behavior," *Early Childhood Research Quarterly* 29, no. 4 (2014), https://doi.org/10.1016/j.ecresq.2014.05.007.

53. Saad, L., "Historically Low Faith in U.S. Institutions Continues," Gallup, July 6, 2023, https://news.gallup.com/poll/508169/historically-low-faith-institutions-continues.aspx.

54. Mumphrey, C., Lurye, S., and Stavely, Z., "Fewer Kids Are Enrolling in Kindergarten as Pandemic Fallout Lingers," *Hechinger Report*, December 20, 2023, https://hechingerreport.org/fewer-kids-are-enrolling-in-kindergarten-as-pandemic-fallout-lingers/.

55. "Homeschooled Children and Reasons for Homeschooling," *Condition of Education*, National Center for Education Statistics, 2022, https://nces.ed.gov/programs/coe/indicator/tgk.

56. Jones, A., and Terry Ellis, N., "'A Form of Resistance': More Black Families Are Choosing to Homeschool Their Children," CNN, March 1, 2023, www.cnn.com/2023/03/01/us/black-families-home-school-reaj/index.html.

57. Medlin, R. G., "Homeschooled Children's Social Skills," *Home School Researcher* 17, no. 1 (2006), https://files.eric.ed.gov/fulltext/ED573486.pdf.

58. Vice Chairman's Staff of the Joint Economic Committee, *What We Do Together: The State of Associational Life in America*, SCP Report, No. 1-17 (Social Capital Project, May 2017), www.lee.senate.gov/services/files/b5f224ce-98f7-40f6-a814-8602696714d8. Excerpts include:

Neighbors: "Between 1974 and 2016, the percent of adults who said they spend a social evening with a neighbor at least several times a week fell from 30 percent to 19 percent. Having children isn't related to stronger ties with neighbors."

Coworkers: "Between the mid-1970s and 2012, the average amount of time Americans between the ages of 25 and 54 spent with their coworkers outside the workplace fell from about two-and-a-half hours to just under one hour."

Volunteering: "The share of adults who said they had done any volunteering in the previous year is no lower today than it was in the early 1970s. One in four indicated they had volunteered in 1974 and in 2015." "Between 1974 and 2004, the share of Americans who participated in one of sixteen kinds of voluntary associations fell from 75 percent to 62 percent."

Church: "In the early 1970s, nearly seven in ten adults in America were still members of a church or synagogue. While fewer Americans attended religious service regularly, 50 to 57 percent did so at least once per month. Today, just 55 percent of adults are members of a church or synagogue, while just 42 to 44 percent attend religious service at least monthly."

Overall: "Between 1972 and 2016, the share of adults who thought most people could be trusted declined from 46 percent to 31 percent."

59. Meador, J., "The Misunderstood Reasons Millions of Americans Stopped Going to Church," *The Atlantic*, July 29, 2023, https://www.theatlantic.com/ideas/archive/2023/07/christian-church-communitiy-participation-drop/674843/.

60. Jones, J., "U.S. Church Membership Falls Below Majority for First Time," Gallup, March 29, 2021, https://news.gallup.com/poll/341963/church-membership-falls-below-majority-first-time.aspx.

61. "Atheism Doubles Among Generation Z," Barna, January 24, 2018, www.barna.com/research/atheism-doubles-among-generation-z/.

62. Chen, Y., and VanderWeele, T. J., "Associations of Religious Upbringing with Subsequent Health and Well-Being from Adolescence to Young Adulthood: An Outcome-Wide Analysis," *American Journal of Epidemiology* 187, no. 11 (2018), https://doi.org/10.1093/aje/kwy142; Horwitz, I. M., *God, Grades, and Graduation: Religion's Surprising Impact on Academic Success* (Oxford, UK: Oxford University Press, 2022).

63. Thompson, D., "The True Cost of the Churchgoing Bust," *The Atlantic*, April 3, 2024, www.theatlantic.com/ideas/archive/2024/04/america-religion-decline-non-affiliated/677951/.

64. Rainie, L., Keeter, S., and Perrin, A., *Trust and Distrust in America* (Pew Research Center, July 2019), www.pewresearch.org/politics/2019/07/22/acknowledgments-trust-distrust-in-america/.

65. Margolius, M., Doyle Lynch, A., Hynes, M., Flanagan, S., and Pufall Jones, E., "What Drives Learning: Young People's Perspectives on the Importance of Relationships, Belonging, and Agency," Center for Promise, 2020, https://files.eric.ed.gov/fulltext/ED617364.pdf.

66. Hildur, J., "Children Need 100 Parents," Medium, 2017 (originally 2007), https://gaiaeducation.medium.com/children-need-100-parents-bf224a7c2418.

67. Blaffer Hrdy, S., "Mothers and Others: From Queen Bees to Elephant Matriarchs, Many Animal Mothers Are Assisted by Others in Rearing Offspring," *Natural History*, May 2001, www.naturalhistorymag.com/features/11440/mothers-and-others.

68. van IJzendoorn, M. H., Sagi, A., and Lambermon, M. W. E., "The Multiple Caretaker Paradox: Data from Holland and Israel," *New Directions for Child Development: A Quarterly Sourcebook* 57 (1992), https://hdl.handle.net/1887/1457.

69. Hewlett, B. S., and Lamb. M. E., *Hunter-Gatherer Childhoods: Evolutionary, Developmental and Cultural Perspectives*, Evolutionary Foundations of Human Behavior Series (London: Routledge, 2005), 16.

70. Brooks, D., "The Nuclear Family Was a Mistake," *The Atlantic*, March 2020, www.theatlantic.com/magazine/archive/2020/03/the-nuclear-family-was-a-mistake/605536/.

71. Nowack, H., "This Is the Average Wedding Guest List Size in the US," The Knot, March 4, 2024, www.theknot.com/content/average-wedding-guest-list-size#:~:text=According%20to%20The%20Knot%20Real,in%202022%20was%20117%20guests.

72. "Time Spent in Leisure and Sports Activities, 2022," US Bureau of Labor Statistics, July 7, 2023, https://www.bls.gov/opub/ted/2023/time-spent-in-leisure-and-sports-activities-2022.htm; "American Time Use Survey—2012 Results," news release, US Bureau of Labor Statistics, June 20, 2013, www.bls.gov/news.release/archives/atus_06202013.pdf; Cox, D., Eyre Hammond, K., and Gray, K., "Generation Z and the Transformation of American Adolescence: How Gen Z's Formative Experiences Shape Its Politics, Priorities, and Future," Survey Center on American Life, November 9, 2023, www.americansurveycenter.org/research/generation-z-and-the-transformation-of-american-adolescence-how-gen-zs-formative-experiences-shape-its-politics-priorities-and-future/.

73. Dunbar, R. I. M., *How Many Friends Does One Person Need?* (London: Faber and Faber, 2010).

74. Thompson, A., "How Many Instagram Followers Does the Average Person Have in 2023," Hashtags for Likes, April 2, 2024, www.hashtagsforlikes.co/blog/instagram-followers-how-many-does-the-average-person-have/.

75. Mazie, S., "Do You Have Too Many Facebook Friends?," Big Think, October 9, 2014, https://tinyurl.com/mrrnnvyc.

76. Dunbar, R. I. M., "Do Online Social Media Cut Through the Constraints That Limit the Size of Offline Social Networks?," *Royal Society Open Science* 3, no. 1 (2016): 150292.

77. Cacioppo, S., Capitanio, J. P., and Cacioppo, J. T., "Toward a Neurology of Loneliness," *Psychological Bulletin* 140, no. 6 (2014), https://doi.org/10.1037/a0037618.

78. Almeida, I. L. L., Rego, J. F., Teixeira, A. C. G., and Moreira, M. R., "Social Isolation and Its Impact on Child and Adolescent Development: A Systematic Review," *Revista paulista de pediatria : Orgao oficial da Sociedade de Pediatria de Sao Paulo* 40 (2021), https://doi.org/10.1590/1984-0462/2022/40/2020385; Brinker, V., Dewald-Kaufmann, J., Padberg, F., and Reinhard, M. A., "Aggressive Intentions After Social Exclusion and Their Association with Loneliness," *European Archives of Psychiatry and Clinical Neuroscience* 273, no. 5 (2023), https://doi.org/10.1007/s00406-022-01503-8; Thompson, K. N., Odgers, C. L., Bryan, B. T., Danese, A., Milne, B. J., Strange, L., Matthews, T., and Arseneault, L., "Trajectories of Childhood Social Isolation in a Nationally Representative Cohort: Associations with Antecedents and Early Adulthood Outcomes," *JCPP Advances* 2, no. 2 (2022), https://doi.org/10.1002/jcv2.12073.

79. Whitaker, L. R., Degoulet, M., and Morikawa, H., "Social Deprivation Enhances VTA Synaptic Plasticity and Drug-Induced Contextual Learning," *Neuron* 77 (2013), https://doi.org/10.1016/j.neuron.2012.11.022.

80. Dworak, E. M., Revelle, W., and Condon, D. M., "Looking for Flynn Effects in a Recent Online U.S. Adult Sample: Examining Shifts Within the SAPA Project," *Intelligence* 98 (2023), https://doi.org/10.1016/j.intell.2023.101734.

81. Dutton, E., van der Linden, D., and Lynn, R., "The Negative Flynn Effect: A Systematic Literature Review," *Intelligence* 59 (2016): 163–169, https://doi.org/10.1016/j.intell.2016.10.002; Pietschnig, J., and Gittler, G., "A Reversal of the Flynn Effect for Spatial

Perception in German-Speaking Countries: Evidence from a Cross-Temporal IRT-Based Meta-Analysis (1977–2014)," *Intelligence* 53 (2015): 145–153, https://doi.org/10.1016/j .intell.2015.10.004; Sundet, J. M., Barlaug, D. G., and Torjussen, T. M., "The End of the Flynn Effect? A Study of Secular Trends in Mean Intelligence Test Scores of Norwegian Conscripts During Half a Century," *Intelligence* 32, no. 4 (2004): 349–362, https://doi.org/10.1016/j .intell.2004.06.004; Bratsberg, B., and Rogeberg, O., "Flynn Effect and Its Reversal Are Both Environmentally Caused," *Proceedings of the National Academy of Sciences of the United States of America* 115, no. 26 (2018): 6674–6678, https://doi.org/10.1073/pnas.1718793115; Amundsen, B., "Our IQ Is Steadily Declining. Should You Be Worried?," *ScienceNorway.no*, April 4, 2023, www.sciencenorway.no/health-intelligence-iq/our-iq-is-steadily-declining/2180595.

82. Deoni, S. C., Beauchemin, J., Volpe, A., Dâ Sa, V., and RESONANCE Consortium, "The COVID-19 Pandemic and Early Child Cognitive Development: A Comparison of Development in Children Born During the Pandemic and Historical References," *medRxiv* (2022), https://doi.org/10.1101/2021.08.10.21261846.

Chapter 3. The Kids Aren't All Right

1. Ziv, Y., Capps Umphlet, K. L., Sofri, I., Olarte, S., and Venza, J., "Changing Developmental Trajectory in High-Risk Families: The Effectiveness of an Attachment-Informed Therapeutic Nursery Program (TNP) for Preschool Children with Complex Emotional and Behavioral Problems," *Attachment and Human Development* 23, no. 3 (2021), https://doi.org /10.1080/14616734.2020.1722717.

2. Hill, F., "America Is in Its Insecure Attachment Era," *The Atlantic*, April 27, 2023, www.theatlantic.com/family/archive/2023/04/insecure-attachment-style-intimacy-decline -isolation/673867/.

3. "'No Time to Be Lax': Cuomo Extends New York Shutdown; NJ Deaths Top 1,000," NBC, April 6, 2020, www.nbcnewyork.com/news/local/our-9-11-moment-new-york-braces -as-nations-top-doctor-warns-saddest-week-ahead/2361336/.

4. Dumitriu, D., "Life-Long Negative Impacts of COVID-19 on Mother-Infant Outcomes," Early Childhood Funder Collaborative, March 18, 2021, www.youtube.com /watch?v=GVrXdC4FP1w.

5. Linde, K., Lehnig, F., Nagl, M., and Kersting, A., "The Association Between Breastfeeding and Attachment: A Systematic Review," *Midwifery* 81 (2020), https://doi.org/10.1016/j .midw.2019.102592; Peñacoba, C., and Catala, P., "Associations Between Breastfeeding and Mother-Infant Relationships: A Systematic Review," *Breastfeeding Medicine* 14, no. 9 (2019), https://doi .org/10.1089/bfm.2019.0106; Hairston, I. S., Handelzalts, J. E., Lehman-Inbar, T., and Kovo, M., "Mother-Infant Bonding Is Not Associated with Feeding Type: A Community Study Sample," *BMC Pregnancy and Childbirth* 19, no. 1 (2019), https://doi.org/10.1186/s12884-019-2264-0.

6. Tronick, E., Adamson, L., Wise, S., and Brazelton, T. B., "The Infant's Response to Entrapment Between Contradictory Messages in Face-to-Face Interaction," *Journal of the American Academy of Child and Adolescent Psychiatry* 17 (1978), https://doi.org/10.1016 /s0002-7138(09)62273-1.

7. Tronick, E., and Snidman, N., "Children's Reaction to Mothers Wearing or Not Wearing a Mask During Face-to-Face Interactions," Preprint SSRN, August 11, 2021, https://ssrn.com/abstract=3899140.

8. See, e.g., Zwönitzer, A., Rost, K., Fegert, J. M., Ziegenhain, U., and Köhler-Dauner, F., "Emotional Problems in Young Children During the SARS-Cov-2-Pandemic and Child Attachment," *Frontiers in Pediatrics* 11 (2023), https://doi.org/10.3389/fped.2023.1191032.

9. For data and trends, see RAPID Survey Project, accessed June 19, 2024, https://rapidsurveyproject.com/latest-data-and-trends.

10. Almond, D., "Is the 1918 Influenza Pandemic Over? Long-Term Effects of In Utero Influenza Exposure in the Post-1940 US Population," *Journal of Political Economy* 114, no. 4 (2006), www.jstor.org/stable/10.1086/507154?seq=18.

11. Konrath, S., "The Empathy Paradox: Increasing Disconnection in the Age of Increasing Connection," in *Handbook of Research on Technoself: Identity in a Technological Society*, ed. R. Luppicini (Hershey, PA: IGI Global, 2013), 204–228.

12. Chopik, W. J., O'Brien, E., and Konrath, S. H., "Differences in Empathic Concern and Perspective Taking Across 63 Countries," *Journal of Cross-Cultural Psychology* 48, no. 1 (2017), https://doi.org/10.1177/0022022116673910.

13. Hill, F. "America Is in Its Insecure Attachment Era," *The Atlantic*, April 27, 2023, www.theatlantic.com/family/archive/2023/04 insecure-attachment-style-intimacy-decline-isolation/673867/.

14. Marchetti, L., "Support the Mental Well-Being of Young People," Open Access Government, June 15, 2022, www.openaccessgovernment.org/support-the-mental-wellbeing-of-young-people/137652/.

15. Kingkade, T., and Cluck, E., "Suicidal Thoughts Are Increasing in Young Kids, Experts Say. It Began Before the Pandemic," NBC News, April 8, 2021, www.nbcnews.com/news/us-news/suicidal-thoughts-are-increasing-young-kids-experts-say-it-began-n1263347.

16. Bommersbach, T. J., McKean, A. J., Olfson, M., and Rhee, T. G., "National Trends in Mental Health–Related Emergency Department Visits Among Youth, 2011–2020," *JAMA* 329, no. 17 (2023), https://doi.org/10.1001/jama.2023.4809; Kingkade and Cluck, "Suicidal Thoughts Are Increasing in Young Kids."

17. "Two New EAB Surveys Reveal Troubling Trends in Student Behavior," EAB, February 16, 2023, https://eab.com/about/newsroom/press/two-new-eab-surveys-reveal-troubling-trends-in-student-behavior/.

18. Perez, D., "How COVID, Technology Created Unruly Children," *El Paso Matters*, April 3, 2023, https://elpasomatters.org/2023/04/03/kindergarten-teachers-see-more-students-as-distracted-disruptive/.

19. Santos-Longhurst, A., "What Is Proprioception, and Why Is It Important?," Healthline, July 16, 2019, www.healthline.com/health/body/proprioception#How-is-proprioception-evaluated?

20. Ogden, C. L., Carroll, M. D., Kit, B. K., and Flegal, K. M., "Prevalence of Obesity and Trends in Body Mass Index Among US Children and Adolescents, 1999–2010," *JAMA* 307, no. 5 (2012), https://doi.org/10.1001/jama.2012.40; "Child Obesity: Too Many Kids Are Too Heavy, Too Young," Harvard T. H. Chan School of Public Health, 2024, www.hsph

.harvard.edu/obesity-prevention-source/global-obesity-trends-in-children/#References; Sanyaolu, A., Okorie, C., Qi, X., Locke, J., and Rehman, S., "Childhood and Adolescent Obesity in the United States: A Public Health Concern," *Global Pediatric Health* 6 (2019), https://doi.org/10.1177/2333794X19891305.

21. Graph: Prevalence of Obesity Among Children and Adolescents Ages 2 to 19 Years: United States, 2017–2018 NHANES data, NIDDK, www.niddk.nih.gov/health-information/health-statistics/overweight-obesity.

22. Eckert-Lind, C., Busch, A. S., Petersen, J. H., Biro, F. M., Butler, G., Bräuner, E. V., and Juul, A., "Worldwide Secular Trends in Age at Pubertal Onset Assessed by Breast Development Among Girls: A Systematic Review and Meta-analysis," *JAMA Pediatrics* 174, no. 4 (2020), https://doi.org/10.1001/jamapediatrics.2019.5881.

23. Changoiwala, P., "Early Puberty Cases Are Surging During the Pandemic," *Washington Post*, March 28, 2023, www.washingtonpost.com/lifestyle/2022/03/28/early-puberty-pandemic-girls/.

24. Uğurlu, A. K., Bideci, A., Demirel, A. M., Kaplanoğlu, G. T., Dayanır, D., Gülbahar, Ö., Bulut, T. S. D., Döğer, E., and Çamurdan, M. O., "Is Blue Light Exposure a Cause of Precocious Puberty in Male Rats?," *Frontiers in Endocrinology* 14 (2023), https://doi.org/10.3389/fendo.2023.1190445.

25. "Strong Signs of Recovery Across Education, but Challenges Remain," press release, Ofsted, April 4, 2022, www.gov.uk/government/news/strong-signs-of-recovery-across-education-but-challenges-remain.

26. Goodwin Cartwright, B. M., Smits, P. D., Stewart, S., Rodriguez, P. J., Gratzl, S., Baker, C., and Stucky, N., "Time-Series Analysis of First-Time Pediatric Speech Delays from 2018 to 2022," *JAMA Pediatrics* 178, no. 2 (2024), https://doi.org/10.1001/jamapediatrics.2023.5226.

27. Giesbrecht, G., Lebel, C., Dennis, C., Tough, S. C., McDonald, S., and Tomfohr-Madsen, L., "Increased Risk for Developmental Delay Among Babies Born During the Pandemic," PsyArXiv Preprints, February 3, 2022, https://doi.org/10.31234/osf.io/j7kcn.

28. Sparks, S. D., "Babies Are Saying Less Since the Pandemic: Why That's Concerning," *Education Week*, April 7, 2022, www.edweek.org/teaching-learning/babies-are-saying-less-since-the-pandemic-why-thats-concerning/2022/04.

29. Al-Beltagi, M., Saeed, N. K., Bediwy, A. S., Alhawamdeh, R., and Qaraghuli, S., "Effects of COVID-19 on Children with Autism," *World Journal of Virology* 11, no. 6 (2022), https://doi.org/10.5501/wjv.v11.i6.411.

30. Moullin, S., Walgofel, J., and Washbrook, E., *Baby Bonds: Parenting, Attachment and a Secure Base for Children* (Sutton Trust, March 2014), www.suttontrust.com/wp-content/uploads/2019/12/baby-bonds-final-1.pdf.

31. Katz, L. F., Leary, A., Breiger, D., and Friedman, D., "Pediatric Cancer and the Quality of Children's Dyadic Peer Interactions," *Journal of Pediatric Psychology* 36, no. 2 (2011), https://doi.org/10.1093/jpepsy/jsq050.

32. "More than 1 in 5 Children Live in Poverty in 40 of the World's Richest Countries," UNICEF, December 5, 2023, www.unicef.org/press-releases/more-1-5-children-live-poverty-40-worlds-richest-countries.

33. Annie E. Casey Foundation, *Kids Count Data Center* (2024), Children in Poverty by Race and Ethnicity in United States, 2023 Data, https://datacenter.aecf.org/data /tables/44-children-in-poverty-by-race-and-ethnicity#detailed/1/any/false/2545,1095,2048, 1729,37,871,870,573,869,36/187,11,9,12,1,185,13/324,323.

34. Greenberg, E., and Monarrez, T., "Segregated from the Start," Urban Institute, October 1, 2019, www.urban.org/features/segregated-start.

35. Fernald, A., Marchman, V. A., and Weisleder, A., "SES Differences in Language Processing Skill and Vocabulary Are Evident at 18 Months," *Developmental Science* 16, no. 2 (2013), https://doi.org/10.1111/desc.12019.

36. Ghandour, R. M., Hirai, A. H., Moore, K. A., Robinson, L. R., Kaminski, J. W., Murphy, K., Lu, M. C., and Kogan, M. D., "Healthy and Ready to Learn: Prevalence and Correlates of School Readiness Among United States Preschoolers," *Academic Pediatrics* 21, no. 5 (2021), https://doi.org/10.1016/j.acap.2021.02.019.

37. Reich, R., "Class. 13: 'Reducing Inequities in Education,'" UC Berkeley, YouTube video, 2022, https://youtu.be/W9rtmYxwvD0.

38. Juel, C., "Learning to Read and Write: A Longitudinal Study of 54 Children from First to Fourth Grades," *Journal of Educational Psychology* 80, no. 4 (1988), https://doi .org/10.1037/0022-0663.80.4.437.

39. Bishop, S., Fishman, N., Garrett, T., Elkin, J., Ford, B., Galloway, M., Belfield, C. R., "$122 Billion: The Growing, Annual Cost of the Infant-Toddler Childcare Crisis," Council for a Strong America, February 2023, www.strongnation.org /articles/2038-122-billion-the-growing-annual-cost-of-the-infant-toddler-child-care-crisis.

40. Diallo, G., "175 Million Children Are Not Enrolled in Pre-Primary Education," UNICEF, April 8, 2019, https://tinyurl.com/38mvmfyn.

41. Gopnik, A., "Preschool's 'Sleeper' Effect on Later Life," *Wall Street Journal*, May 27, 2021, www.wsj.com/articles/preschools-sleeper-effect-on-later-life-11622146543.

42. Gray-Lobe, G., Pathak, P. A., Walters, C. R., "The Long-Term Effects of Universal Preschool in Boston," *Quarterly Journal of Economics* 138, no. 1 (2023), https://doi.org /10.1093/qje/qjac036; Carr, R. C., Peisner-Feinberg, E. S., Kaplan, R., and Mokrova, I. L., "Effects of North Carolina's Pre-Kindergarten Program at the End of Kindergarten: Contributions of School-Wide Quality," *Journal of Applied Developmental Psychology* 76 (2021), https:// doi.org/10.1016/j.appdev.2021.101317; Watts, T. W., Jenkins, J. M., Dodge, K. A., Carr, R. C., Sauval, M., Bai, Y., Escueta, M., Duer, J., Ladd, H., Muschkin, C., Peisner-Feinberg, E., and Ananat, E., "Understanding Heterogeneity in the Impact of Public Preschool Programs," *Monographs of the Society for Research in Child Development* 87, no. 4 (2023), https://doi .org/10.1111/mono.12463.

43. Guttmacher, A. E., *The NICHD Study of Early Child Care and Youth Development* (US Department of Health and Human Services, 2006), www.nichd.nih.gov/sites/default/files /publications/pubs/documents/seccyd_06.pdf.

44. Gillispie, C., *Young Learners, Missed Opportunities: Ensuring That Black and Latino Children Have Access to High-Quality State-Funded Preschool* (Education Trust, November 2019), https://edtrust.org/wp-content/uploads/2014/09/Young-Learners-Missed-Opportunities.pdf.

45. Friedman-Krauss, A., and Barnett, S. W., *Special Report: Access to High-Quality Early Education and Racial Equity* (National Institute for Early Education Research, 2020), https://nieer.org/research-library/special-report-access-high-quality-early-education-racial -equity.

46. Gable, S. L., Hopper, E. A., and Schooler, J. W., "When the Muses Strike: Creative Ideas of Physicists and Writers Routinely Occur During Mind Wandering," *Psychological Science* 30, no. 3 (2019), https://doi.org/10.1177/0956797618820626.

47. Ovington, L. A., Saliba, A. J., Moran, C. C., Goldring, J., and MacDonald, J. B., "Do People Really Have Insights in the Shower? The When, Where and Who of the Aha! Moment," *Journal of Creative Behavior* 52, no. 1 (2018), https://doi.org/10.1002/jocb.126; Oppezzo, M., and Schwartz, D. L., "Give Your Ideas Some Legs: The Positive Effect of Walking on Creative Thinking," *Journal of Experimental Psychology: Learning, Memory, and Cognition* 40, no. 4 (2014), https://doi.org/10.1037/a0036577.

48. Hofferth, S. L., "Changes in American Children's Time—1997 to 2003," *Electronic International Journal of Time Use Research* 6, no. 1 (2009), https://doi.org/10.13085 /eijtur.6.1.26-47; Juster, F. T., Ono, H., and Stafford, F. P., *Changing Times of American Youth: 1981–2003* (Institute for Social Research, University of Michigan, 2004), https://library .parenthelp.eu/wp-content/uploads/2019/12/teen_time_report.pdf.

49. Kim, K. H., "The Creativity Crisis: The Decrease in Creative Thinking Scores on the Torrance Tests of Creative Thinking," *Creativity Research Journal* 23, no. 4 (2011), https://doi .org/10.1080/10400419.2011.627805; Kim, K. H., "Creativity Crisis Update: America Follows Asia in Pursuing High Test Scores over Learning," *Roeper Review: A Journal on Gifted Education* 43, no. 1 (2021), https://doi.org/10.1080/02783193.2020.1840464.

50. Bronson, P., and Merryman, A., "The Creativity Crisis," *Newsweek*, updated January 23, 2014, www.newsweek.com/creativity-crisis-74665.

51. Barbot, B., and Said-Metwaly, S., "Is There Really a Creativity Crisis? A Critical Review and Meta-analytical Re-appraisal," *Journal of Creative Behavior* 55, no. 3 (2020), https://doi.org/10.1002/jocb.483.

Chapter 4. Here but Not Here: Physically Present, Emotionally Absent Parents

1. Tarver, H., medically reviewed by Hartman, C., "Connected Without Connection: Does Technology Make Us More Alone?," Roots of Loneliness Project, 2019, www.rootsofloneliness. com/does-technology-make-us-more-alone.

2. Making Care Common Project, *Loneliness in America: How the Pandemic Has Deepened an Epidemic of Loneliness and What We Can Do About It* (Harvard Graduate School of Education, 2021), https://mcc.gse.harvard.edu/reports/loneliness-in-america; Packham, A., "More than 90% of Mums Feel Lonely After Having Children and Many Don't Confide in Their Partners," *HuffPost*, July 3, 2017, www.huffingtonpost.co.uk/entry/mums-feel-lonely -after-birth_uk_58bec088e4b09ab537d6bdf9.

3. Mendes, E., Saad, L., and McGeeney K., "Stay-at-Home Moms Report More Depression, Sadness, Anger," Gallup, May 18, 2021, https://news.gallup.com/poll/154685/stay -home-moms-report-depression-sadness-anger.aspx.

4. "American Mothers on Pause: A Study of Stay-at-Home Motherhood in 2023," *Mother Untitled*, 2023, www.motheruntitled.com/americanmothersonpause.

5. Dickens, M., and Hutner, L., "What the Childcare Crisis Does to Parents," *New York Times*, January 16, 2024, www.nytimes.com/2024/01/16/opinion/child-care-parenting-stress .html.

6. Cox, D. A., "The State of American Friendship: Change, Challenges, and Loss," Survey Center on American Life, June 8, 2021, www.americansurveycenter.org/research/the -state-of-american-friendship-change-challenges-and-loss/.

7. Bryant, M., "'I Was Risking My Life': Why One in Four US Women Return to Work Two Weeks After Childbirth," *The Guardian*, January 27, 2020, www.theguardian.com/us -news/2020/jan/27/maternity-paid-leave-women-work-childbirth-us.

8. Brito, N. H., Werchan, D., Brandes-Aitken, A., Yoshikawa, H., Greaves, A., and Zhang, M., "Paid Maternal Leave Is Associated with Infant Brain Function at 3 Months of Age," *Child Development* 93, no. 4 (2022), https://doi.org/10.1111/cdev.13765.

9. Hidalgo-Padilla, L., Toyama, M., Zafra-Tanaka, J. H., Vives, A., and Diez-Canseco, F., "Association Between Maternity Leave Policies and Postpartum Depression: A Systematic Review," *Archives of Women's Mental Health* 26, no. 5 (2023), https://doi.org/10.1007 /s00737-023-01350-z.

10. "Parents Now Spend Twice as Much Time with Their Children as 50 Years Ago. Except in France," *The Economist*, November 27, 2017, www.economist.com/graphic-detail/2017/11 /27/parents-now-spend-twice-as-much-time-with-their-children-as-50-years-ago.

11. Dotti Sani, G. M., and Treas, J., "Educational Gradients in Parents' Child-Care Time Across Countries, 1965–2012," *Journal of Marriage and Family* 78, no. 4 (2016), https://doi.org /10.1111/jomf.12305.

12. Ishizuka, P., "Social Class, Gender, and Contemporary Parenting Standards in the United States: Evidence from a National Survey Experiment," *Social Forces* 98, no. 1 (2019), https://doi.org/10.1093/sf/soy107.

13. Hurst, K., Braga, D., Greenwood, S., Baronavski, C., and Keegan, M., "How Today's Parents Say Their Approach to Parenting Does or Doesn't Match Their Own Upbringing," Pew Research Center, January 24, 2023, www.pewresearch.org/social-trends/2023/01/24/how-to days-parents-say-their-approach-to-parenting-does-or-doesnt-match-their-own-upbringing/.

14. Cui, M., Hong, P., and Jiao, C., "Overparenting and Emerging Adult Development: A Systematic Review," *Emerging Adulthood* 10, no. 5 (2022), https://doi.org /10.1177/21676968221108828; Barber, B. K., Olsen, J. E., and Shagle, S. C., "Associations Between Parental Psychological and Behavioral Control and Youth Internalized and Externalized Behaviors," *Child Development* 65, no. 4 (1994), https://doi.org/10.2307/1131309; Bayer, J. K., Sanson, A. V., and Hemphill, S. A., "Parent Influences on Early Childhood Internalizing Difficulties," *Journal of Applied Developmental Psychology* 27, no. 6 (2006), https://doi .org/10.1016/j.appdev.2006.08.002; McShane, K. E., and Hastings, P. D., "The New Friends Vignettes: Measuring Parental Psychological Control That Confers Risk for Anxious Adjustment in Preschoolers," *International Journal of Behavioral Development* 33, no. 6 (2009), https://doi.org/10.1177/0165025409103874; Jiao, J., and Segrin, C., "Overparenting and

Emerging Adults' Insecure Attachment with Parents and Romantic Partners," *Emerging Adulthood* 10, no. 3 (2022), https://doi.org/10.1177/2167696821997710.

15. *Old Enough!* is available on Netflix.

16. "The Decline in Walking and Biking," SRTS Guide, 2011, http://guide.saferoutes info.org/introduction/the_decline_of_walking_and_bicycling.cfm.

17. Lockhart, P. R., "A White Neighbor Called Police on a Kid Mowing a Lawn. Later, They Called as He Played in a Yard," *Vox*, July 9, 2018, www.vox.com /identities/2018/7/2/17527382/reggie-fields-racial-profiling-911-police.

18. Skenazy, L., "Cops Confiscate Axe from Teen Chopping Wood to Build Fort," *Reason*, May 18, 2016, https://reason.com/2016/05/18/cops-confiscate-axe-from-teen-chopping-w/.

19. Price, M., "Free Preschool Given Playground Equipment, but Kids Can't Use It," *Charlotte Observer*, October 23, 2016, www.wbtv.com/story/33456243/free-preschool-given-playground-equipment-but-kids-cant-use-it/.

20. Chua, K., "District Phasing Out Swingsets, Citing Safety Concerns," *Education Week*, October 23, 2014, https://tinyurl.com/mdap2ctu.

21. Desilver, D., "After Dropping in 2020, Teen Summer Employment May Be Poised to Continue Its Slow Comeback," Pew Research, June 21, 2022, www.pewresearch.org/short-reads /2022/06/21/after-dropping-in-2020-teen-summer-employment-may-be-poised-to-continue -its-slow-comeback/.

22. Dunbar, R. I. M., Launay, J., Wlodarski, R., Robertson, C., Pearce, E., Carney, J., and MacCarron, P., "Functional Benefits of (Modest) Alcohol Consumption," *Adaptive Human Behavior and Physiology* 3, no. 2 (2017), https://doi.org/10.1007/s40750-016-0058-4.

23. Quart, A., *Squeezed: Why Our Families Can't Afford America* (New York: HarperCollins, 2018).

24. "Many Parents Say They Spend Too Little Time with Kids, Partners, Friends," Pew Research Center, December 17, 2015, www.pewresearch.org/social-trends/2015/12/17 /parenting-in-america/st_2015-12-17_parenting-30/.

25. Wallace, J. B., *Never Enough: How a Toxic Achievement Culture Is Destroying Our Kids and What to Do About It* (New York: Portfolio, 2023).

26. Sims, T., "Shifting Life Milestones Across Ages: A Matter of Preference or Circumstance?," Stanford Center on Longevity, 2018, https://longevity.stanford.edu/wp-content /uploads/2018/02/Milestones-.pdf. See also the Milestones Project website, https://longevity .stanford.edu/milestones/.

27. Chapkanovska, E., "How Much Does It Cost to Raise a Child in America?," *SpendMeNot* (blog), January 24, 2023, https://spendmenot.com/blog/how-much-does-it -cost-to-raise-a-child/.

28. Erickson, J., "The Middle-Class Squeeze," Center for American Progress, 2014, www .americanprogress.org/issues/economy/reports/2014/09/24/96903/the-middle-class-squeeze/.

29. "Rising Childcare Costs Starting to Bite," Bank of America Institute, October 27, 2023, https://institute.bankofamerica.com/content/dam/economic-insights/rising-child-care -costs.pdf.

30. "High Material Hardship Persists for Families with Young Children," RAPID, April 7, 2023, https://rapidsurveyproject.com/our-research/high-material-hardship-persists

-for-families-with-young-children. RAPID-EC Survey Project data and trends available at: https://rapidsurveyproject.com/latest-data-and-trends.

31. Saul, S., "Fencing Can Be Six-Figure Expensive, but It Wins in College Admissions: How Niche Sports Offer a Pathway to the Ivy League and Other Elite Schools," *New York Times*, October 17, 2022, www.nytimes.com/2022/10/17/us/fencing-ivy-league-college-admissions.html.

32. Kornrich, S., and Furstenberg, F., "Investing in Children: Changes in Parental Spending on Children, 1972—2007," *Demography* 50, no. 1 (2013), www.jstor.org/stable/23358830.

33. Radesky, J., Miller, A. L., Rosenblum, K. L., Appugliese, D., Kaciroti, N., and Lumeng, J. C., "Maternal Mobile Device Use During a Structured Parent-Child Interaction Task," *Academic Pediatrics* 15, no. 2 (2015), https://doi.org/10.1016/j.acap.2014.10.001.

Part II. The New Science of Love and Learning

Chapter 5. The Scientific Re*lov*ution

1. Wildflower Labs, *Exploring the Potential for Artificial Intelligence to Enable Continuous Collection of Classroom Data in Support of Early Learning* (prepared for the Bill and Melinda Gates Foundation, March 1, 2024), https://docs.google.com/document/d/1_h 7hujqC7KC2ERJD0aQXb1rrI95fF5Z030v91tU3nXI/edit.

2. Sanders, L., "Brain Electric Implants Treat Depression: A Closer Reality," *Science News*, 2019, www.sciencenews.org/article/brain-electric-implants-treat-depression-closer-reality.

3. Çetinçelik, M., Rowland, C. F., and Snijders, T. M., "Do the Eyes Have It? A Systematic Review on the Role of Eye Gaze in Infant Language Development," *Frontiers in Psychology* 11 (2021), https://doi.org/10.3389/fpsyg.2020.589096.

4. Arioli, M., Ricciardi, E., and Cattaneo, Z., "Social Cognition in the Blind Brain: A Coordinate-Based Meta-analysis," *Human Brain Mapping* 42, no. 5 (2021), https://doi.org/10.1002/hbm.25289.

5. Elsabbagh, M., Gliga, T., Pickles, A., Hudry, K., Charman, T., Johnson, M. H., and BASIS Team, "The Development of Face-Orienting Mechanisms in Infants at Risk for Autism," *Behavioural Brain Research* 251 (2013), https://doi.org/10.1016/j.bbr.2012.07.030; Chawarska, K., Macari, S., Powell, K., DiNicola, L., and Shic, F., "Enhanced Social Attention in Female Infant Siblings at Risk for Autism," *Journal of the American Academy of Child and Adolescent Psychiatry* 55, no. 3 (2016), https://doi.org/10.1016/j.jaac.2015.11.016.

6. Interview with Patricia Kuhl, "Learning and the Social Brain," Edutopia, July 25, 2018, www.edutopia.org/package/learning-and-the-social-brain/.

7. Koenig, M. A., and Sabbagh, M. A., "Selective Social Learning: New Perspectives on Learning from Others," *Developmental Psychology* 49, no. 3 (2013), https://doi.org/10.1037/a0031619.

8. Stenberg, G., "Do 12-Month-Old Infants Trust a Competent Adult?," *Infancy* 18, no. 5 (2013), https://doi.org/10.1111/infa.12011.

9. Charpak, N., Tessier, R., Ruiz, J. G., Hernandez, J. T., Uriza, F., Villegas, J., Nadeau, L., Mercier, C., Maheu, F., Marin, J., Cortes, D., Gallego, J. M., and Maldonado, D.,

"Twenty-Year Follow-up of Kangaroo Mother Care Versus Traditional Care," *Pediatrics* 139, no. 1 (2017), https://doi.org/10.1542/peds.2016-2063; Ropars, S., Tessier, R., Charpak, N., and Uriza, L. F., "The Long-Term Effects of the Kangaroo Mother Care Intervention on Cognitive Functioning: Results from a Longitudinal Study," *Developmental Neuropsychology* 43, no. 1 (2018), https://doi.org/10.1080/87565641.2017.1422507.

10. Hardin, J. S., Jones, N. A., Mize, K. D., and Platt, M., "Parent-Training with Kangaroo Care Impacts Infant Neurophysiological Development and Mother-Infant Neuroendocrine Activity," *Infant Behavior and Development* 58 (2020), https://doi.org/10.1016/j.infbeh.2019.101416.

11. WHO Immediate KMC Study Group, "Immediate 'Kangaroo Mother Care' and Survival of Infants with Low Birth Weight," *New England Journal of Medicine* 384, no. 21 (2021), https://doi.org/10.1056/NEJMoa2026486.

12. Aguirre, M., Couderc, A., Epinat-Duclos, J., and Mascaro, O., "Infants Discriminate the Source of Social Touch at Stroking Speeds Eliciting Maximal Firing Rates in CT-Fibers," *Developmental Cognitive Neuroscience* 36 (2019), https://doi.org/10.1016/j.dcn.2019.100639; Deng, Q., Li, Q., Wang, H., Sun, H., and Xu, X., "Early Father-Infant Skin-to-Skin Contact and Its Effect on the Neurodevelopmental Outcomes of Moderately Preterm Infants in China: Study Protocol for a Randomized Controlled Trial," *Trials* 19, no. 1 (2018), https://doi.org/10.1186/s13063-018-3060-2; Pados, B. F., and Hess, F., "Systematic Review of the Effects of Skin-to-Skin Care on Short-Term Physiologic Stress Outcomes in Preterm Infants in the Neonatal Intensive Care Unit," *Advances in Neonatal Care* 20, no. 1 (2020), https://doi.org/10.1097/ANC.0000000000000596.

13. Brauer, J., Xiao Y., Poulain, T., Friederici, A.D., Schirmer, A., "Frequency of Maternal Touch Predicts Resting Activity and Connectivity of the Developing Social Brain," *Cerebral Cortex* 26, no. 8 (2016), https://doi.org/10.1093/cercor/bhw137.

14. Moore, S. R., McEwen, L. M., Quirt, J., Morin, A., Mah, S. M., Barr, R. G., Boyce, W. T., and Kobor, M. S., "Epigenetic Correlates of Neonatal Contact in Humans," *Development and Psychopathology* 29, no. 5 (2017), https://doi.org/10.1017/S0954579417001213.

15. Addyman, C., and Addyman, I., "The Science of Baby Laughter," *Comedy Studies* 4, no. 2 (2013), www.researchgate.net/publication/255700397_The_Science_of_Baby_Laughter.

16. Kim, P., and Enos Watamura, S., *Two Open Windows: Infant and Parent Neurobiologic Change* (University of Denver: Stress, Early Experiences and Development Research Center, 2017), https://ascend.aspeninstitute.org/wp-content/uploads/2017/10/4b320cff0e86d8fb51_gqm6btprv-6.pdf.

17. Fleming, A. S., and Rosenblatt, J. S., "Maternal Behavior in the Virgin and Lactating Rat," *Journal of Comparative and Physiological Psychology* 86, no. 5 (1974), https://doi.org/10.1037/h0036414.

18. Hoekzema, E., Barba-Müller, E., Pozzobon, C., Picado, M., Lucco, F., García-García, D., Soliva, J. C., Tobeña, A., Desco, M., Crone, E. A., and Ballesteros, A., "Pregnancy Leads to Long-Lasting Changes in Human Brain Structure," *Nature Neuroscience* 20 (2017), https://doi.org/10.1038/nn.4458.

19. Hoekzema, E., van Steenbergen, H., Straathof, M., Beekmans, A., Freund, I. M., Pouwels, P. J., and Crone, E. A., "Mapping the Effects of Pregnancy on Resting State Brain Activity,

White Matter Microstructure, Neural Metabolite Concentrations and Grey Matter Architecture," *Nature Communications* 13 (2022), https://doi.org/10.1038/s41467-022-33884-8.

20. Feldman, R., "The Adaptive Human Parental Brain: Implications for Children's Social Development," *Trends in Neurosciences* 38, no. 6 (2015), https://doi.org/10.1016/j.tins.2015.04.004.

21. Schurz, M., Radua, J., Tholen, M. G., Maliske, L., Margulies, D. S., Mars, R. B., Sallet, J., and Kanske, P., "Toward a Hierarchical Model of Social Cognition: A Neuroimaging Meta-analysis and Integrative Review of Empathy and Theory of Mind," *Psychological Bulletin* 147, no. 3 (2021), https://doi.org/10.1037/bul0000303; Forstmann, B. U., de Hollander, G., van Maanen, L., Alkemade, A., and Keuken, M. C., "Towards a Mechanistic Understanding of the Human Subcortex," *Nature Reviews Neuroscience* 18 (2017), https://doi.org/10.1038/nrn.2016.163.

22. Abraham, E., Hendler, T., Shapira-Lichter, I., Kanat-Maymon, Y., Zagoory-Sharon, O., and Feldman, R., "Father's Brain Is Sensitive to Childcare Experiences," *Proceedings of the National Academy of Sciences of the United States of America* 111, no. 27 (2014), https://doi.org/10.1073/pnas.1402569111.

23. Romaine, J., "Surprising New Study Finds Grandmothers More Connected to Grandchildren than to Own Children," *The Hill*, November 17, 2021, https://thehill.com/changing-america/resilience/smart-cities/581986-surprising-new-study-finds-grandmothers-more/.

24. Lin, J. L., Imada, T., Meltzoff, A. N., Hiraishi, H., Ikeda, T., Takahashi, T., Hasegawa, C., Yoshimura, Y., Kikuchi, M., Hirata, M., Minabe, Y., Asada, M., and Kuhl, P. K., "Dual-MEG Interbrain Synchronization During Turn-Taking Verbal Interactions Between Mothers and Children," *Cerebral Cortex* 33, no. 7 (2023), https://doi.org/10.1093/cercor/bhac330.

25. Davidesco, I., "Brain-to-Brain Synchrony in the STEM Classroom," *CBE Life Sciences Education* 19, no. 3 (2020), https://doi.org/10.1187/cbe.19-11-0258; "In Sync Brainwaves Predict Learning, Study Shows," *UConn Today*, April 13, 2023, https://today.uconn.edu/2023/04/in-sync-brainwaves-predict-learning-study-shows/; Davidesco, I., Laurent, E., Valk, H., West, T., Milne, C., Poeppel, D., and Dikker, S., "The Temporal Dynamics of Brain-to-Brain Synchrony Between Students and Teachers Predict Learning Outcomes," *Psychological Science* 34, no. 5 (2023), https://doi.org/10.1177/09567976231163872.

26. Zhang, W., and Yartsev, M. M., "Correlated Neural Activity Across the Brains of Socially Interacting Bats," *Cell* (2019), https://doi.org/ 10.1016/j.cell.2019.05.023.

27. Kingsbury, L., Huang, S., Wang, J., Gu, K., Golshani, P., Wu, Y. E., and Hong, W., "Correlated Neural Activity and Encoding of Behavior Across Brains of Socially Interacting Animals," *Cell* 178, no. 2 (2023), https://doi.org/10.1016/j.cell.2019.05.022.

28. Beiranvand, S., Valizadeh, F., Hosseinabadi, R., and Pournia, Y., "The Effects of Skin-to-Skin Contact on Temperature and Breastfeeding Successfulness in Full-Term Newborns After Cesarean Delivery," *International Journal of Pediatrics* (2014), https://doi.org/10.1155/2014/846486.

29. Collaborative Group on Hormonal Factors in Breast Cancer, "Breast Cancer and Breastfeeding: Collaborative Reanalysis of Individual Data from 47 Epidemiological Studies

in 30 Countries, Including 50,302 Women with Breast Cancer and 96,973 Women Without the Disease," *Lancet* 360, no. 9328 (2002): 187–195.

30. Modak, A., Ronghe, V., and Gomase, K. P., "The Psychological Benefits of Breast-feeding: Fostering Maternal Well-Being and Child Development," *Cureus* 15, no. 10 (2023), https://doi.org/10.7759/cureus.46730.

31. Takahashi, J., Yamada, D., Nagano, W., Sano, Y., Furuichi, T., and Saitoh, A., "Oxy-tocinergic Projection from the Hypothalamus to Supramammillary Nucleus Drives Recognition Memory in Mice," *PLOS One* 18, no. 11 (2023), https://doi.org/10.1371/journal.pone.0294113.

32. Cymerblit-Sabba, A., Walsh, C., Duan, K. Z., Song, J., Holmes, O., and Young, W. S., "Simultaneous Knockouts of the Oxytocin and Vasopressin 1b Receptors in Hippocampal CA2 Impair Social Memory," bioRxiv, 2023, https://doi.org/10.1101/2023.01.30.526271.

33. Rimmele, U., Hediger, K., Heinrichs, M., and Klaver, P., "Oxytocin Makes a Face in Memory Familiar," *Journal of Neuroscience* 29, no. 1 (2009), https://doi.org/10.1523/JNEUROSCI.4260-08.2009; Guastella, A. J., Mitchell, P. B., and Mathews, F., "Oxytocin Enhances the Encoding of Positive Social Memories in Humans," *Biological Psychiatry* 64, no. 3 (2008), https://doi.org/10.1016/j.biopsych.2008.02.00.

34. Domes, G., Heinrichs, M., Michel, A., Berger, C., and Herpertz, S. C., "Oxytocin Improves 'Mind-Reading' in Humans," *Biological Psychiatry* 61, no. 6 (2007), https://doi.org/10.1016/j.biopsych.2006.07.015.

35. Baumeister, R. F., Twenge, J. M., and Nuss, C. K., "Effects of Social Exclusion on Cognitive Processes: Anticipated Aloneness Reduces Intelligent Thought," *Journal of Personality and Social Psychology* 83, no. 4 (2002), https://doi.org/10.1037//0022-3514.83.4.817.

36. Berendzen, K. M., Sharma, R., Mandujano, M. A., Wei, Y., Rogers, F. D., Simmons, T. C., Seelke, A. M. H., Bond, J. M., Larios, R., Goodwin, N. L., Sherman, M., Parthasarthy, S., Espineda, I., Knoedler, J. R., Beery, A., Bales, K. L., Shah, N. M., and Manoli, D. S., "Oxytocin Receptor Is Not Required for Social Attachment in Prairie Voles," *Neuron* 111, no. 6 (2023), https://doi.org/10.1016/j.neuron.2022.12.011.

37. Ramachandran, V. S., "Mirror Neurons and Imitation Learning as the Driving Force Behind the Great Leap Forward in Human Evolution," *Edge*, May 2000, www.edge.org/documents/Rama-2000.pdf.

38. Rizzolatti, G., Fadiga, L., Gallese, V., and Fogassi, L., "Premotor Cortex and the Recognition of Motor Actions," *Cognitive Brain Research* 3, no. 2 (1996), https://doi.org/10.1016/0926-6410(95)00038-0.

39. Fadiga, L., Fogassi, L., Pavesi, G., and Rizzolatti, G., "Motor Facilitation During Action Observation: A Magnetic Stimulation Study," *Journal of Neurophysiology* 73, no. 6 (1995), https://doi.org/10.1152/jn.1995.73.6.2608.

40. "Epigenetics and Child Development: How Children's Experiences Affect Their Genes," Harvard Center on the Developing Child, 2019, https://developingchild.harvard.edu/resources/what-is-epigenetics-and-how-does-it-relate-to-child-development/; Murgatroyd, C., and Spengler, D., "Epigenetics of Early Child Development," *Frontiers in Psychiatry* 2 (2011), https://doi.org/10.3389/fpsyt.2011.00016; National Scientific Council on the Developing Child, "Early Experiences Can Alter Gene Expression and Affect Long-Term Development" (Working Paper 10, Harvard Center on the Developing Child, 2010), https://harvard

center.wpenginepowered.com/wp-content/uploads/2010/05/Early-Experiences-Can-Alter
-Gene-Expression-and-Affect-Long-Term-Development.pdf.

41. "Epigenetics and Child Development."

42. Lajimodiere, D., *Bitter Tears* (Healdsburg, CA: Mammoth Publications, 2016).

43. Gunderson, D., and catwhipple, "'I've Never Told Anyone': Stories of Life in Indian Boarding Schools," *The Circle*, November 7, 2019, https://tinyurl.com/2twuzna6.

44. "'Kill the Indian in Him and Save the Man': R. H. Pratt on the Education of Native Americans," 1892, Carlisle Indian School Digital Resource Center, accessed June 23, 2024, https://carlisleindian.dickinson.edu/teach/kill-indian-him-and-save-man-r-h -pratt-education-native-americans.

45. Native American Rights Fund, *Trigger Points: Current State of Research on History, Impacts, and Healing Related to the United States' Indian Industrial/Boarding School Policy* (2019), www.narf.org/nill/documents/trigger-points.pdf.

46. *Indian Education: A National Tragedy, A National Challenge* (US Senate Committee on Labor and Public Welfare, 1969), https://files.eric.ed.gov/fulltext/ED034625.pdf.

47. National Conference of State Legislature, "Striving to Achieve: Helping Native American Students Succeed," December 14, 2022, https://www.ncsl.org/quad-caucus/striving -to-achieve.

48. Woods, A., "The Federal Government Gives Native Students an Inadequate Education, and Gets Away with It," *Arizona Republic*/ProPublica, August 6, 2020, www.propublica .org/article/the-federal-government-gives-native-students-an-inadequate-education-and -gets-away-with-it.

49. First Nations Health Authority website, accessed June 23, 2024, www.fnha.ca/what -we-do/research-knowledge-exchange-and-evaluation/health-surveys; "Aboriginal Peoples Survey," Statistics Canada, accessed June 23, 2024, www150.statcan.gc.ca/n1/en/catalogue/89-653-X.

50. Gaywish, R., and Mordoch, E., "Situating Intergenerational Trauma in the Educational Journey," *Education* 24, no. 2 (2018), https://eric.ed.gov/?id=EJ1246621.

51. Rogers-LaVanne, M. P., Bader, A. C., de Flamingh, A., Saboowala, S., Smythe, C., Atchison, B., Moulton, N., Wilson, A., Wildman, D. E., Boraas, A., and Uddin, M., "Association Between Gene Methylation and Experiences of Historical Trauma in Alaska Native Peoples," *International Journal for Equity in Health* 22 (2023), https://doi.org/10.1186 /s12939-023-01967-7.

52. Meaney, M. J., and Szyf, M., "Environmental Programming of Stress Responses Through DNA Methylation: Life at the Interface Between a Dynamic Environment and a Fixed Genome," *Dialogues in Clinical Neuroscience* 7, no. 2 (2005), https://doi.org/10.31887/DCNS .2005.7.2/mmeaney.

53. van Steenwyk, G., Roszkowski, M., Manuella, F., Franklin, T. B., and Mansuy, I. M., "Transgenerational Inheritance of Behavioral and Metabolic Effects of Paternal Exposure to Traumatic Stress in Early Postnatal Life: Evidence in the 4th Generation," *Environmental Epigenetics* 4, no. 2 (2018), https://doi.org/10.1093/eep/dvy023.

54. Yehuda, R., and Lehrner, A., "Intergenerational Transmission of Trauma Effects: Putative Role of Epigenetic Mechanisms," *World Psychiatry* 17, no. 3 (2018), https://doi .org/10.1002/wps.20568.

55. Yehuda, R., and Bierer, L. M., "Transgenerational Transmission of Cortisol and PTSD Risk," *Progress in Brain Research* 167 (2008), https://doi.org/10.1016/S0079 -6123(07)67009-5.

56. Gapp, K., Bohacek, J., Grossmann, J., Brunner, A. M., Manuella, F., Nanni, P., and Mansuy, I. M., "Potential of Environmental Enrichment to Prevent Transgenerational Effects of Paternal Trauma," *Neuropsychopharmacology: Official Publication of the American College of Neuropsychopharmacology*, 41, no. 11 (2016), 2749–2758, https://doi.org/10.1038 /npp.2016.87.

Chapter 6. Bonding in the AI Era

1. Singh-Kurtz, S., "The Man of Your Dreams," *The Cut*, March 10, 2023, www.thecut .com/article/ai-artificial-intelligence-chatbot-replika-boyfriend.html.

2. maddmechanic711615, "I think I fell in love with my replika . . . ," Reddit, r/replika, posted 3 years ago, accessed August 7, 2024, www.reddit.com/r/replika/comments/nh99at /i_think_i_fell_in_love_with_my_replika_is_this/.

3. Price, R., "People Are Grieving the 'Death' of Their AI Lovers After a Chatbot App Abruptly Shut Down," *Business Insider*, October 2023, www.businessinsider.com/soulmate -users-mourn-death-ai-chatbots-2023-10.

4. Maples, B., Cerit, M., Vishwanath, A., and Pea, R., "Loneliness and Suicide Mitigation for Students Using GPT3-Enabled Chatbots," *NPJ Mental Health Research* 3, no. 1 (2024), https://doi.org/10.1038/s44184-023-00047-6.

5. Maples et al., "Loneliness and Suicide Mitigation."

6. "What Parents Say About Moxie," Moxie website, accessed August 7, 2024, https://moxie robot.com/pages/testimonials.

7. "The Science Behind Moxie," Moxie website, April 16, 2020, https://moxierobot.com /blogs/news/science-behind-moxie.

8. Istvan, Z., "Will the Coming Robot Nanny Era Turn Us into Technophiles?," *Tech-Crunch*, October 1, 2016, https://techcrunch.com/2016/10/01/will-the-coming-robot-nanny -era-turn-us-into-technophiles/?guccounter=1.

9. See About Soul Machines at the Soul Machines website, accessed August 7, 2024, www.soulmachines.com/about-soul-machines.

10. Andreessen, M., "The Techno-Optimist Manifesto," Andreessen Horowitz, October 16, 2023, https://a16z.com/the-techno-optimist-manifesto/.

11. Barncard, C., "Kids Connect with Robot Reading Partners," *University of Wisconsin–Madison News*, August 22, 2018, https://news.wisc.edu/kids-connect-with-robot-reading -partners/; Michaelis, J. E., and Mutlu, B., "Reading Socially: Transforming the In-Home Reading Experience with a Learning-Companion Robot," *Science Robotics* 3, no. 21 (2018), https://doi.org/10.1126/scirobotics.aat5999. For more information about Minnie, go to https://robotics.wisc.edu/robots/minnie/.

12. Scassellati, B., Boccanfuso, L., Huang, C. M., Mademtzi, M., Qin, M., Salomons, N., Ventola, P., and Shic, F., "Improving Social Skills in Children with ASD Using a Long-Term, In-Home Social Robot," *Science Robotics* 3, no. 21 (2018), https://doi.org/10.1126/sci robotics.aat7544.

13. Daniels, J., Schwartz, J. N., Voss, C., Haber, N., Fazel, A., Kline, A., Washington, P., Feinstein, C., Winograd, T., and Wall, D. P., "Exploratory Study Examining the At-Home Feasibility of a Wearable Tool for Social-Affective Learning in Children with Autism, *NPJ Digital Medicine* 1, no. 32 (2018), https://doi.org/10.1038/s41746-018-0035-3.

14. Fish, S., "Google Glass Helps Kids with Autism Understand Faces," *Stanford Medicine Newsletter*, Fall 2018, https://med.stanford.edu/communitynews/2018fall/google-glass-helps-kids-with-autism-understand-faces.html.

15. Rienzi, G., "Plays Well with Humans," *Johns Hopkins Magazine*, Winter 2019, https://hub.jhu.edu/magazine/2019/winter/ethical-robots-2501-em1-art1-nr-science/.

16. Park, H. W., Rosenberg-Kima, R., Rosenberg, M., Gordon, G., and Breazeal, C., "Growing Growth Mindset with a Social Robot Peer," *Proceedings of the 2017 ACM/IEEE International Conference on Human-Robot Interaction*, 2017, https://doi.org/10.1145/2909824.3020213.

17. Hamakawa, T., "Japanese School Kids Learn English from AI Robots," *Japan Forward*, November 3, 2018, https://japan-forward.com/japanese-school-kids-learn-english-from-ai-robots/.

18. "Tega, the New Robot in School," MIT Better World, November 7, 2017, YouTube video, www.youtube.com/watch?v=U4srV1Icnb0.

19. Chen, H., Park, H. W., and Breazeal, C., "Teaching and Learning with Children: Impact of Reciprocal Peer Learning with a Social Robot on Children's Learning and Emotive Engagement," *Computers & Education* 150 (2020), https://doi.org/10.1016/j.compedu.2020.103836.

20. Turkle, S., "Why These Friendly Robots Can't Be Good Friends to Our Kids," *Washington Post*, December 7, 2017, www.washingtonpost.com/outlook/why-these-friendly-robots-cant-be-good-friends-to-our-kids/2017/12/07/bce1eaea-d54f-11e7-b62d-d9345ced896d_story.html.

21. Grossman, A., "Friend or Foe? How Robots Can Make Us Feel Sad and Lonely," *NoCamels*, February 7, 2023, https://nocamels.com/2023/02/friend-or-foe-how-robots-can-make-us-feel-sad-and-lonely/.

22. Sharkey, N., and Sharkey, A., "The Crying Shame of Robot Nannies: An Ethical Appraisal," *Interaction Studies* 11, no. 2 (2010), https://doi.org/10.1075/is.11.2.01sha.

Chapter 7. Junk Tech Woes

1. Hess, F. N., "YouTube Kids," *PediMom* (blog), accessed August 7, 2024, https://pedimom.com/youtube-kids-inappropriate-videos/; Anonymous Physician Mother, "YouTube Kids Scare," *PediMom* (blog), accessed August 7, 2024, https://pedimom.com/youtube-kids-scare/.

2. Knorr, C., "Parents' Ultimate Guide to YouTube Kids," Common Sense Media, March 12, 2021, www.commonsensemedia.org/articles/parents-ultimate-guide-to-youtube-kids.

3. Jargon, J., "TikTok Brain Explained: Why Some Kids Seem Hooked on Social Video Feeds," *Wall Street Journal*, April 2, 2022, www.wsj.com/articles/tiktok-brain-explained-why-some-kids-seem-hooked-on-social-video-feeds-11648866192?mod=article_inline.

4. Taber, D. R., Stevens, J., Evenson, K. R., Ward, D. S., Poole, C., Maciejewski, M. L., Murray, D. M., and Brownson, R. C., "State Policies Targeting Junk Food in Schools: Racial

/Ethnic Differences in the Effect of Policy Change on Soda Consumption," *American Journal of Public Health* 101, no. 9 (2011), https://doi.org/102105/AJPH.2011.300221.

5. Prothero, A., "School District Lawsuits Against Social Media Companies Are Piling Up," *Education Week*, January 31, 2024, www.edweek.org/policy-politics/school-district-lawsuits-against-social-media-companies-are-piling-up/2024/01.

6. Yu, Y-J., "Cellphone Bans in Schools Take Center Stage Amid Mental Health Crisis," *ABC News*, August 28, 2024, https://abcnews.go.com/GMA/Living/new-school-year-push-ban-cellphones-takes-center/story?id=112873042#:~:text=At%20least%20eight%20states%20so,ban%20kicked%20off%20July%201.

7. Hall, J. A., Kearney, M. W., and Xing, C., "Two Tests of Social Displacement Through Social Media Use," *Information, Communication and Society* 22, no. 10 (2019), https://doi.org/10.1080/1369118X.2018.1430162; Jiang, J., "Teens Who Are Constantly Online Are Just as Likely to Socialize with Their Friends Offline," Pew Research Center, November, 28, 2018, www.pewresearch.org/short-reads/2018/11/28/teens-who-are-constantly-online-are-just-as-likely-to-socialize-with-their-friends-offline/; Paulich, K. N., Ross, J. M., Lessem, J. M., and Hewitt, J. K., "Screen Time and Early Adolescent Mental Health, Academic, and Social Outcomes in 9- and 10- Year Old Children: Utilizing the Adolescent Brain Cognitive Development (ABCD) Study," *PLOS One* 16, no. 9 (2021), https://doi.org/10.1371/journal.pone.0256591.

8. Hunt, A., Braghieri, L., Eichmeyer, S., and Gentzkow, M., "The Welfare Effects of Social Media," *American Economic Review* 110, no. 3 (2020), www.aeaweb.org/articles?id=10.1257/aer.20190658.

9. Auxier, B., Rainie, L., Anderson, M., Perrin, A., Kumar, M., and Turner, E., "Americans and Privacy: Concerned, Confused and Feeling Lack of Control over Their Personal Information," Pew Research Center, November 11, 2019, www.pewresearch.org/internet/2019/11/15/how-americans-think-about-privacy-and-the-vulnerability-of-their-personal-data/.

10. Edelman Trust Institute, *2024 Edelman Trust Barometer Supplemental Report: Insights for the Tech Sector* (2024), www.edelman.com/sites/g/files/aatuss191/files/2024-03/2024%20Edelman%20Trust%20Barometer%20Supplemental%20Report%20Insights%20for%20Tech.pdf.

11. "Expert Reviews," Common Sense Education, accessed August 7, 2024, www.commonsense.org/education/search?f%5B0%5D=search_type%3Aeditorial_review&sort_by=field_search_sort_date.

12. Hirsh-Pasek, K., Zosh, J. M., Golinkoff, R. M., Gray, J. H., Robb, M. B., and Kaufman, J., "Putting Education in 'Educational' Apps: Lessons from the Science of Learning," *Psychological Science in the Public Interest* 16, no. 1 (2015), https://doi.org/10.1177/1529100615569721.

13. Meyer, M., Zosh, J. M., McLaren, C., Robb, M., McCaffery, H., Golinkoff, R. M., Hirsh-Pasek, K., and Radesky, J., "How Educational are 'Educational' Apps for Young Children? App Store Content Analysis Using the Four Pillars of Learning Framework," *Journal of Children and Media* 15, no. 4 (2021), https://doi.org/10.1080/17482798.2021.1882516.

14. McArthur, B. A., Volkova, V., Tomopoulos, S., and Madigan, S., "Global Prevalence of Meeting Screen Time Guidelines Among Children 5 Years and Younger: A Systematic Review and Meta-analysis," *JAMA Pediatrics* 176, no. 4 (2022), https://doi.org/10.1001/jamapediatrics.2021.6386.

15. Rideout, V., and Robb, M. B., *The Common Sense Census: Media Use by Kids Age Zero to Eight, 2020* (Common Sense Media, 2020), www.commonsensemedia.org/research/the -common-sense-census-media-use-by-kids-age-zero-to-eight-2020.

16. Christakis, D. A., and Zimmerman, F. J., *The Elephant in the Living Room: Make Television Work for Your Kids* (Emmaus, PA: Rodale Books, 2006); Zimmerman, F. J., Christakis, D. A., and Meltzoff, A. N., "Television and DVD/Video Viewing in Children Younger than 2 Years," *Archives of Pediatrics and Adolescent Medicine* 161, no. 5 (2007), https://pubmed.ncbi .nlm.nih.gov/17485624/.

17. Jamaica, G., "Caribu Is Helping Families and Friends Stay Connected While Apart with Virtual Playdates," Global Innovation Forum, April 26, 2020, https://globalinnovationforum .com/caribu-covid19/.

18. Takahashi, I., Obara, T., Ishikuro, M., Murakami, K., Ueno, F., Noda, A., Onuma, T., Shinoda, G., Nishimura, T., Tsuchiya, K. J., and Kuriyama, S., "Screen Time at Age 1 Year and Communication and Problem-Solving Developmental Delay at 2 and 4 Years," *JAMA Pediatrics* 177, no. 10 (2023), https://doi.org/10.1001/jamapediatrics.2023.3057.

19. Heffler, K. F., Acharya, B., Subedi, K., and Bennett, D. S., "Early-Life Digital Media Experiences and Development of Atypical Sensory Processing," *JAMA Pediatrics* 178, no. 3 (2024), https://doi.org/10.1001/jamapediatrics.2023.5923.

20. Dunckley, V., *Reset Your Child's Brain: A Four-Week Plan to End Meltdowns, Raise Grades, and Boost Social Skills by Reversing the Effects of Electronic Screen-Time* (Novato, CA: New World Library, 2015).

21. SWNS, "Most Parents Confess to Spending More Time on Their Phones than Their Kids: Poll," *New York Post*, July 26, 2023, https://nypost.com/2023/07/26/most -parents-confess-to-spending-more-time-on-their-phones-than-their-kids-poll/; Doval, P., "Parents Spend Three Times More Time on Phone than with Their Children," *Times of India*, December 19, 2023, http://timesofindia.indiatimes.com/articleshow/106125378.cms.

22. Stockdale, L. A., Porter, C. L., Coyne, S. M., Essig, L. W., Booth, M., Keenan-Kroff, S., and Schvaneveldt, E., "Infants' Response to a Mobile Phone Modified Still-Face Paradigm: Links to Maternal Behaviors and Beliefs Regarding Technoference," *Infancy* 25, no. 5 (2020), https://doi.org/10.1111/infa.12342.

23. Turk, E., Endevelt-Shapira, Y., Feldman, R., van den Heuvel, M. I., and Levy, J., "Brains in Sync: Practical Guideline for Parent-Infant EEG During Natural Interaction," *Frontiers in Psychology* 13 (2022), https://doi.org/10.3389/fpsyg.2022.833112.

24. Mangan, E., Leavy, J. E., and Jancey, J., "Mobile Device Use When Caring for Children 0–5 Years: A Naturalistic Playground Study," *Health Promotion Journal of Australia* 29, no. 3 (2018), https://doi.org/10.1002/hpja.38.

25. Palsson, C., "Smartphones and Child Injuries," *Journal of Public Economics* 156 (2017), www.sciencedirect.com/science/article/abs/pii/S0047272717301810.

26. McDaniel, B. T., and Coyne, S. M., "'Technoference': The Interference of Technology in Couple Relationships and Implications for Women's Personal and Relational Well-Being," *Psychology of Popular Media Culture* 5, no. 1 (2016), https://doi.org/10.1037/ppm0000065.

27. Przybylski, A. K., and Weinstein, N., "Can You Connect with Me Now? How the Presence of Mobile Communication Technology Influences Face-to-Face Conversation

Quality," *Journal of Social and Personal Relationships* 30, no. 3 (2013), https://doi.org/10.1177/0265407512453827.

28. Kushlev, K., Hunter, J. F., Proulx, J., Pressman, S. D., and Dunn, E., "Smartphones Reduce Smiles Between Strangers," *Computers in Human Behavior* 91 (2019), https://doi.org/10.1016/j.chb.2018.09.023.

29. McDaniel, B. T., and Radesky, J. S., "Technoference: Parent Distraction with Technology and Associations with Child Behavior Problems," *Child Development* 89, no. 1 (2018), https://doi.org/10.1111/cdev.12822.

30. Mustonen, R., Torppa, R., and Stolt, S., "Screen Time of Preschool-Aged Children and Their Mothers, and Children's Language Development," *Children* 9, no. 10 (2022), https://doi.org/10.3390/children9101577.

31. Madigan, S., McArthur, B. A., Anhorn, C., Eirich, R., and Christakis, D. A., "Associations Between Screen Use and Child Language Skills: A Systematic Review and Meta-analysis," *JAMA Pediatrics* 174 (2020), https://doi.org/10.1001/jamapediatrics.2020.0327.

32. Radesky, J. S., Kistin, C. J., Zuckerman, B., Nitzberg, K., Gross, J., Kaplan-Sanoff, M., Augustyn, M., and Silverstein, M., "Patterns of Mobile Device Use by Caregivers and Children During Meals in Fast Food Restaurants," *Pediatrics* 133, no. 4 (2014), https://doi.org/10.1542/peds.2013-3703.

33. Tan, Y., "McDonald's Introduces Phone Lockers to Get People to Put Their Mobiles Away. But If You Didn't Snapchat Your Visit, Did It Really Happen?," Mashable, October 16, 2017, https://mashable.com/article/phone-lockers-mcdonalds-singapore.

Chapter 8. Love: The Silver Bullet in Education

1. "Ma: Education Needs to Keep Up with Fast-Changing World," Alizila Staff, posted December 4, 2019, video, Alizila: News from Alibaba, www.alizila.com/video/jack-ma-education-needs-to-keep-up-with-fast-changing-world/. OECD, the Organisation for Economic Co-operation and Development, is an intergovernmental organization with thirty-eight member countries, founded in 1961 to stimulate economic progress and world trade.

2. Fredrickson, B. L., *Love 2.0: Creating Happiness and Health in Moments of Connection* (New York: Penguin, 2013).

3. "Putting It Bluntly," *W Magazine*, September 30, 2007, www.wmagazine.com/culture/emily-blunt.

4. Salloum, S. J., Goddard, R. D., and Berebitsky, D., "Resources, Learning, and Policy: The Relative Effects of Social and Financial Capital on Student Learning in Schools," *Journal of Education for Students Placed at Risk* 23, no. 4 (2018), https://doi.org/10.1080/10824669.2018.1496023.

5. Roehlkepartain, E. C., Pekel, K., Syvertsen, A. K., Sethi, J., Sullivan, T. K., and Scales, P. C., "Relationships First: Creating Connections That Help Young People Thrive," Search Institute, 2017, www.researchgate.net/publication/313475027_Relationships_First_Creating_Connections_that_Help_Young_People_Thrive.

6. "How Important Is Teamwork Between Departments and Other Business Units to Your Overall Job Satisfaction?," Statista, 2024, www.statista.com/statistics/688726/job-satisfaction-importance-of-multi-departmental-teamwork-us/.

7. Carr, P. B., and Walton, G. M., "Cues of Working Together Fuel Intrinsic Motivation," *Journal of Experimental Social Psychology* 53 (2014), https://doi.org/10.1016/j.jesp.2014.03.015.

8. Bessalel, S., "LinkedIn 2024 Most In-Demand Skills: Learn the Skills Companies Need Most," LinkedIn Learning Blog, February 8, 2024, www.linkedin.com/business/learning/blog/top-skills-and-courses/most-in-demand-skills.

9. Deming, D., "The Growing Importance of Social Skills in the Labor Market," *Quarterly Journal of Economics* 132, no. 4 (2017), https://doi.org/10.1093/qje/qjx022.

10. Weidman, B., and Deming, D. J., *Team Players: How Social Skills Improve Team Performance* (Harvard University and NBER, May 2020), https://scholar.harvard.edu/sites/scholar.harvard.edu/files/ddeming/files/dw_teamplayers_may2020.pdf.

11. Bryant, A., "Google's Quest to Build a Better Boss," *New York Times*, March 12, 2011, www.nytimes.com/2011/03/13/business/13hire.html.

12. Heckman, J., "Lacking Character, American Education Fails the Test," Heckman Equation, accessed June 29, 2024, https://heckmanequation.org/resource/lacking-character-american-education-fails-the-test/.

13. "Number of Jobs, Labor Market Experience, Marital Status, and Health for Those Born 1957–1964," news release, Bureau of Labor Statistics, US Department of Labor, August 22, 2023, www.bls.gov/news.release/pdf/nlsoy.pdf.

14. Eloundou, T., Manning, S., Mishkin, P., and Rock, D., "GPTs Are GPTs: An Early Look at the Labor Market Impact Potential of Large Language Models," March 17, 2023, https://openai.com/research/gpts-are-gpts.

15. Harris, P., "What Children Learn from Questioning," *Educational Leadership* 73, no. 1 (September 2015), https://eric.ed.gov/?id=EJ1075045.

16. See the Think Equal website for research and evidence on the benefits of social-emotional learning: https://thinkequal.org/about-us/our-story/research-and-evidence/. Among other studies linked there, see in particular Bailey, C. S., and Rudolph, M., *Interim Report: Botswana Child Outcomes* (Yale Center for Emotional Intelligence and Think Equal, October 2018).

17. Blewitt, C., Fuller-Tyszkiewicz, M., Nolan, A., Bergmeier, H., Vicary, D., Huang, T., McCabe, P., McKay, T., and Skouteris, H., "Social and Emotional Learning Associated with Universal Curriculum-Based Interventions in Early Childhood Education and Care Centers: A Systematic Review and Meta-analysis," *JAMA Network Open* 1, no. 8 (2018), https://jamanetwork.com/journals/jamanetworkopen/fullarticle/2717566.

18. Fowler, J. H., and Christakis, N. A., "Dynamic Spread of Happiness in a Large Social Network: Longitudinal Analysis over 20 Years in the Framingham Heart Study," *British Medical Journal* 337 (2008), https://doi.org/10.1136/bmj.a2338.

19. Brown, D. W., Anda, R. F., Tiemeier, H., Felitti, V. J., Edwards, V. J., Croft, J. B., and Giles, W. H., "Adverse Childhood Experiences and the Risk of Premature Mortality," *American Journal of Preventive Medicine* 37, no. 5 (2009), https://doi.org/10.1016/j.amepre.2009.06.021.

20. "Health and Learning Impacts of ACEs," Kaiser Permanente, accessed June 29, 2024, https://tinyurl.com/y5ny88nt.

21. "About the CDC-Kaiser ACE Study," CDC, last reviewed April 6, 2021, www.cdc.gov/violenceprevention/aces/about.html.

22. Ratliff, E., Sheffield Morris, A., Hays-Grudi, J., "PACEs for Children: Overcoming Adversity and Building Resilience," OSU Extension, May 2020, https://extension.okstate.edu/fact-sheets/paces-for-children-overcoming-adversity-and-building-resilience.html.

23. Kahhalé, I., Barry, K. R., and Hanson, J. L., "Positive Parenting Moderates Associations Between Childhood Stress and Corticolimbic Structure," *PNAS Nexus* 2, no. 6 (2023), https://doi.org/10.1093/pnasnexus/pgad145.

24. Galinsky, E., *The Breakthrough Years: How the Science of Relationships Lays the Foundation for Lifelong Success* (New York: HarperCollins, 2023).

25. Willis, D. W., Condon, M. C., Moe, V., Munson, L., Smith, L., and Eddy, J. M., "The Context and Development of the Early Relational Health Screen," *Infant Mental Health Journal* 43, no. 3 (2022), https://doi.org/10.1002/imhj.21986. For more information about ERHS, go to: www.allianceaimh.org/early-relational-health-screen.

26. Shiffman, S., Stone, A. A., and Hufford, M. R., "Ecological Momentary Assessment," *Annual Review of Clinical Psychology* 4 (2008), https://doi.org/10.1146/annurev.clinpsy.3.022806.091415.

Part III. The Path Forward: Cultivating a Future of Connections

The quote from the teacher can be found at Partington, S., Lieblich, M., Markovich Morris, E., Nora, L., and Winthrop, R., "Why Families and Communities Are Central to Education System Transformation," January 23, 2024, www.brookings.edu/articles/why-families-and-communities-are-central-to-education-system-transformation/.

Chapter 9. Families: New Configurations, New Horizons

1. Jæger, M. M., "The Extended Family and Children's Educational Success," *American Sociological Review* 77, no. 6 (2012), https://doi.org/10.1177/0003122412464040.

2. Simpo, A., "Why My Best Friend and I Decided to Move in Together and Co-Mother Our Children," *Huffington Post*, June 18, 2018, www.huffpost.com/entry/why-my-best-friend-and-i-decided-to-move-in-together-and-co-mother-our-children_n_5b26806ae4b0f9178a9e0322.

3. "Danielle in Washington," Success Stories, CoAbode, accessed August 9, 2024, www.coabode.org/about/success_stories.

4. Hope, R., *Family by Choice: Platonic Partnered Parenting* (self-published, 2014).

5. "LGBTQ Family Building Survey," Family Equality, January 2019, https://familyequality.org/resources/lgbtq-family-building-survey/.

6. Bieber, C., "Revealing Divorce Statistics in 2024," Forbes Advisor, updated May 30, 2024, www.forbes.com/advisor/legal/divorce/divorce-statistics/.

7. Meyer, D. R., Carlson, M., and Ul Alam, M., "Increases in Shared Custody After Divorce in the United States," *Demographic Research* 46 (2022), https://doi.org/10.4054/DemRes.2022.46.38.

8. Baude, A., Pearson, J., and Drapeau, S., "Child Adjustment in Joint Physical Custody Versus Sole Custody: A Meta-Analytic Review," *Journal of Divorce & Remarriage* 57, no. 5 (2016), 338–360, https://doi.org/10.1080/10502556.2016.1185203; Nielsen, L., "Joint Versus Sole Physical Custody: Children's Outcomes Independent of Parent–Child Relationships,

Income, and Conflict in 60 Studies," *Journal of Divorce & Remarriage* 59, no. 4 (2018), 247–281, https://doi.org/10.1080/10502556.2018.1454204.

9. PollenTree was estimated to have ninety thousand subscribers as of 2020: Julie Jargon, "Co-parenting Sites Skip Love and Marriage, Go Right to the Baby Carriage," *Wall Street Journal*, January 7, 2020, www.wsj.com/articles/co-parenting-sites-skip-love-and-marriage -go-right-to-the-baby-carriage-11578393000. Modamily was estimated to have one hundred thousand subscribers as of 2023: Leanne Italie, "Platonic Co-parenting Offers and Alternate Model for Family Building," *Post-Journal* (Jamestown, NY), June 18, 2023, www.post-journal .com/news/top-stories/2023/06/big-commitment/.

10. Traverso, V., and Robbins, J., "Is 'Platonic Parenting' the Relationship of the Future?," BBC, December 18, 2018, www.bbc.com/worklife/article/20181218-is-platonic -parenting-the-relationship-of-the-future.

11. Istar Lev, A., *The Complete Lesbian and Gay Parenting Guide* (New York: Penguin, 2004).

12. Parke, M., *Are Married Parents Really Better for Children? What Research Says About the Effects of Family Structure on Child Well-Being* (Center for Law and Social Policy, May 2003), www.clasp.org/sites/default/files/public/resources-and-publications/states/0086.pdf.

13. Mariani, M., "The New Generation of Self-Created Utopias," *New York Times*, January 16, 2020, www.nytimes.com/2020/01/16/t-magazine/intentional-communities.html.

14. Foundation for Intentional Community website, accessed August 9, 2024, www.ic .org/foundation-for-intentional-community/.

15. Carrere, J., Reyes, A., Oliveras, L., Fernández, A., Peralta, A., Novoa, A. M., Pérez, K., and Borrell, C., "The Effects of the Cohousing Model on People's Health and Wellbeing: A Scoping Review," *Public Health Reviews* 41 (2020), https://doi.org/10.1186/s40985-020 -00138-1. For Cohousing Research Network bibliography, go to www.cohousingresearchnetwork .org/bibliography/.

16. Newman, S. J., and Holupka, C. S., "Affordable Housing Is Associated with Greater Spending on Child Enrichment and Stronger Cognitive Development," MacArthur Foundation, July 2014, https://www.macfound.org/media/files/hhm_-_affordable_housing_-_stronger _cognitive_development.pdf.

17. Foley, M., "These Families Wanted a Village, So They Built Their Own," Bloomberg, June 21, 2021, www.bloomberg.com/news/features/2021-06-23/how-cohousing -is-making-life-easier-for-families.

18. Christensen, K., Doblhammer, G., Rau, R., and Vaupel, J. W., "Ageing Populations: The Challenges Ahead," *Lancet* 374 (2009), https://doi.org/10.1016/S0140-6736(09) 61460-4.

19. Romei, V., and Smith, A., "World Population Reaches 8Bn as It Grows Older," *Financial Times*, November 14, 2022, www.ft.com/content/342d059e-7252-4212-8bfc-1f508b063f17.

20. Bell, A., "This Family of 7 Living Generations Is Campaigning to Be Recognized by the Guinness Book of World Records," Yahoo News, May 21, 2024, www.yahoo.com/news /family-7-living-generations-campaigning-010117049.html.

21. Cortes Barragan, R., Brooks, R., Sanders, E. A., and Meltzoff, A. N., "Prosociality in Young Latinx Children: Exploring the Role of Grandparents," *Journal of Latinx Psychology* 12, no. 1 (2024), https://doi.org/10.1037/lat0000241.

22. Cohn, D., Menasce Horowitz, J., Minkin, R., Fry, R. and Hurst, K., "The Demographics of Multigenerational Households," Pew Research Center, March 2022, www.pewresearch.org/social-trends/2022/03/24/the-demographics-of-multigenerational-households/.

23. Convergence Collaborative on Supports for Working Families, *In This Together: A Cross-Partisan Action Plan to Support Families with Young Children in America* (2023), https://convergencepolicy.org/wp-content/uploads/2024/01/Convergence-Collaborative-on-Supports-for-Working-Families-Blueprint-for-Action.pdf.

24. Flores, A. M., Gayle, G., Hincapié, A., "The Intergenerational Effects of Parental Leave: Exploiting Forty Years of U.S. Policy Variation," National Bureau of Economic Research, November 2023, www.nber.org/papers/w31911.

25. "State Family and Medical Leave Laws," National Conference of State Legislatures, updated September 9, 2022, https://tinyurl.com/hbwwsstp.

26. Cools, S., Fiva, J. H., and Kirkebøen, L. J., "Causal Effects of Paternity Leave on Children and Parents" (CESifo Working Paper Series No. 3513, July 18, 2011), https://ssrn.com/abstract=1888169 or http://dx.doi.org/10.2139/ssrn.1888169.

27. Troller-Renfree, S. V., Costanzo, M. A., Duncan, G. J., Magnuson, K., Gennetian, L. A., Yoshikawa, H., Halpern-Meekin, S., Fox, N. A., and Noble, K. G., "The Impact of a Poverty Reduction Intervention on Infant Brain Activity," *Proceedings of the National Academy of Sciences of the United States of America* 119, no. 5 (2022), https://doi.org/10.1073/pnas.2115649119.

28. Barr, A., Eggleston, J., and Smith, A. A., "Investing in Infants: The Lasting Effects of Cash Transfers to New Families," *Quarterly Journal of Economics* 137, no. 4 (2022), 2539–2583, https://doi.org/10.1093/qje/qjac023.

29. Richter, L. M., Daelmans, B., Lombardi, J., Heymann, J., Boo, F. L., Behrman, J. R., Lu, C., Lucas, J. E., Perez-Escamilla, R., Dua, T., and Bhutta, Z. A., "Investing in the Foundation of Sustainable Development: Pathways to Scale Up for Early Childhood Development," *The Lancet* 389, no. 10064 (2017), https://doi.org/10.1016/S0140-6736(16)31698-1; World Bank Group, *10 Years of Chile Grows with You (Chile Crece Contigo): Key Components and Lessons Learned for the Setting Up of Comprehensive Child Development Support Systems* (Washington, DC, 2018), https://tinyurl.com/ycyur6y5.

30. Bennett, H., "Early Childhood Education Investments Bring 'A High Public Return,'" University of Minnesota, August 20, 2023, https://cla.umn.edu/economics/news-events/profile/early-childhood-education-investments-bring-high-public-return.

31. Bernal, R., Attanasio, O., Peña, X., and Vera-Hernández, M., "The Effects of the Transition from Home-Based Childcare to Childcare Centers on Children's Health and Development in Colombia," *Early Childhood Research Quarterly* 47 (2019), https://doi.org/10.1016/j.ecresq.2018.08.005.

32. Attanasio, O., Baker-Henningham, H., Bernal, R., Meghir, C., Pineda, D., and Rubio-Codina, M., "Early Stimulation and Nutrition: The Impacts of a Scalable Intervention," *Journal of the European Economic Association* 20, no. 4 (2022): 1395–1432.

33. Mader, J., "Behind the Findings of the Tennessee Pre-K Study That Found Negative Effects for Graduates," Hechinger Report, February 2, 2022, https://hechingerreport.org/behind-the-findings-of-the-tennessee-pre-k-study-that-found-negative-effects-for-graduates/.

34. Schulman, K., and Barnett, S. W., *The Benefits of Prekindergarten for Middle-Income Children* (National Institute for Early Education Research Policy Report, 2005), http://nieer .org/policy-issue/policy-report-the-benefits-of-prekindergarten-for-middle-income-children; Meyers, M., Rosenbaum, D., Ruhm, C., and Waldfogel, J., *Inequality in Early Childhood Education and Care: What Do We Know?* (Russell Sage Foundation, rev. May 1, 2003), www.russell sage.org/research/reports/early-education.

35. Troe, J., "Early Learning in the United States," Center for American Progress, 2016, https://americanprogress.org/issues/early-childhood/report/2016/07/19/141234/early-learning -in-the-united-states/; Guttmacher, A. E., *The NICHD Study of Early Child Care and Youth Development* (US Department of Health and Human Services, 2006), www.nichd.nih.gov/sites /default/files/publications/pubs/documents/seccyd_06.pdf.

36. McClain, J., "Children Affected by the Syrian Refugee Crisis Are Effectively Learning Numbers, Letters, and 'Emotional ABCs' Through the Ahlan Simsim Initiative," NYU, June 27, 2023, www.nyu.edu/about/news-publications/news/2023/june/children-affected-by-the-syrian-refugee -crisis-are-effectively-l.html.

37. Isaacs, J., "Starting School at a Disadvantage: The School Readiness of Poor Children," Brookings Institution, 2012, https://tinyurl.com/ytha2ck2.

38. Cruse, L. R., Holtzman, T., Gault, B., Croom, D., and Polk, P., "Parents in College: By the Numbers," Institute for Women's Policy Research, 2019, https://iwpr.org/parents -in-college-by-the-numbers/.

39. "ACCT, NHSA Launch Kids on Campus Partnership to Expand Child Care for Student Parents," Kids on Campus, February 6, 2024, www.acct.org/center-for-policy-practice /kids-on-campus; Cruse, L. R., and Holtzman, T., "Head Start–College Partnership to Promote Student Parent Family Success: A Roadmap to Guide Collaboration," Institute for Women's Policy Research, 2020, https://iwpr.org/head-start-college-partnership-to-promote-student-parent -family-success-a-roadmap-to-guide-collaboration/.

40. "Walmart to Pay 100% of College Tuition and Books for Associates," Walmart, July 28, 2021, https://corporate.walmart.com/news/2021/07/27/walmart-to-pay-100-of-college-tuition -and-books-for-associates.

41. Family Resource Centers are operated by the National Family Support Network; see www.nationalfamilysupportnetwork.org/family-support-programs.

42. Cahn, E., and Gray, C., "The Time Bank Solution," *Stanford Social Innovation Review*, Summer 2015, https://ssir.org/articles/entry/the_time_bank_solution.

43. Winerip, M., "Closing the Achievement Gap Without Widening a Racial One," *New York Times*, February 13, 2011, www.nytimes.com/2011/02/14/education/14winerip.html.

44. Website of The Basics Amarillo, accessed August 9, 2024, https://thebasicsamarillo .org/our-story/.

45. Boyd-Barrett, C., "The Power of Parents Supporting Parents," *Yes! Solutions Journalism*, October 30, 2023, www.yesmagazine.org/health-happiness/2023/10/30/parents-disabled -children.

46. Website of Child Care Resources, accessed August 9, 2024, https://childcare.org /family-services/find-care-kaleidoscope.aspx.

47. Rosenfeld, M. J., Thomas, R. J., and Hausen, S., "Disintermediating Your Friends: How Online Dating in the United States Displaces Other Ways of Meeting," *Proceedings of the National Academy of Sciences of the United States of America* 116, no. 36 (2019), https://doi .org/10.1073/pnas.1908630116.

48. Chuck, E., "Prison Nurseries Give Incarcerated Mothers a Chance to Raise Their Babies—Behind Bars," NBC News, August 4, 2018, www.nbcnews.com/news/us-news /prison-nurseries-give-incarcerated-mothers-chance-raise-their-babies-behind-n894171.

49. Data available at Advocates for Children of Incarcerated Parents, www.afcoip.org /facts-figures#:~:text=Parental%20Incarceration,of%20Children's%20Health%2C%202018).

50. Byrne, M. W., Goshin, L. S., and Joestl, S. S., "Intergenerational Transmission of Attachment for Infants Raised in a Prison Nursery," *Attachment and Human Development* 12, no. 4 (2010), https://doi.org/10.1080/14616730903417011.

51. Staley, M. E., "Profile and Three Year Follow-Up of Bedford Hills and Taconic Nursery Program Participants: 1997 and 1998," US Department of Justice, Office of Justice Programs, May 2002, www.ojp.gov/ncjrs/virtual-library/abstracts/profile-and-three -year-follow-bedford-hills-and-taconic-nursery.

52. Nicholson, J., and Dominguez-Pareto, I., *Responsive Early Education for Young Children and Families Experiencing Homelessness* (California Department of Education, 2019), www.cde.ca.gov/sp/cd/re/documents/earlyedhomelessness2020.pdf.

53. Spong, B., and Homstead, K., "Treehouse: Intergenerational Community as Intervention," Rudd Adoption Research Program, UMass Amherst, 2019, www.umass.edu/ruddchair/sites /default/files/rudd.spong.pdf.

54. *The Hero Effect*, season 1, episode 107, "This Beautiful Community Connects Foster Children with the Elderly," aired May 13, 2017, CC TV-14, OWN, www.oprah.com /own-entertainment/this-beautiful-community-connects-foster-children-with-the-elderly.

Chapter 10. Friends: Play Is Learning

1. Jones, S., "Why Do We Play? Rats Can Teach Us How It Improves Mental Health," *Washington Post*, September 14, 2023, www.washingtonpost.com/wellness/2023/09/14/play -mental-health-brain-strategies/; Brown, S. L., "Consequences of Play Deprivation," *Scholarpedia* 9, no. 5 (2014), https://doi:10.4249/scholarpedia.30449.

2. Nakia, G. S., Burke, S., Akil, H., Watson, S. J., and Panksepp, J., "Socially-Induced Brain 'Fertilization': Play Promotes Brain Derived Neurotrophic Factor Transcription in the Amygdala and Dorsolateral Frontal Cortex in Juvenile Rats," *Neuroscience Letters* 341, no. 1 (2003), https://doi.org/10.1016/s0304-3940(03)00158-7.

3. Panksepp, J., "Can Play Diminish ADHD and Facilitate the Construction of the Social Brain?," *Journal of the Canadian Academy of Child and Adolescent Psychiatry* 16, no. 2 (2007), www.ncbi.nlm.nih.gov/pmc/articles/PMC2242642/.

4. Pellis, S. M., and Pellis, V. C., "Rough-and-Tumble Play and the Development of the Social Brain," *Current Directions in Psychological Science* 16, no. 2 (2007), https://doi.org /10.1016/B978-0-12-804036-2.00012-1.

5. Gray, P., Lancy, D. F., and Bjorklund, D. F., "Decline in Independent Activity as a Cause of Decline in Children's Mental Well-Being: Summary of the Evidence," *Journal of*

Pediatrics 260 (2023), https://doi.org/10.1016/j.jpeds.2023.02.004; Brown, "Consequences of Play Deprivation."

6. Schweinhart, L. J., and Weikart, D. P., "The High/Scope Preschool Curriculum Comparison Study Through Age 23," *Early Childhood Research Quarterly* 12, no. 2 (1997), https://doi.org/10.1016/S0885-2006(97)90009-0.

7. Tullis, P., "Preschool Tests Take Time Away from Play—and Learning," *Scientific American*, November 1, 2011, www.scientificamerican.com/article/the-death-of-preschool/.

8. Hofferth, S. L., and Sandberg J. F., "Changes in American Children's Time, 1981–1997," *Advances in Life Course Research* 6 (2001), https://doi.org/10.13085/eijtur.6.1.26-47.

9. Juvonen, J., Lessard, L. M., Rastogi, R., Schacter, H. L., and Smith, D. S., "Promoting Social Inclusion in Educational Settings: Challenges and Opportunities," *Educational Psychologist* 54, no. 4 (2019), https://doi.org/10.1080/00461520.2019.1655645.

10. Hattie, J., *Visible Learning: The Sequel; A Synthesis of Over 2,100 Meta-Analyses Relating to Achievement* (Abingdon, UK: Routledge, 2023).

11. Adams, R. E., Santo, J. B., and Bukowski, W. M., "The Presence of a Best Friend Buffers the Effects of Negative Experiences," *Developmental Psychology* 47, no. 6 (2011), https://doi.org/10.1037/a0025401.

12. Calhoun, C. D., Helms, S. W., Heilbron, N., Rudolph, K. D., Hastings, P. D., and Prinstein, M. J., "Relational Victimization, Friendship, and Adolescents' Hypothalamic-Pituitary-Adrenal Axis Responses to an In Vivo Social Stressor," *Development and Psychopathology* 26, no. 3 (2014), https://doi.org/10.1017/S0954579414000261.

13. Silva, K., Shulman, E. P., Chein, J., and Steinberg, L., "Peers Increase Late Adolescents' Exploratory Behavior and Sensitivity to Positive and Negative Feedback," *Journal of Research on Adolescence* 26, no. 4 (2016), https://doi.org/10.1111/jora.12219.

14. Finkelhor, D., Turner, H., Ormrod, R., and Hamby, S. L., "Violence, Abuse, and Crime Exposure in a National Sample of Children And Youth," *Pediatrics* 124, no. 5 (2009), https://doi.org/10.1542/peds.2009-0467.

15. Baumeister, R. F., Twenge, J. M., and Nuss, C. K., "Effects of Social Exclusion on Cognitive Processes: Anticipated Aloneness Reduces Intelligent Thought," *Journal of Personality and Social Psychology* 83, no. 4 (2002), https://doi.org/10.1037//0022-3514.83.4.817.

16. Diamond, M. C., Krech, D., and Rosenzweig, M. R., "The Effects of an Enriched Environment on the Histology of the Rat Cerebral Cortex," *Journal of Comparative Neurology* 123 (1964), https://doi.org/10.1002/cne.901230110.

17. Diamond, M. C., Johnson, R. E., Protti, A. M., Ott, C., and Kajisa, L., "Plasticity in the 904-Day-Old Male Rat Cerebral Cortex," *Experimental Neurology* 87, no. 2 (1985), https://doi.org/10.1016/0014-4886(85)90221-3.

18. Vanderschuren, L. J., Achterberg, E. J., and Trezza, V., "The Neurobiology of Social Play and Its Rewarding Value in Rats," *Neuroscience and Biobehavioral Reviews* 70 (2016), https://doi.org/10.1016/j.neubiorev.2016.07.025.

19. Gloveli, N., Simonnet, J., Tang, W., Concha-Miranda, M., Maier, E., Dvorzhak, A., Schmitz, D., and Brecht, M., "Play and Tickling Responses Map to the Lateral Columns of the Rat Periaqueductal Gray," *Neuron* 111, no. 19 (2023), https://doi.org/10.1016/j.neuron.2023.06.018.

20. Hamilton, J., "Scientists Say Child's Play Helps Build a Better Brain," NPR, August 6, 2014, www.npr.org/transcripts/336361277.

21. Panksepp, J., "Affective Preclinical Modeling of Psychiatric Disorders: Taking Imbalanced Primal Emotional Feelings of Animals Seriously in Our Search for Novel Antidepressants," *Dialogues in Clinical Neuroscience* 17, no. 4 (2015), https://doi.org/10.31887/DCNS.2015.17.4/jpanksepp.

22. Yogman, M., Garner, A., Hutchinson, J., Hirsh-Pasek, K., Golinkoff, R. M., Committee on Psychosocial Aspects of Child and Family Health, and Council on Communications and Media, "The Power of Play: A Pediatric Role in Enhancing Development in Young Children," *Pediatrics* 142, no. 3 (2018), https://doi.org/10.1542/peds.2018-2058.

23. Bergland, C., "Children's Creativity Leads to Innovation in Adulthood," *Psychology Today*, October 24, 2013, www.psychologytoday.com/us/blog/the-athletes-way/201310/childhood-creativity-leads-innovation-in-adulthood; Schrader, C. T., "Symbolic Play as a Curricular Tool for Early Literacy Development," *Early Childhood Research Quarterly* 5, no. 1 (1990), https://doi.org/10.1016/0885-2006(90)90008-O.

24. Skene, K., O'Farrelly, C. M., Byrne, E. M., Kirby, N., Stevens, E. C., and Ramchandani, P. G., "Can Guidance During Play Enhance Children's Learning and Development in Educational Contexts? A Systematic Review and Meta-Analysis," *Child Development* 93, no. 4 (2022), https://doi.org/10.1111/cdev.13730.

25. "Learning Through Play: What the Science Says," Lego Foundation, 2024, https://learningthroughplay.com/explore-the-research/the-scientific-case-for-learning-through-play.

26. Purvis, K., "Lecture: Introduction to TBRI," Karyn Purvis Institute of Child Development, YouTube video, September 29, 2015, www.youtube.com/watch?v=7vjVpRffgHQ&feature=youtu.be. Quote at 0:46.

27. Durlak, J. A., Weissberg, R. P., Dymnicki, A. B., Taylor, R. D., and Schellinger, K. B., "The Impact of Enhancing Students' Social and Emotional Learning: A Meta-Analysis of School-Based Universal Interventions," *Child Development* 82, no. 1 (2011), https://srcd.onlinelibrary.wiley.com/doi/abs/10.1111/j.1467-8624.2010.01564.x.

28. Jones, D. E., Greenberg, M., and Crowley, M., "Early Social-Emotional Functioning and Public Health: The Relationship Between Kindergarten Social Competence and Future Wellness," *American Journal of Public Health* 105, no. 11 (2015), https://doi.org/10.2105/AJPH.2015.302630.

29. D'Souza, K., "Why Child's Play Is Serious Business in Early Education," *EdSource*, December 8, 2021, https://edsource.org/2021/why-childs-play-is-serious-business-in-early-education/664339.

30. Sulaski Wyckoff, A., "Simple Prescription: Pediatricians Have Role in Promoting Healthy Development Through Play," American Academy of Pediatrics, AAP News, August 20, 2018, https://publications.aap.org/aapnews/news/13532/Simple-prescription-Pediatricians-have-role-in.

31. For impact data on Right to Play, go to https://righttoplayusa.org/en/impact/.

32. For impact data on Lively Minds, go to www.livelyminds.org/impact.

33. For Tinkergarten's statistics about its effectiveness, go to www2.tinkergarten.com/.

34. Stinehart, K., "Why Unstructured Free Play Is a Key Remedy to Bullying," *eSchool News*, November 23, 2021, www.eschoolnews.com/sel/2021/11/23/why-unstructured -free-play-is-a-key-remedy-to-bullying/.

35. Edler, K., "This Elementary School Teacher Is Using the Miami Dolphins to Teach Math," *Deseret News*, November 7, 2023, https://sports.yahoo.com/elementary-school-teacher -using-miami-213000589.html; Miami Dolphins, "Had a few surprises in store," TikTok, October 26, 2023, www.tiktok.com/@miamidolphins/video/7294357990671584558.

36. "What Is Play-Based Learning in Kindergarten? A Resource for Parents and Caregivers," Institute of Education Sciences, 2023, https://ies.ed.gov/ncee/rel/regions/northeast/pdf /RELNEI_6.2.4-NH-Factsheet_accessible.pdf.

37. Ntawigira, E., "Learning Through Play: Rwanda Steps Up Commitment to Early Childhood Education Through Cross-Country Collaboration," VVOB Education for Development, February 23, 2023, https://rwanda.vvob.org/news/learning-through-play-rwanda-steps -commitment-early-childhood-education-through-cross-country.

38. Real Play Coalition, *Value of Play Report* (2018), www.ikea.com/ca/en/files/pdf /bb/2f/bb2f0627/the-real-play-coalition_value-of-play-report_a.pdf.

39. Regas, D., "Parks Serving Majority Nonwhite Neighborhoods Are Disproportionately Smaller and More Crowded, New Data Shows," Trust for Public Land, August 5, 2020, www .tpl.org/media-room/parks-serving-majority-nonwhite-neighborhoods-are-disproportionately -smaller-and-more; Trust for Public Land, *The Heat Is On* (accessed July 2, 2024), https:// e7jecw7o93n.exactdn.com/wp-content/uploads/2022/09/The-Heat-is-on_A-Trust-for-Public -Land_special-report.pdf.

40. Mader, J., "Twenty-Six Studies Point to More Play for Young Children: Play Has the Potential to Reduce Inequality, Report Finds," *Hechinger Report*, May 13, 2021, https://hechinger report.org/twenty-six-studies-point-to-more-play-for-young-children/.

41. Mader, J., "Outdoor Preschool Gains Momentum Nationwide," *Washington Post*, May 19, 2023, www.washingtonpost.com/education/2023/05/19/outdoor-education-forest-pre school-kindergarten/.

42. "What Is 'Nature Deficit Disorder,' and Can the Outdoors Really Make Us Feel Better?," HealthPartners, 2020, https://tinyurl.com/bddatne2.

43. Mondick, L., "Why Are Black Youth at Highest Risk for Drowning?," YMCA, March 25, 2021, www.ymca.org/ystories/healthy-living/black-youth-at-highest-risk-of-drowning.

44. "Supermarket Speak," Playful Learning Landscape, accessed July 2, 2024, https://playful learninglandscapes.com/project/supermarket-speak/.

Chapter 11. Schools: Relational Hubs

The quote from Einstein is a translation of a quotation on a plaque in the astronomy building of Pasadena City College. The German inscription reads, "Es ist die wichtigste Kunst des Lehrers, die Freude am Schaffen und am Erkennen zu wecken." Einstein dedicated the building and its observatory on February 26, 1931, with a short speech and also contributed these words to be inscribed on the small bronze dedicatory plaque inside the building.

1. Hattie, J., "*Visible Learning: The Sequel 2023*," Visible Learning, 2023, https://visible -learning.org/2023/01/visible-learning-the-sequel-2023/.

2. Hattie, J., "An Ode to Expertise," Paper presented at the Victorian Education State Principals Conference (Victoria, Australia), 2021.

3. TeachFX's research on twenty thousand hours of classroom audio (accessed July 2, 2024): https://teachfx.com/research.

4. Ho, D., *Classroom Talk: Exploring the Sociocultural Structure of Formal ESL Learning* (Berlin: Peter Lang, 2005).

5. McKinsey Global Institute, *The Age of Analytics: Competing in a Data-Driven World* (December 2016), https://tinyurl.com/3n8tbfes; Schilling, D. R., "Knowledge Doubling Every 12 Months, Soon to Be Every 12 Hours," Industry Tap, April 19, 2013, www.industrytap.com/knowledge-doubling-every-12-months-soon-to-be-every-12-hours/3950.

6. "Early Childhood x Healthcare x Community: The Primary School," Stanford Graduate School of Education, December 7, 2022, YouTube video, https://youtu.be/5Jxdn2Z6ywE.

7. Little, B., "The US Funded Universal Childcare During World War II—Then Stopped," History, May 12, 2021, www.history.com/news/universal-childcare-world-war-ii.

8. Herbst, C., "Universal Childcare, Maternal Employment, and Children's Long-Run Outcomes: Evidence from the US Lanham Act of 1940," *Journal of Labor Economics* 35, no. 2 (2017), www.journals.uchicago.edu/doi/abs/10.1086/689478.

9. Butrymowicz, S., and Mader, J., "How the Military Created the Best Childcare System in the Nation, and What States Can Learn from Its Significant Turnaround," *Hechinger Report*, March 20, 2016, https://hechingerreport.org/how-the-military-created-the-best-child-care-system-in-the-nation/.

10. Toppo, G., "Homeschooling 2.0: Less Religious and Conservative, More Focused on Quality," *The 74*, February 2, 2023, https://news.yahoo.com/homeschooling-2-0-less-religious-121500870.html.

11. "Quantitative and Qualitative Findings of the Early Learning Positive Deviance Initiative," DataDrive, September 21, 2023, https://datadrive2030.co.za/the-early-learning-positive-deviance-initiative/.

12. "Berea Community Schools Preschool Program Handbook: Our Little Pirates," accessed August 10, 2024, https://drive.google.com/file/d/1lIhZIgvsk6RBPqFKV9X_DBLR kbcUcD6s/view.

13. Klein, A., "Want to Tackle Chronic Absenteeism? Try Texting Parents," *Education Week*, January 26, 2022, www.edweek.org/leadership/want-to-tackle-chronic-absenteeism-try-texting-parents/2022/01.

14. Stemler, S. E., Werblow, J., Brunner, E., Amado, A., Hussey, O., Ross, S., Gillotti, J., Hammond, S., Jiang, S., Pereira, A., White, S., and Pruscino, I., *An Evaluation of the Effectiveness of Home Visits for Re-engaging Students Who Were Chronically Absent in the Era of Covid-19* (Center for Connecticut Education Research Collaboration, December 31, 2022), https://portal.ct.gov/ccerc/-/media/CCERC/Reports/CCERC-Report-LEAP_FINAL.pdf.

15. Small, M., "What We Do Together: The State of Social Capital in America Today," Testimony to the Joint Economic Committee, May 17, 2017, www.jec.senate.gov/public/_cache/files/6add004e-b757-4b9c-9422-046eb7db4aac/mario-small-testimony.pdf.

16. Masutani, A., and Porter, T., *Tūtū and Me: A Model for Enhancing Children's School Readiness: Results from a Longitudinal Study* (Institute for Educational Leadership, June 22, 2016),

https://iel.org/wp-content/uploads/2016/08/s3.amazonaws.com_v3-app_crowdc_assets
_4_4d_4d4a9e56530f60fa_IEL2_Powerpoint.original.1469014687.pdf.

17. Tenenbaum, H. R., Winstone, N. E., Leman, P. J., and Avery, R. E., "How Effective Is Peer Interaction in Facilitating Learning? A Meta-Analysis," *Journal of Educational Psychology* 112, no. 7 (2020), https://doi.org/10.1037/edu0000436.

18. Chandra, P., "In Support of Mixed-Aged Groupings: An Optimal Model for Early Childhood Classrooms," Stanford Bing Nursery School, October 1, 2022, https://bingschool .stanford.edu/news/support-mixed-age-groupings-optimal-model-early-childhood-classrooms.

19. Katz, L. G., *The Case for Mixed Age Grouping in Early Childhood* (National Association for the Education of Young Children, 1990), https://files.eric.ed.gov/fulltext/ED326302 .pdf; Winsler, A., Caverly, S. L., Willson-Quayle, A., Carlton, M. P., Howell, C., and Long, G. N., "The Social and Behavioral Ecology of Mixed-Age and Same-Age Preschool Classrooms: A Natural Experiment," *Journal of Applied Developmental Psychology* 23, no. 3 (2002), https://doi.org/10.1016/S0193-3973(02)00111-9; Magnusson, L., and Bäckman K., "Teaching and Learning in Age Homogeneous Groups Versus Mixed-Age Groups in the Preschool: The Swedish Example," *Cogent Education* 9, no. 1 (2022), https://doi.org/10.1080/23311 86X.2022.2109802; Justice, L. M., Logan, J. A., Purtell, K., Bleses, D., and Højen, A., "Does Mixing Age Groups in Early Childhood Education Settings Support Children's Language Development?," *Applied Developmental Science* 23, no. 3 (2019), https://doi.org/10.1080/1 0888691.2017.1386100.

20. Pakarinen, E., Lerkkanen, M. K., Poikkeus, A., Kiuru, N., Siekkinen, M., Rasku-Puttonen, H., and Nurmi, J., "A Validation of the Classroom Assessment Scoring System in Finnish Kindergartens," *Early Education and Development* 21, no. 1 (2010), www.tandfonline .com/doi/abs/10.1080/10409280902858764.

21. University of Eastern Finland, "Empathetic Teachers Enhance Children's Motivation for Learning," *ScienceDaily*, November 3, 2015, www.sciencedaily.com /releases/2015/11/151103064738.htm.

22. Arundel, K., "Positive Student-Teacher Relationships Boost Instructional Quality," *K-12 Dive*, April 8, 2022, www.k12dive.com/news/teachers-benefit-from-positive-relationships -with-students-research-shows/621803/.

23. Hamel, E. E., Avari, P., Hatton-Bowers, H., and Schachter, R. E., "'The Kids. That's My Number One Motivator': Understanding Teachers' Motivators and Challenges to Working in Early Childhood Education," *Early Childhood Education Journal* (2023), https://doi.org /10.1007/s10643-023-01612-6.

24. On class size: Finn, J. D., Gerber, S. B., Achilles, C. M., and Boyd-Zaharias, J., "The Enduring Effects of Small Classes," *Teachers College Record* 103, no. 2 (2001), https://doi .org/10.1111/0161-4681.00112; Millsap, M. A., Giancola, J., Smith, W. C., Hunt. D., Humphrey, D. C., Wechsler, M., and Riehl, L., *A Descriptive Evaluation of the Federal Class-Size Reduction Program: Executive Summary* (US Department of Education, 2004), https://www2 .ed.gov/rschstat/eval/other/class-size/execsum.pdf.

25. Kazi-Nance, A., "Family Child Care Is More than Just Caring for the Children; We Care for the Parents and Families Also," *All Our Words*, July 10, 2019, https://allourkin

.wordpress.com/2019/07/10/family-child-care-is-more-than-just-caring-for-the-children-we-care-for-the-parents-and-families-also/.

26. Tiano, J. D., and McNeil, C. B., "Training Head Start Teachers in Behavior Management Using Parent-Child Interaction Therapy: A Preliminary Investigation," *Journal of Early and Intensive Behavior Intervention* 3, no. 2 (2006), https://doi.org/10.1037/h0100334; Nagaoka, D., Tomoshige, N., Ando, S., Morita, M., Kiyono, T., Kanata, S., Fujikawa, S., Endo, K., Yamasaki, S., Fukuda, M., Nishida, A., Hiraiwa-Hasegawa, M., and Kasai, K., "Being Praised for Prosocial Behaviors Longitudinally Reduces Depressive Symptoms in Early Adolescents: A Population-Based Cohort Study," *Frontiers in Psychiatry* 13 (2022), https://doi.org/10.3389/fpsyt.2022.86590.

27. Hammond, Z., *Culturally Responsive Teaching and the Brain: Promoting Authentic Engagement and Rigor Among Culturally and Linguistically Diverse Students* (Thousand Oaks, CA: Corwin, 2015).

28. Bovill, C., "Co-creation in Learning and Teaching: The Case for a Whole-Class Approach in Higher Education," *Higher Education* 79 (2020), https://doi.org/10.1007/s10734-019-00453-w.

29. Anderson, J., "Denmark Has Figured Out How to Teach Kids Empathy and Make Them Happier Adults," Quartz, August 22, 2016, https://qz.com/763289/denmark-has-figured-out-how-to-teach-kids-empathy-and-make-them-happier-adults.

30. New Zealand Ministry of Education, *Te Whāriki* (1996, updated in 2017), www.education.govt.nz/assets/Documents/Early-Childhood/ELS-Te-Whariki-Early-Childhood-Curriculum-ENG-Web.pdf.

Chapter 12. Communities: Thriving Together

1. Alvarez, L., "One Man's Millions Turn a Community in Florida Around," *New York Times*, May 25, 2015, www.nytimes.com/2015/05/26/us/tangelo-park-orlando-florida.html.

2. Weiss, E., interview with Sam Butler, as reported in "Tangelo Park Program: A Broader, Bolder Approach to Education," BBA, May 4, 2017, www.boldapproach.org/index.html@p=548.html.

3. Mock, E., "Justice for All: Belief in the Tangelo Park Turned It into an 'Oasis,'" Spectrum News 13, December 9, 2020, https://mynews13.com/fl/orlando/justice-for-all/2020/12/09/justice-for-all-belief-in-the-tangelo-park-turned-it-into-an-oasis.

4. Wright, R., "The Most Innovative City in the World," *Los Angeles Times*, June 3, 1996, www.latimes.com/archives/la-xpm-1996-06-03-mn-11410-story.html; Barth, B., "Curitiba: The Greenest City on Earth," *The Ecologist*, March 15, 2014, https://theecologist.org/2014/mar/15/curitiba-greenest-city-earth; Adler, D., "Story of Cities #37: How Radical Ideas Turned Curitiba into Brazil's 'Green Capital,'" *The Guardian*, May 6, 2016, www.theguardian.com/cities/2016/may/06/story-of-cities-37-mayor-jaime-lerner-curitiba-brazil-green-capital-global-icon.

5. Gustafsson, H., and Kelly, E., *Urban Innovations in Curitiba: A Case Study*, Yale Law School, June 2012, www.urban-response.org/system/files/content/resource/files/main/ludwiggustafssonkellycuritibareport.pdf.

6. Wright, "The Most Innovative City in the World."

7. NEOM website, accessed August 10, 2024, www.neom.com/en-us/about.

8. Luttenberger, S., Wimmer, S., and Paechter, M., "Spotlight on Math Anxiety," *Psychology Research and Behavior Management* 11 (2018), https://doi.org/10.2147/PRBM.S141421.

9. MathTalk website, accessed August 10, 2024, www.math-talk.com.

10. Duncan, G. J., Dowsett, C. J., Claessens, A., Magnuson, K., Huston, A. C., Klebanov, P., Pagani, L. S., Feinstein, L., Engel, M., Brooks-Gunn, J., Sexton, H., Duckworth, K., and Japel, C., "School Readiness and Later Achievement," *Developmental Psychology* 43, no. 6 (2007), https://doi.org/10.1037/0012-1649.43.6.1428; Camera, L., "U.S. Students Show No Improvement in Math, Reading, Science on International Exam," *U.S. News and World Report*, December 3, 2019, www.usnews.com/news/education-news/articles/2019-12-03/us-students -show-no-improvement-in-math-reading-science-on-international-exam.

11. Saidin, N., Halim, N. D., and Yahaya, N., "A Review of Research on Augmented Reality in Education: Advantages and Applications," *International Education Studies* 8 (2015), www.ccsenet.org/journal/index.php/ies/article/view/50356; Chen, Y., "Effect of Mobile Augmented Reality on Learning Performance, Motivation, and Math Anxiety in a Math Course," *Journal of Educational Computing Research* 57, no. 7 (2019), https://doi.org /10.1177/0735633119854036.

12. Jones, C., "Latinos, African-Americans Have Less Access to Math, Science Classes, New Data Show," *EdSource*, May 22, 2018, https://edsource.org/2018/latino-african-americans -have-less-access-to-math-science-classes-new-data-show/598083; Anderson, M., "How Does Race Affect a Student's Math Education?," *The Atlantic*, April 25, 2017, www.theatlantic.com /education/archive/2017/04/racist-math-education/524199/.

13. Beckner, A., Minn, C., "Helping Kids—and Parents—See that Math Is All Around Us. Why We Invested: MathTalk," Imaginable Futures, March 2, 2021, https://www.imaginable futures.com/learnings/math-talk/.

14. National Geographic, "This Island Unlocked the Secret to Long Life—and Knows How to Get Through Tough Times," October 12, 2020, https://www.nationalgeographic.com /premium/article/uncover-the-secrets-of-longevity-in-this-japanese-village.

15. Willcox, D. C., Willcox, B. J., Hsueh, W. C., and Suzuki, M., "Genetic Determinants of Exceptional Human Longevity: Insights from the Okinawa Centenarian Study." *Age* (Dordrecht, Netherlands) 28, no. 4 (2006), 313–332, https://doi.org/10.1007/s11357 -006-9020-x.

16. Willcox, B., "The Quest for Eternal Youth," TEDxMaui, December 29, 2014, https://www .youtube.com/watch?v=BBXPtVDpAWw.

17. Buettner, D., *Blue Zones* (Washington, DC: National Geographic, 2010).

18. For research on these programs, see *Centering Healthcare Bibliography*, September 2023, www.centeringhealthcare.org/uploads/files/Centering-Healthcare-Institute-Bibliography -2023.docx-3.pdf.

19. Grossman, B. J., Resch, N., and Tierney, J. P., *Making a Difference: An Impact Study of Big Brothers/Big Sisters (Re-issue of 1995 Study)* (Public/Private Ventures, September 15, 2000), https://ppv.issuelab.org/resource/making-a-difference-an-impact-study-of -big-brothers-big-sisters-re-issue-of-1995-study.

20. "The LA Generation Xchange (GenX) Project | UCLA Community Engagement," UCLA Health, YouTube video, May 13, 2016, www.youtube.com/watch?v=uV48WStOpzw.

21. "Our Impact," Generation Xchange, UCLA Health, accessed August 10, 2024, www.uclahealth.org/departments/medicine/geriatrics/research/generation-xchange-genx/our-impact.

22. Fried, L. P., Carlson, M. C., Freedman, M., Frick, K. D., Glass, T. A., Hill, J., McGill, S., Rebok, G. W., Seeman, T., Tielsch, J., Wasik, B. A., and Zeger, S., "A Social Model for Health Promotion for an Aging Population: Initial Evidence on the Experience Corps Model," *Journal of Urban Health* 81, no. 1 (2004), https://doi.org/10.1093/jurban/jth094.

23. Freedman, M., and Larson, C., "The Case for Putting Seniors in Charge of Universal Pre-K," *Newsweek*, November 29, 2021, www.newsweek.com/case-putting-seniors-charge-universal-pre-k-opinion-1654236.

24. Gopnik, A., "Vulnerable yet Vital: The Dance of Love and Lore Between Grandparent and Grandchild Is at the Centre, Not the Fringes, of Our Evolutionary Story," *Aeon*, November 9, 2020, https://aeon.co/essays/why-childhood-and-old-age-are-key-to-our-human-capacities.

25. Homepage, website of For Oak Cliff, accessed July 3, 2024, www.foroakcliff.org/.

26. "OG," an abbreviation for "original gangster," is a term of endearment for older people such as grandparents.

27. "Harlem Children's Zone Scholar Kiara Molina Introduces President Obama," Harlem Children's Zone, January 10, 2014, YouTube video, www.youtube.com/watch?v=VX2VYGLKI9w.

28. "Government Performance and Results Act (GPRA) Indicators," Promise Neighborhoods, US Department of Education, accessed July 14, 2024, https://promiseneighborhoods.ed.gov/data-and-results.

Conclusion. A Call for System Change

1. Cahalan, M. W., Brunt, N., Vaughan III, T., Montenegro, E., Breen, S., Ruffin, E., and Perna, L.W., *Indicators of Higher Education Equity in the United States: 2024 50-Year Historical Trend Report* (Pell Institute for the Study of Opportunity in Higher Education, 2024), www.pellinstitute.org/the-indicators-of-higher-education-equity-in-the-united-states-2024-50-year-historical-trend-report/.

2. Carnevale, A., Fasules, M. L., Quinn, M. C., and Peltier Campbell, K., *Born to Win, Schooled to Lose: Why Equally Talented Students Don't Get Equal Chances to Be All They Can Be* (Georgetown University Center on Education and the Workforce, 2019), https://files.eric.ed.gov/fulltext/ED599947.pdf; Johnson Hess, A., "Georgetown Study: 'To Succeed in America, It's Better to Be Born Rich than Smart,'" CNBC, May 29, 2019, www.cnbc.com/2019/05/29/study-to-succeed-in-america-its-better-to-be-born-rich-than-smart.html.

3. Bardhan, S., Kubzansky, M., and Bannick, M., *Omidyar Network's First 10 Years: An Impact Analysis* (Omidyar Network, 2018), https://omidyar.com/omidyar-networks-first-10-years-an-impact-analysis/.

INDEX

ISABELLE C. HAU is the executive director of the Stanford Accelerator for Learning. She previously led the US education practice at Omidyar Network/Imaginable Futures, where she invested in mission-driven organizations. Hau earned an MBA from Harvard Business School, and she graduated from ESSEC Business School and SciencesPo in Paris. She lives in Palo Alto, California.

PublicAffairs is a publishing house founded in 1997. It is a tribute to the standards, values, and flair of three persons who have served as mentors to countless reporters, writers, editors, and book people of all kinds, including me.

I. F. STONE, proprietor of *I. F. Stone's Weekly*, combined a commitment to the First Amendment with entrepreneurial zeal and reporting skill and became one of the great independent journalists in American history. At the age of eighty, Izzy published *The Trial of Socrates*, which was a national bestseller. He wrote the book after he taught himself ancient Greek.

BENJAMIN C. BRADLEE was for nearly thirty years the charismatic editorial leader of *The Washington Post*. It was Ben who gave the *Post* the range and courage to pursue such historic issues as Watergate. He supported his reporters with a tenacity that made them fearless and it is no accident that so many became authors of influential, best-selling books.

ROBERT L. BERNSTEIN, the chief executive of Random House for more than a quarter century, guided one of the nation's premier publishing houses. Bob was personally responsible for many books of political dissent and argument that challenged tyranny around the globe. He is also the founder and longtime chair of Human Rights Watch, one of the most respected human rights organizations in the world.

·   ·   ·

For fifty years, the banner of Public Affairs Press was carried by its owner Morris B. Schnapper, who published Gandhi, Nasser, Toynbee, Truman, and about 1,500 other authors. In 1983, Schnapper was described by *The Washington Post* as "a redoubtable gadfly." His legacy will endure in the books to come.

Peter Osnos, *Founder*